The United Nations and its Future in the 21st Century

To Siru Mewle

Together we can make a difference

Jigeep Mehta

The United Nations and its Future in the 21st Century

Editor
Vijay Mehta

SPOKESMAN
for
Action for UN Renewal

First published in 2005 by
Spokesman
Russell House, Bulwell Lane
Nottingham
NG6 0BT
Phone 0115 970 8318. Fax 0115 942 0433
e-mail elfeuro@compuserve.com
www.spokesmanbooks.com

All rights reserved. No part of this publication may be reproduced, stored in a retrieval system or transmitted in any form or by means, electronic, mechanical, photocopying, recording or otherwise, without prior permission of the publishers.

ISBN 0 85124 707 5

A CIP Catalogue is available from the British Library.

Printed by the Russell Press Ltd (phone 0115 978 45050)

The United Nations and its Future in the 21st Century

Contents

Acknowledgements	iv
Glossary	v
Notes on Contributors	x
Introduction *Vijay Mehta*	1
Foreword *Jayantha Dhanapala*	13
Erskine Childers (1929-1996): UN Free-thinker, Critic and Constructive Analyst *Richard Jolly*	32
The United Nations at the Crossroads of Ideals and Reality *Ramesh Thakur*	36

The Erskine Childers Lectures 1997 – 2004

The United Nations in the Twenty-First Century: Prospects for Reform *Razali Ismail*	52
Who Rules? The United Nations: Democratic and Representative? *Patricia McKenna*	64
'To Save Succeeding Generations from the Scourge of War': the Role of the International Court of Justice	84

The United Nations and its Future in the 21st Century

Rosalyn Higgins

The UN in Crisis? 102
Margaret Anstee

The United Nations and the Promotion of Peace 115
Paul Rogers

The United Nations: the Embarrassment of International Law 132
Denis Halliday

Crisis in the UN, NATO and the EU 144
Caroline Lucas

After Kosovo, Afghanistan and Iraq- What is the Future for the UN? 158
Jenny Tonge

Afterword 166

Appendices

A More Secure World: Our Shared Responsibility 168
Recommendations of the Secretary – General's High-level Panel on Threats, Challenges and Change

We the Peoples: Civil Society, the UN and Global Governance
Recommendations of the Panel of Eminent Persons on UN-Civil Society Relationships 195

Charter of the United Nations 205

Universal Declaration of Human Rights 251

UN Millennium Development Goals 258

The United Nations and its Future in the 21st Century

The Hague Agenda for Peace and Justice for the 21st Century	263
Further Reading	269
Some Useful Websites	273
Index	275
About Action for UN Renewal	283

Acknowledgements

The birth of this project came from a decision by Action for UN Renewal to incorporate the annual Erskine Childers lectures into a book. The lectures were started after the untimely death of Erskine Childers, who was a long-standing, distinguished, UN diplomat and a staunch supporter of the organisation and its ideals, and wrote extensively for its reform.

We would like to thank all the contributors for their permission to reproduce the lectures in book form, Jayantha Dhanapala for writing the foreword, and Richard Jolly for his biography of Erskine Childers. Furthermore, we would like to thank Ramesh Thakur for his article titled *'The UN at the Crossroads of Ideals and Reality.'*

We would also like to thank Routledge, Taylor & Francis, now publishers of the journal *Medicine, Conflict and Survival*, where these lectures appeared first, for permission to republish.

Action for UN Renewal gratefully acknowledges the financial contribution by INLAP (Institute for Law and Peace) for their assistance in the project. We would also like to thank Mary and Douglas Holdstock for their efforts in getting the copyright permission for the lectures and preparing the Index, and Abdul Muhib for his assistance in producing this book.

Vijay Mehta

The United Nations and its Future in the 21st Century

Glossary

ABM Anti-Ballistic Missile Treaty

AIDS Acquired Immune Deficiency Syndrome

ASEAN Association of Southeast Asian Nations

BTWC Biological and Toxin Weapons Convention

CD Conference on Disarmament

CFC Chlorofluorocarbons

CIA Central Intelligence Agency

CTBT Comprehensive (Nuclear) Test Ban Treaty

CTC Counter Terrorism Committee

DfID Department for International Development

DPRK Democratic People's Republic of Korea

ECOSOC United Nations Economic and Social Council

ENDC Eighteen Nation Disarmament Commission

EU European Union

The United Nations and its Future in the 21st Century

FAO Food and Agricultural Organization

FCO Foreign and Commonwealth Office

FMCT Fissile Material Cut-off Treaty

GA General Assembly

GATT General Agreement on Tariffs and Trade

GNP Gross National Product

G7 Group of Seven

G8 Group of Eight

HDI Human Development Index

IAEA International Atomic Energy Agency

ICC International Criminal Court

ICJ International Court of Justice

ILO International Labour Organization

IMF International Monetary Fund

IRA Irish Republican Army

MAD Mutually Assured Destruction

MAI Multilateral Agreement on Investment

MDG Millennium Development Goals

MEP Member of European Parliament

NAM Non-aligned Movement

NATO North Atlantic Treaty Organization

NGO Non-Governmental Organisation

NPT Nuclear Non-Proliferation Treaty

OAU Organization for African Unity

OSCE Organization for Security and Cooperation in Europe

PfP Partnership for Peace

P-5 Permanent Five Members of the Security Council: the United States, United Kingdom, Russian Federation, France and China

SALW Small Arms and Light Weapons

SAP Structural Adjustment Program

SARS Severe Acute Respiratory Syndrome

SC Security Council

SSOD Special Session of the General Assembly on Disarmament

START Strategic Arms Reduction Treaty

TNC Transnational Corporation

UN United Nations

UNA United Nations Association

UNAVEM United Nations Angola Verification Mission

UNCTAD United Nations Conference on Trade and Development

UNDP United Nations Development Programme

UNEP United Nations Environmental Programme

UNESCO United Nations Educational, Scientific and Cultural Organization

UNICEF United Nations Children's Fund

UNITA National Union for the Total Independence of Angola

UNSCOM United Nations Special Commission for Iraq

WFUNA World Federation of United Nations Associations

WEU Western European Union

The United Nations and its Future in the 21st Century

WHO World Health Organization

WMD Weapons of Mass Destruction

WTO World Trade Organization

Notes on Contributors

Dame Margaret Joan Anstee served in the UN from 1952 to 1993. As Under Secretary-General, she was Director General of the UN Office in Vienna from 1987 to 1992. She was special representative of the Secretary General in Angola and Head of UNAVEM II from 1992-3. Her published works include *'Orphan of the Cold War: The Inside Story of the Collapse of the Angolan Peace Process 1992-3'* (Macmillan, 1996) and *'Never Learn to Type: A Woman at the United Nations'* (Wiley, 2003).

Jayantha Dhanapala is the former United Nations Under-Secretary-General for Disarmament Affairs and a former Ambassador for Sri Lanka in the USA. He is currently Secretary-General of the Sri Lanka Peace Secretariat and a Senior Adviser to the President of Sri Lanka.

Denis J. Halliday worked for the United Nations for 34 years, becoming Assistant Secretary-General. For several years he was UN Humanitarian Co-ordinator in Iraq, resigning in protest at the impact of sanctions on the country's economy and health services.

Judge Rosalyn Higgins, DBE, QC has been a member of the International Court of Justice since July 1995. She was former Professor of International Law at the London School of Economics and a member of the UN Human Rights committee. She is a Member of the Institut de Droit International, and is author of numerous publications on international law, including *The Development of International Law through the Political Organs of the UN; UN Peacekeeping: Documents and commentary (4 Vols.); Problems and*

The United Nations and its Future in the 21st Century

Process (Hague Academy Lectures).

H.E. Razali Ismail has been the Permanent Representative of Malaysia to the United Nations since 1988, and was President of the 51st Session of the UN General Assembly. He has held a number of posts on behalf of Malaysia's Ministry of Foreign Affairs since 1962 and has served in various capacities in the United Nations. In 1993 he was the first Chairman of the Commission on Sustainable Development. He has been actively involved in several academic and other bodies dealing with development, environment, human rights and UN reform, and has spoken and written widely on these issues.

Sir Richard Jolly is the former Special Adviser to the Administrator of UNDP and became a Trustee in 2001. He was the architect of the Human Development Report. Before this he was Deputy Executive Director of UNICEF, responsible for programmes in 130 countries. Now an Honorary Professorial Fellow at the Institute of Development Studies at the University of Sussex and the author of publications, including: *Development with a Human Face, Adjustment with a Human Face* and *Planning Education for African Development*.

Caroline Lucas is Member of the European Parliament for South-east England She was elected as one of the Green Party's first MEPs in June 1999 and is Member of the Committee for Trade, Industry, Energy and Research and of the Environment Committee. Her professional background is in research and policy analysis on trade, development and environment issues. In 1993 Caroline won the Green Party's second County Council seat in the UK (Oxfordshire County Council, 1993-97) and has held many positions in the party, including National Press Officer (1987-89), Co-Chair (1989-90), and National Speaker on various occasions.

Patricia McKenna was a Member of the European Parliament for the

Green Party from 1994 to 2004, topping the poll in the Dublin area. Before becoming an MEP she worked for the Green Party on a variety of issues, including organising a campaign against the Single European Act, opposing the Gulf War, and resisting the proposal for an underground nuclear waste facility near Sellafield. As an MEP, she emphasised environmental issues related to Dublin, such as working for a light rail link and highlighting the lack of cycle lanes in the city. She is concerned that the Amsterdam Treaty is inadequate on civil liberties, human rights and unemployment.

Vijay Mehta MA is a writer and a anti-nuclear campaigner. He is Co-Chairman: World Disarmament Campaign; Co-Chairman: Arms Reduction Coalition; Vice Chairman: Action for United Nations Renewal; Secretary: London CND (Campaign for Nuclear Disarmament); Editor: INLAP TIMES (Institute for Law and Peace). He has served on various advisory bodies on peace and disarmament and was a member of the team of international experts who met in Greece for the creation of the School of Athens. He travels widely to give talks on international relations, peace, disarmament, UN reforms and the global arms trade in all its aspects from small arms to nuclear weapons and WMD. He regularly writes for various journals and newsletters.

Paul Rogers is Professor of Peace Studies at Bradford University UK and consultant to Oxford Research Group. He trained originally as a biologist and later developed a research interest in resource conflict and the politics of North-South relations. He chaired the UK Alternative Defence Commission from 1984 – 1987 and has written several books on international peace and security issues including, with Malcolm Dando, *A Violent Peace: Global Security after the Cold War* (London: Brassey's, 1992).

The United Nations and its Future in the 21st Century

Prof. Dr. Ramesh Thakur is the Senior Vice-Rector of the United Nations University and Assistant Secretary-General of the United Nations. He was Professor of International Relations and Director of Asian Studies at the University of Otago in New Zealand and Professor and Head of the Peace Research Centre at the Australian National University in Canberra before joining UNU in 1998. He was a Commissioner on the International Commission on Intervention and State Sovereignty which published the report *The Responsibility to Protect*, and Senior Advisor on Reforms and Principal Writer of the UN Secretary-General's second reform report. Educated in India and Canada. He is author/editor of some twenty books and 200 journal articles and book chapters, and writes regularly for the national and international quality press.

Dr. Jenny Tonge was Liberal Democrat MP for Richmond Park from 1997 to 2005, and was party spokesperson for International Development until 2003. She qualified in medicine from University College London in 1964, and worked in general practice and in local authority health and community services in West London. Her political interests also include Third World issues, health, the environment, Europe and constitutional reform.

The UN and its Future in the 21st Century

Introduction

Vijay Mehta

Two decades ago, the world was swept with a wave of hope. Inspired by the popular movements for peace, freedom, democracy and solidarity, the nations of the world worked together to end the cold war. Yet the opportunities opened up by that historic change are slipping away. The global community is gravely concerned with the resurgent nuclear and conventional arms race, disrespect for international law and the failure of the world's governments to address adequately the challenges of poverty and environmental degradation. A culture of violence is spreading globally, eroding the opportunity to build a culture of peace, advocated by the United Nations.

Alongside the challenges inherited from the past there are new ones, which, if not properly addressed, could cause a clash of civilisations, religions and cultures. The inevitability of such a conflict must be rejected. The recent spate of terrorism in all its forms is an issue that should be pursued with determination. Only by reaffirming our shared ethical values -- respect for human rights and fundamental freedoms -- and by observing democratic principles, within and amongst countries, can terrorism be defeated. We must address the root causes of terrorism -- poverty, ignorance and injustice - rather than responding to violence with violence.

This book has been compiled in the light of the international situation we face today. In recent times, the United States has become reluctant to use the UN process, and in particular the Security Council, as the primary organ for international peace and security. It would appear to many that it

The UN and its Future in the 21st Century

will co-operate with the UN only as long as it furthers the US foreign policy agenda and strategic interest.

After the failure to secure a second UN Security Council resolution authorising war, the US-led intervention seriously undermined international law and thus sidelined the United Nations. In his address to the General Assembly in September 2003, United Nations Secretary-General Kofi Annan warned Member States that the United Nations had reached a fork in the road. It could rise to the challenge of meeting new threats or it could risk erosion in the face of mounting discord between States and unilateral action by them.

A More Secure World: Our Shared Responsibility

As the legitimacy of the UN was challenged, Secretary-General Kofi Annan, appointed a high-level UN Panel to study global threats and challenges and come up with radical reforms. The report, *A More Secure World: Our Shared Responsibility* (Report of the Secretary-General's High-level Panel on Threats, Challenges and Change), explores the possibility of collective responses to our global problems, and generates new ideas and solutions for the 21st century. It recommends far-reaching changes to boost the ability of the UN to deal effectively with future threats caused by poverty and environmental degradation, terrorism, civil war, conflict between states, weapons of mass destruction (WMD) and organised crime.

The panel's Chair, former Prime Minister Anand Panyarachun of Thailand, says the 95-page report 'puts forward a new vision of collective security, one that addresses all of the major threats to international peace and security felt around the world.' The panel included Gro Harlem Brundtland, former Prime Minister of Norway, and prominent diplomats and politicians as well as former senior UN officials drawn from all regions of the world.

The report affirms the right of States to defend themselves, including preemptively when an attack is truly imminent, and says that, in cases involving terrorists and WMDs, the Security Council may have to act earlier, more pro-actively, and more decisively than in the past.

The panel also endorses the idea of collective responsibility to protect civilians from genocide, ethnic cleansing and comparable atrocities, saying that the wider international community should intervene - acting preventively where possible - when countries are unwilling or unable to fulfil their responsibility to their citizens. However, if force is needed, it should be used as a last resort and authorised by the Security Council. Experts identify five criteria to guide the Council in its decisions over whether to authorise force:

- the seriousness of the threat;
- proper purpose;
- whether it is a last resort;
- whether proportional means are used; and
- whether military action is likely to have better or worse results than inaction.

The panel also came up with an unambiguous definition of terrorism, encompassing 'any definition that is intended to cause death or serious bodily harm to civilians or non-combatants, when the purposes of such an action . . . is to intimidate a population [or sway] a government or international organisation.' If the definition secures agreement, it can be counted as a step forward.

It also urges the creation of a Peacebuilding Commission under the Security Council to identify countries at risk of violent conflicts, organise prevention efforts and sustain international peacebuilding efforts.

The report notes that major changes are needed in UN bodies to make them more effective, efficient and equitable, including universal membership of the Geneva-based Commission on Human Rights. Such a move would

The UN and its Future in the 21st Century

underscore the commitment of all members to the promotion of human rights, and might help focus attention back on the substantive issues rather than the politicking currently engulfing the Commission.

Also included in the report's 101 recommendations are proposals to strengthen development efforts, public health capacity and the current nuclear non-proliferation regime. The panel says this is a less effective constraint than previously because of lack of compliance, threats to withdraw from the Nuclear Non-Proliferation Treaty, the changing security environment, and the diffusion of technology. It endorses the idea of collective responsibility to protect civilians from harm, and spurring economic and social development in order to ward off potential problems.

It calls for increasing the credibility and effectiveness of the Security Council by making its composition better reflect today's realities. Two formulas for an enlarged Security Council increase the membership to 24 from the current 15, but differ on allowing more permanent seats. The first provides for six new permanent seats without veto power in addition to the five that currently hold it, and three more two-year rotating seats divided among the UN's regional groupings.

The second plan envisages no new permanent seats but creates a new category of eight four-year renewable-term seats and one new two-year non-permanent, non- renewable seat, all without veto power. Both documents are intended to provide a basis for discussions at the proposed high-level summit in September 2005 before the Assembly's next session, which coincides with the UN's Sixtieth Anniversary.

In its report, the High-level Panel sets out a bold, new vision of collective security for the 21st century. We live in a world of new and evolving threats, threats that could not have been anticipated when the UN was founded in 1945 – threats like nuclear terrorism, and State collapse from the witches' brew of poverty, disease and civil war.

The UN and its Future in the 21st Century

In today's world, a threat to one is a threat to all. Globalisation means that a major terrorist attack anywhere in the industrial world would have devastating consequences for the well-being of millions in the developing world. Any one of 700 million international airline passengers every year can be an unwitting carrier of a deadly infectious disease. And the erosion of State capacity anywhere in the world weakens the protection of every State against transnational threats such as terrorism and organised crime. Every State requires international co-operation to make it secure.

There are six clusters of threats with which the world must be concerned now and in the decades ahead:

- war between States;
- violence within States, including civil wars, large-scale human rights abuses and genocide;
- poverty, infectious disease and environmental degradation;
- nuclear, radiological, chemical and biological weapons;
- terrorism; and
- transnational organised crime.

The good news is that the United Nations and our collective security institutions have shown that they *can* work. More civil wars ended through negotiation in the past 15 years than the previous 200. In the 1960s, many believed that by now 15 to 25 States would possess nuclear weapons; the Nuclear Non-Proliferation Treaty (NPT) has helped prevent this. The World Health Organization (WHO) helped to stop the spread of Severe Acute Respiratory Syndrome (SARS) before it killed tens of thousands, perhaps more. But these accomplishments can be reversed. There is a real danger that they will be, unless we act soon to strengthen the United Nations, so that in future it responds effectively to the full range of threats that confront us.

The panel concluded that the threat agenda we faced was not a narrow one limited to international terrorism and to the proliferation of weapons of mass destruction, real though these threats certainly are. It is much wider, including the phenomena of the failure of states often leading to major regional instability and conflicts, and a whole range of issues which have not traditionally been considered as part of the peace and security nexus at all - poverty, environmental degradation, pandemic diseases and the spread of organised crime - to mention the most prominent. They reached this conclusion not simply because in many parts of the world, notably in Africa, and Latin America, these so-called 'soft' threats are often seen as even more menacing and imminent than the 'hard' threats of the narrower agenda, but also because they became increasingly aware of the inter-connections and overlap between the different categories of threat which rendered the whole 'hard/soft' categorisation misleading and inadequate.

After all, the greatest terrorist outrage in recent times was launched from a failed state, Afghanistan, and the greatest genocide occurred in another, Rwanda. Organised crime has frequently undermined international efforts at post-conflict peacebuilding. Pandemic diseases like AIDS threaten the stability of many states, in Africa in particular. The correlation between poverty and insecurity leaps at you from the report. All these threats require a universal response if they are to be effectively combated. Only a broad, common agenda provides any hope of mustering such a universal response.

The panel came to examine responses to these threats and challenges and rapidly found themselves at risk of being drawn into something of an ideological, almost a theological, battle - between those who believed in unilateral responses and those who believed in multilateral ones. The fact remains that a collective response is essential for implementing the recommendations made by the panel. No single country, even the world's current single super-power, could mount an adequate response to all the threats it faces on its own.

For instance, in dealing with terrorism or the proliferation of weapons of mass destruction, it is fairly obvious that states, and their intelligence and law enforcement capabilities, are essential to any effective action and cannot be replaced by multilateral institutions. But it is just as obvious that the normative capacity of international organisations and their scope for organising co-operation on a wide-ranging basis are essential for dealing with a range of threats and challenges which do not respect national boundaries and which have often seized on globalisation as an ally in the pursuit of their objectives. From this the panel concluded that a collective response was needed to every one of these challenges, but that dealing with each effectively would require a judicious blend between the national and the international when it came to action.

Besides dealing with the harder end of the peace and security agenda, the panel was very conscious that, so far as the rest of the agenda was concerned - poverty, environmental degradation, epidemic disease, organised crime – there exist a broader network of organisations and civil society which is working in unison with the UN. The Secretary-General has recently put forward separately his definitive views on these issues in the context of his review of progress on the Millennium Development Goals. Substantially greater financial resources will be needed to fuel development programmes and to counter AIDS and other epidemic diseases. It is critically important to bring the Doha Development Round of trade negotiations to a conclusion at the latest by 2006. It is high time to start thinking about and negotiating a post-Kyoto set of arrangements which will bring both the United States and the main developing countries within its ambit and provide a more effective response to global warming than what has been attempted so far.

Policies for Prevention

Meeting the challenge of today's threats means getting serious about prevention; the consequences of allowing latent threats to become manifest, or of allowing existing threats to spread, are simply too severe. Development has to be the first line of defence for a collective security system that takes prevention seriously. Combating poverty will not only

The UN and its Future in the 21st Century

save millions of lives but also strengthen States' capacity to combat terrorism, organised crime and proliferation. Development makes everyone more secure. There is an agreed international framework for how to achieve these goals, set out in the Millennium Declaration and the Monterrey Consensus, but implementation lags.

Biological security must be at the forefront of prevention. International response to HIV/AIDS was shockingly late and shamefully ill-resourced. It is urgent that we halt and roll back this pandemic.

A UN for the 21st Century

To meet these challenges, the UN needs its existing institutions to work better. This means revitalising the General Assembly and the Economic and Social Council (ECOSOC), to make sure they play the role intended for them, and restoring credibility to the Commission on Human Rights.

Outside the UN, a forum bringing together the heads of the 20 largest economies, developed and developing, would help the coherent management of international monetary, financial, trade and development policy. Better collaboration with regional organisations is also crucial, and the report sets out a series of principles that govern a more structured partnership between them and the UN.

The report recommends strengthening the Secretary-General's critical role in peace and security. To be more effective, the Secretary-General should be given substantially more latitude to manage the Secretariat, and be held accountable. He also needs better support for his mediation role, and new capacities to develop effective peacebuilding strategy. He currently has one Deputy Secretary-General; with a second, responsible for peace and security, he would have the capacity to ensure oversight of both the social, economic and development functions of the UN, and its many peace and security functions.

The UN and its Future in the 21st Century

We the Peoples: Civil Society, the UN and Global Governance

A second report has been released which looked at the importance of civil society *vis-à-vis* the United Nations, called *We the Peoples: Civil Society, the UN and Global Governance* (Report of the Panel of Eminent Persons on UN-Civil Society Relationships). The report made some key recommendations that are instrumental for the efficient functioning of the United Nations.

The panel's report presents 30 proposals for reform, some of which the Secretary-General himself would have authority to act on, while others would require intergovernmental debate and decision. These proposals largely stem from four underlying priorities or principles for the UN that the panel identified over the course of its deliberations:

- the UN must become an outward looking organisation: giving more emphasis to convening and facilitating rather than 'doing;' putting the needs, not the institution, at the centre;
- the UN must embrace a plurality of constituencies: many actors may be relevant to an issue;
- the UN must connect the local with the global: putting countries first by starting engagement at the country level for both operational and deliberative processes. Global norms should drive the operations, and country realities should mould those norms; civil society is vital for both;
- the UN must help re-shape democracy for the 21st century, accepting a more explicit role in strengthening global governance and tackling the democratic deficits it is prone to, emphasising participatory democracy and deeper accountability of institutions to the global public.

The report points out that the UN is not starting from scratch: 'There is much to be proud of in its existing strategies and recent measures to enhance engagement. These proposals are largely intended to expand, deepen and protect them, not replace them'. Similarly, it recognises that the UN's main civil society partners 'have already done a great deal to help strengthen the outward orientation of the UN and would be invaluable allies in helping to implement the suggested strategy'.

A Time to Change and the Way Forward

The publication of this book is well-timed as the UN is going through a crucial period of self examination and needs reforming to make itself more relevant to the challenges of the 21st century. It coincides with the recent UN High-level Panel Report discussed above. These cannot be confronted without reform, which makes the report and its recommendations even more pertinent.

The report is the start, not the end, of a process. The United Nations 60th anniversary in 2005 will be a crucial opportunity for Member States to discuss and build on the recommendations in the report, some of which will be considered by a summit of Heads of State. But building a more secure world takes much more than a report or a summit. It will take resources commensurate with the scale of the challenges ahead; commitments that are long-term and sustained; and, most of all, it will take leadership – from within States, and between them.

The UN and its Future in the 21st Century

The challenges of security, poverty and environmental crisis can only be met successfully through multilateral efforts based on the rule of law. All nations must strictly fulfil their treaty obligations and reaffirm the indispensable role of the United Nations and the primary responsibility of the UN Security Council for maintaining peace.

To benefit from humankind's new, unprecedented opportunities and to counter the dangers confronting us there is a need for better global governance. Therefore, the United Nations and its institutions need strengthening and reforming

The United Nations is clearly at a pivotal moment in its history. As it faces the emerging challenges of global terrorism and nuclear proliferation, member-states must decide whether to adhere to the UN processes to solve their common problems or face the consequences.

If the recommendations of the report are taken up in earnest, we can have a new and revitalised United Nations and Security Council. It will heal some of the North-South divide. On the other hand, if the report is thought of as a scripture and away from the realities on the ground, then it will simply gather dust like countless other UN reports. After the report was published, Kofi Annan said:

> In his last annual address to Congress in January 1945, Franklin Roosevelt, then America's president, alluded to his plans to create a new collective security institution, the United Nations, and gave warning that: 'In our disillusionment after the last war, we gave up the hope of achieving a better peace because we had not the courage to fulfil our responsibilities in an admittedly imperfect world.'

Almost exactly 60 years later, we once again find ourselves mired in disillusionment, in an all too imperfect world. It is easy to stand at the sidelines and criticise, we could talk endlessly about UN reform. But our

The UN and its Future in the 21st Century

world no longer has that luxury. The time has come to adapt our collective security system, so that it works efficiently, effectively and equitably.

In 2005, UN member states will be reviewing progress in implementing the 2000 Millennium Declaration, culminating in a summit of world leaders in New York in September. This will be an appropriate moment for them to act on some of the most important recommendations in the panel's report, which require decisions at the highest levels of government.

I hope that world leaders will rise to this challenge. In the past three years we have all lived through a period of deep division and sombre reflection. We must make 2005 a year of bold decision. As the panel puts it: 'We all share responsibility for each other's security.' Let us summon the courage to fulfil that responsibility.

Foreword

Jayantha Dhanapala

I never had the privilege of knowing Erskine Childers. To my mind he represents a significant part of the rich Irish contribution to international peace and security in general and the United Nations (UN) in particular together with Frederick Boland, Conor Cruise O'Brien and others. It was the famous Irish UN General Assembly Resolution that formed the genesis of the Treaty for the Non-Proliferation of Nuclear Weapons (NPT). The reputation of Childers both within the UN system and in the sphere of international relations was formidable enough for me to follow his writings with close interest - especially on the UN. In view of my own commitment to multilateralism and deep convictions on the need to strengthen the UN, I had avidly read the report on *'Renewing the United Nations System'* which he had co-authored with another redoubtable UN veteran – the distinguished Sir Brian Urquhart. Its remarkable clarity, the holistic scope of the recommendations and the fusion of idealism and practicality stood out. On the eve of the report of the Secretary-General's High Level Panel on *'Threats, Challenges and Change'* and our celebration of the 60th anniversary of the UN it is appropriate for us all to revisit the Childers/Urquhart report.

An Ethical Foundation for the UN

It is in this context that we must reflect on how our world body can be reformed to face the challenges of the future based on the experience of the past. We must begin with a foundation of ethical values that we can share. The use of the term 'Ethics' for a set of moral principles presupposes that we are all bound by a common understanding of what we mean. In a very broad sense, we are talking about the absolutely irreducible minimum of humankind's cultural, moral and spiritual achievement over centuries of civilisation. It is not only what distinguishes the human species from other living beings, but also the soul of humankind. It is the quintessence of all religious philosophies and the highest common factor among all cultures.

Ethics *per se* would be of little value if it did not have a practical propensity to be applied to human affairs and the improvement of the human condition. It is widely, but wrongly, assumed that the realm of ethical values and the world of pragmatic politics are wide apart and that never the twain shall meet. The achievements of the UN illustrate that there can be a fusion between ethics and policy, and it is this fusion that contributes to the betterment of mankind and to peace.

We are still in the early years of the first century of a new millennium in the human saga, leaving behind the bloodiest century of all time. There is a unique opportunity for us to use the indisputable authority that the UN wields to shape a world order that is built more solidly on ethics than on the pursuit of individual profit or national self-interest. In the year 2000 the largest ever gathering of Heads of State and Government met at the United Nations in New York and issued the historic Millennium Declaration. Significantly, before the Declaration embarks on setting objectives in respect of the different areas of peace, security and disarmament including the elimination of weapons of mass destruction especially nuclear weapons; development and poverty eradication; human rights, democracy and good governance including the Millennium Development Goals; protecting the vulnerable and meeting the special needs of Africa, it addresses the issue of fundamental values underpinning international relations in the twenty-first century. That demonstrates a remarkably sound judgement of priorities. If the leaders of the world cannot agree on the ethical values that bind them together, they are unlikely to agree on common goals and common strategies to overcome what Secretary-General Kofi Annan has called 'problems without passports'.

It is relevant for us therefore to review these shared values set out in the

The UN and its Future in the 21st Century

United Nations Millennium Declaration as a common ethical base. They comprise six of the most basic aspirations of humankind – *freedom, equality, solidarity, tolerance, respect for nature, and shared responsibility*. From each of these fundamental values we draw our guidance for the specific action plans that the international community committed itself to in the Millennium Declaration. It is a moral compass for us all. Individually these values represent powerful forces that have inspired and motivated humankind throughout millennia of history. They have been accelerators of human progress. Collectively they represent the benchmark against which we must judge our performance as individual nations and as the world community in taking humankind forward to a better and safer world.

- *Freedom* - was the spur that rid the world of slavery, colonialism and apartheid: it is the ethical value that protects men, women and children from fear, exploitation and abuse, from injustice and deprivation and from want and hunger.

- *Equality* - is what drove societies to abolish discrimination on the basis of colour, creed, wealth, ethnicity, aristocratic origin and gender: it is the ethical value that empowers individuals in society and nations in the international community whether big or small, rich or poor, mighty or meek.

- *Solidarity* - is the sense of a common identity as one human family with reciprocal duties and obligations that has led to social contracts and social security within countries and to the aid and assistance of the wealthy and developed countries to those who are stricken with disease, disaster and endemic poverty: it is the ethical value that must ensure the elimination of injustices, asymmetries in globalised development and absolute poverty.

- *Tolerance* - is the glue that has bonded us together as human beings with mutual respect for each other despite our astonishing diversity both within nations and the international community: it is the ethical value that will prevent ethnic and religious conflict within nations and the 'clash of civilisations' on a global scale ensuring instead a 'dialogue among civilisations' and the celebration of human diversity as an endowment.

- *Respect for nature* - is what has preserved the available and potential natural resources of our planet Earth and our ecological system as our common heritage to serve the genuine needs and not the greedy wants of humankind: it is the ethical value that will guide us to sustainable development managing our consumption of resources equitably and wisely so that we pass on the world which we occupy as a trust, to generations to come in at least as healthy and wholesome a state as we received it from preceding generations. Finally,

- *Shared responsibility* – is the common realisation that we are one brotherhood and sisterhood placed together in a world that is more integrated than ever before through the processes of globalisation and that the management of public goods has to be achieved optimally through participatory, people-centred endeavours and good democratic governance at the national level and through multilateralism and international organisations - with the United Nations at its apex - in the collective response to global challenges to international peace and human security: it is the ethical value that will prevent humankind from anarchy and self-destruction through selfishness and profligacy and the insurance policy to achieve a rule based international order founded on the bedrock of international law, human rights, equity and justice.

The translation of these ethical values to the daily world of human interaction – to do the right thing for the right reason - presents all of us with an enormous challenge. No government or group can claim a monopoly over wisdom. Nor can they claim to be the sole interpreters of the national or global interest. Those with experience of working in the UN, with which Erskine Childers and Sir Brian Urquhart were richly endowed, can contribute towards the public discourse on national and international policy by emphasising the ethical dimension. Already there are danger signals that illustrate the erosion of our ethical base. Terrorism, nihilism and anarchism are ominous symptoms. Are they the result of perceptions that the policies pursued in the past have been divorced from ethics? Or are they the emergence of a new threat for which our collective response must not be militarism but a return to implementing our shared value base of ethics - honestly, transparently and consistently?

In his address to the General Assembly in September 2003, United Nations Secretary-General Kofi Annan warned Member States that the United Nations had reached a fork in the road. It could rise to the challenge of meeting new threats or it could risk erosion in the face of mounting discord between States and unilateral action by them. He created the High-level Panel on Threats, Challenges and Change to generate new ideas about the kinds of policies and institutions required for the UN to be effective in the 21st century.

It would help our task if we had a barometer to measure the performance of all our leaders in the achievement of implementing ethics as policy. The world has seen the evolution of numerous indices for human progress. We have economic and social indicators ranging from Gross National Product in quantitative terms to the Human Development Index in qualitative terms. There are other more specific indices such as a Corruption Index from Transparency International, a Freedom Index from Freedom House and there is even a Happiness Index! I would hope that research organisations, think tanks and NGOs would combine their efforts to devise an Ethical Policy Index ranking countries in accordance with their adherence to a commonly accepted set of ethical values such as those enshrined in the Millennium Declaration of the United Nations. That will contribute to some pressure on governments to be accountable to their people in adopting policies that will be of widespread and durable benefit. It is but one of many tools we can propose in the quest for a greater role for ethics in the formulation of policy to respond to the new threats to security and to the other challenges facing humankind today. It is an urgent task to preserve and develop the mainsprings of our common humanity for a new and glorious chapter of human history.

The Concept of Collective Security

In his statement to the United Nations General Assembly on 23 September 2003 Secretary General Kofi Annan described the situation of the UN following the controversy over the invasion of Iraq as ' a fork in the road …. no less decisive than 1945 itself when the United Nations was founded.' While some may disagree with this over-dramatisation of where the world body is today, the Secretary-General used the opportunity to appoint a sixteen member High Level Panel of eminent personalities to examine current challenges to peace and security; identify the contribution collective action can make in addressing these challenges; and recommend changes in the principal organs of the UN and elsewhere to ensure effective collective action.

The concept of collective security forms the bedrock of the United Nations Charter and has served the international community well for several decades. However all concepts and systems must be re-appraised from time to time and adapted to serve new realities.

Secretary General Kofi Annan's primary rationale for the appointment of the High Level Panel is that the consensus underpinning collective security, which had been recently restated in the Millennium Declaration, had broken down in the wake of sharp disagreement over military intervention in Iraq last year. Unilateral military intervention is not new in the post World War II history of global events. What is new is that, after the events of 11 September 2001 and the alarming revelations of clandestine weapons of mass destruction (WMD) proliferation to states that had legally renounced such weapons as well as to non-state actors, pre-emptive unilateral action even with WMD is being asserted as justifiable - ostensibly in the exercise of the right of self-defence. The legitimacy conferred on armed intervention by the Security Council and, consequently, the universal support that such action enjoys is thus sacrificed for the freedom of unilateral action in pursuit of individual national interest. In the pre-UN era nations waged wars self-righteously claiming their justness whatever the circumstances. To do so today without Security Council authority undermines international law and the unity of the UN system and opens the way to an anarchic global society with no internationally accepted norms.

The problem lies perhaps in the evolution of the global system from a bipolar one to a unipolar system and the exceptionalism demanded for some forms of unilateral action. It also arises from the inroads being made into the theory of state sovereignty as an absolute. The controversial 'humanitarian intervention' speech of Secretary General Kofi Annan in 1999 led to the International Commission on Intervention and State Sovereignty whose report was published at the end of 2001.[1] It asserted that state sovereignty implied a responsibility to protect its citizens and that where a state was unwilling or unable to provide that protection the principle of non-intervention yielded to the international responsibility to protect. However guiding principles and criteria were carefully described in terms of international law and the circumstances warranting action and the procedure for obtaining authority set out. The obvious limitation of this approach is that in the selective application of new principles the powerful states will ensure that their state sovereignty will not be compromised thus provoking the charge of double standards.

Any changes that we propose must discourage unilateral action and seek to facilitate multilateral consensus through UN mechanisms that are palpably effective. No one seriously questions the virtue of co-operative action in the defence of collective security. Empowering one state or a group of states to be the global gendarme without Security Council authority undermines this.

The UN and its Future in the 21st Century

How do we therefore strengthen UN institutions to serve collective security in the current context?

I believe it is essential that we agree on three basic principles before we proceed to consider specific institutional reforms.

- Firstly it is my deep conviction that the founders of the UN intended that there should be equilibrium among the principal organs of the UN for the purposes and principles of the world body to be implemented. Admittedly the Security Council is vested with the primary responsibility for maintaining international peace and security but that is a task performed on behalf of the entire membership of the UN, all of whom have citizens with equal human rights even if the principle of the sovereign equality of all its member states (laid down in Article 2:1 of the UN Charter) has become one of the more glorious myths of the UN today. Today the system is in disequilibrium not only because of the Security Council is the overwhelmingly dominant organ but also because of disequilibrium within the Council. How do we restore equilibrium within the system while accepting the realities of power asymmetry in the world?

- Secondly, in the functioning of the UN system for over six decades there has been an unhealthy compartmentalisation of programmes and a lack of co-ordination even after two waves of well-intentioned reforms launched by the present Secretary General. This arises partly from major powers and major contributors to the UN budget demanding that their nationals be placed in positions of authority and that their agendas be implemented if not through the regular budget then through tied extra-budgetary resources (which are actually more than regular budget resources and finance the larger percentage of UN Secretariat posts). It also arises from the bureaucratic corrosion that accumulates in any large organisation. Thus the principal organs of the UN are not adequately linked, depriving the organisation of valuable cross-fertilisation of ideas and sharing of information that could lead to collective action. Cross cutting issues appear to be dealt with on a system wide basis through inputs from the various departments, agencies and programmes which focus on demonstrating what has been achieved individually and not on synergetic action.

- Finally, we are all aware that the concept of security has expanded vastly. It is no longer possible to regard national or international security in purely military terms. We have a wider view which embraces political elements, economic and environmental factors and social and cultural aspects. The Security Council has recognised this by considering women's rights, AIDS and other non-conventional issues as security issues. Clearly more needs to be done to link the Security Council more closely with the Economic and Social Council and other principal organs, with the work of the specialised agencies and regional economic commissions and by calling for action oriented reports on particular aspects of security related issues where the authority of the Security Council could ensure the attainment of goals such as the Millennium Development Goals (MDG).

New Threats – Terrorism

The terrorist attacks in the United States on 11 September 2001, by their unexpected boldness, their diabolically elaborate inter-continental planning and the tragic scale of the death and destruction they wrought, are now widely regarded as a watershed in the global history of terrorism and political violence. This does not minimise the impact of terrorism in other countries prior to 9/11. Nor does it trivialise the importance of the twelve international treaties and conventions on terrorism adopted well before the events of 11 September 2001. It is, however, a realistic assessment of the repercussions of a terrorist attack on the nerve centres of the sole superpower in the world and the global reaction to it. Nothing after 9/11 will be as it was before. A wounded superpower has not only been driven to act globally on the issue of terrorism but the entire world has responded to what is being seen as a global campaign against terrorism. The United Nations (UN) as the only universal global body empowered by its 191 member states to maintain international peace and security has been at the forefront of this renewed effort to combat the scourge of terrorism. This has helped to provide legitimacy and universality to the campaign as well to establish forums to discuss some of its drawbacks and omissions.

Beyond the formal condemnations of the events of 11 September 2001 adopted both by the Security Council one day afterwards (S/RES/1368(2001)) and by the UN General Assembly on 18 September (A/RES/56/10), the United Nations moved swiftly to adopt practical and effective measures through international co-operation to prevent future acts of terrorism. In this connection UN Secretary-General Kofi Annan underlined three important principles when he addressed the opening of the 56th session of the UN General Assembly one day after the tragic events and again on the 1st October:

- '…terrorist acts are never justified no matter what considerations may be invoked.' At the same time the counter-terrorist campaign should not distract from action on other UN principles and purposes the achievement of which could by itself reduce and eliminate terrorism.

- The adoption of preventive measures to be undertaken on a co-operative basis should be 'in accordance with the Charter and other relevant provisions of international law'.

- The search for legal precision must be subordinated to 'moral clarity' on the subject of terrorism.

This approach ensured that the UN reaction was not one of revenge or retribution but based, as to be expected in a norm-based organisation, on legal concepts and values. It also placed the action to be taken in the context of the anti-terrorism conventions already adopted within the UN framework. Moreover the Secretary-General focused on the protection of civilians – a vital theme in the UN - pointing significantly to the indiscriminate nature of terrorist attacks.

I believe this approach is best practised by the UN entrusting the surveillance of terrorism to a broad-based Commission on Terrorism under the aegis of the Economic and Social Council in addition to the Security Council's mandated tasks.

New Threats – Weapons of Mass Destruction

Disarmament, especially the disarmament of WMDs, is at a critical crossroad. It is over a decade since the end of the Cold War led to an illusion of security as the prospect of global nuclear war receded into the background. The disarmament endeavour did lead to positive results in the past. Concrete reductions of nuclear weapons through actual destruction of missiles followed the INF and START I treaties. Reductions (but not destruction) of deployed strategic weapons followed more recently after the Moscow treaty of May 2002, although most experts do not consider this a disarmament treaty. As a result we do have fewer nuclear weapons deployed today than at the height of the Cold War. The Comprehensive Nuclear Test Ban Treaty (CTBT) was signed in 1996 in a dramatic breakthrough for the advocates of nuclear disarmament who had long seen this as a litmus test of the political will to disarm. These apparent successes are now not only under siege but they stand a real danger of being overturned as nuclear weapons are, quite unabashedly, being given a new rationale and the dangers of both indefinite possession and proliferation have acquired a new urgency. Not only has the threshold for the actual use of nuclear weapons been lowered dangerously but also allegations of WMD possession have been trivialised as *casus belli* without verifiable proof. The ideological basis for the continued possession of nuclear weapons existed in some countries before the events of 11 September 2001, but today counter-terrorism has been widely cited as the reason for massive increases in military expenditure.

Before we can revive the disarmament process let us analyse what afflicts it. The problems confronting the world in so far as WMD are concerned are complex. I would like to place them in five categories. The first is the horizontal proliferation of nuclear weapons beyond the five nuclear weapon states recognised in the Nuclear Non-Proliferation Treaty (NPT). With the South Asian nuclear tests of 1998 we have, *de facto*, eight countries with a nuclear weapon capability (not counting the Democratic People's Republic of Korea). A dilemma, both political and moral, lies at the root of the non-recognition of Israel, India and Pakistan as nuclear weapon states. And yet without their active co-operation we are unable to make progress on nuclear disarmament let alone nuclear abolition. In every one of the cases of proliferation since the NPT was signed in 1968, a recognised nuclear weapon state has either wittingly (for *raisons d'etat*) or unwittingly (through careless custody of nuclear material and /or technology or naïve transfer of technology arrangements) been the source of the transfer of this technology. The burden of guilt, whatever the circumstances, is clear. What are worse are the dual standards being adopted towards proliferation, with some proliferation being regarded as benign and others as being downright evil depending on the nature of the ruling regime in the proliferating country. This Manichean judgement is made in terms of the relationship of the proliferating countries towards particular powers, unmindful of the fact that regimes change and with them the relationships forged with the powers.

The proliferation of nuclear weapons to Israel, India and Pakistan, though not formally recognised, is certainly being accepted as inevitable and irreversible. *Realpolitik* has played its role in this notwithstanding Security Council Resolution 1172 in respect of India and Pakistan. Countries who have had the capability of going nuclear and have not done so have witnessed this 'managed proliferation' with concern. Some may even be encouraged to harbour secret ambitions to go nuclear. The publicly declared stance of the Democratic People's Republic of Korea (DPRK) to withdraw from the NPT and announce its nuclear ambitions has raised the fear of proliferation in Northeast Asia beyond DPRK in a sort of domino effect. We cannot forge a principled multilateral response to violations of non-proliferation norms if some members of the international community choose to look the other way. All this is symptomatic of a weakening of the non-proliferation norm and some cynicism regarding the subjective manner with which it has been implemented.

The second category of problems is connected to the first because of the failure of existing nuclear weapon states to fulfil their promises to disarm and to achieve the total elimination of nuclear weapons. As long as nuclear weapon states continue to enjoy the power, deterrence effects and influence derived directly from nuclear weapon possession we cannot realistically expect the non-proliferation norm to hold indefinitely. This is not to cite the record of nuclear weapon states as extenuating circumstances for nuclear proliferation. No WMD proliferation is acceptable. Our moral and indeed our scientific position would, however, not be complete if we did not at the same time deplore the continued possession of nuclear weapons by those who have them.

The brazen withdrawal of DPRK from the NPT and its open admission of a nuclear weapon programme, Libya's admission and subsequent renunciation of its nuclear weapon development programme in violation of its NPT obligations, Iran's enrichment of uranium, the dramatic revelations of Pakistan's Dr AQ Khan's 'Wallmart' - like nuclear bazaar, and the latest discovery of South Korean scientists engaging in clandestine nuclear activities have all left the international community perplexed as to what credible and effective action can be taken. The International Atomic Energy Agency has asked Iran to sign the Additional Protocol on safeguards as a demonstration of good faith on Iran's part and as a means of enabling the IAEA to expand its verification powers. We may well have more countries following the proliferation route either overtly or covertly, especially since it is a moot point whether the invasion of Iraq has encouraged or deterred more countries to acquire WMD. The 'nth country' syndrome that was widely discussed in apocalyptic terms in the 1950s and 1960s has returned to haunt us.

The NPT was expected to be the bulwark to halt the trend towards proliferation and it has served that purpose admirably for three decades with the exception of Iraq and DPRK. Do we need fresh mechanisms now or do we need to end forever the casteism or *apartheid* between the 'haves' and the 'have-nots'? Those who have nuclear weapons regard it as their 'manifest destiny' while those who do not, appear to be under a 'cargo cult' - if I may borrow a term from the cultural anthropologists who write of the mesmerising effect of manufactured goods being brought into developing countries by plane. Assuming that some supernatural force had endowed these developed industrialised countries with manufactured goods, the traditional societies of Melanesia in the 19th century prayed to the spirits of the dead to bring them cargoes of modern goods for distribution and restore their golden age to them. Sadly today the possession of WMD is seen as an attribute of power and development that can ensure independence and sovereignty.

It is a quest to be 'mimic men' of which VS Naipaul writes in one of his early novels or the 'Brown Sahib' syndrome familiar to South Asians like me. The attractions of nuclear weapons in particular acquire greater urgency for medium to large size countries in conflict-ridden regional situations that have a reasonably strong industrial base to sustain a nuclear weapon development programme. That it conflicts with solemn treaty undertakings and international conventions is seen as less important than the overriding national security interest. After all, the same argument of the supremacy of national interest is used by nuclear weapon states to abrogate treaties, to refuse to sign other internationally agreed conventions to protect global welfare and to actually attempt the legal invention of 'unsigning' treaties with impunity.

The third set of problems arises from the serious emergence of the danger that WMD may be used by terrorists or sub-national groups for anarchist, secessionist or other purposes. This danger predated 11 September 2001. It was among the reasons why the break-up of the Soviet Union was viewed with such alarm by those who cared about the safeguarding of nuclear materials and technology in the former Soviet states and the future of the trained nuclear scientists there. It was the first time in history that a nuclear weapon state had imploded and we have not learned any lessons that would make the next break-up of a nuclear weapon state any easier to manage. The visionary Nunn-Lugar Co-operative Threat Reduction programme has contributed greatly towards mitigating the problem, but despite this too many reports of leakages of material continue to be recorded. It proves not only that the safeguards are still inadequate but also that a demand continues for such materials with many shadowy groups in the market.

After 11 September 2001 when the astonishing scale of the terrorist attacks in the USA were revealed, the relief that WMD were not used was quickly replaced by a deeper anxiety that such use was not beyond the reach of the organisational capacity of Al Qaida and similarly well-funded and fanatical groups with their global reach. That anxiety is well founded not only in respect of nuclear weapons and the more likely danger of a 'dirty bomb' (a device to disperse radioactive material through the use of conventional explosives) but also with biological and chemical weapons where the detection of clandestine programmes is more difficult.

A different category of problems exists in the paralysis of the disarmament machinery and the weakening of the multilateral system which provided the context for constructive and result-oriented multilateral disarmament diplomacy. Twenty-five years after the First Special Session of the UN General Assembly devoted to Disarmament (SSOD I) achieved its remarkable Final Document by consensus we find the machinery it set up for the deliberation and negotiation of disarmament issues in disarray. The 66 member Geneva-based Conference on Disarmament (CD) – a direct descendant of the Eighteen Nation Disarmament Commission (ENDC) – has not even been able to agree on a programme of work because of disagreements on the priorities of the disarmament agenda. Some states believe that the CD should resume work on negotiating a Fissile Material Cut-off Treaty (FMCT) for which a mandate – the Shannon Mandate – was agreed upon sometime ago. Others argue that, concurrently with this, work should also begin on the prevention of an arms race in outer space, on nuclear disarmament and on negative security assurances on the basis of mandates that could be non-negotiating if necessary.

An earlier compromise formula by the then Brazilian Ambassador Amorim has now been elaborated as a proposal from five past Presidents of the CD cutting across group loyalties. This has failed to find acceptance and clearly the main actors in the stalemate are the US and China. A lack-lustre debate is held perfunctorily when the CD meets but increasingly member states are losing faith in the process and some have withdrawn the Ambassadors they had specially accredited to this important body. Misguided calls for the abolition of the CD are dangerous. It is easier to destroy multilateral institutions than to create them. The CD has been idle for long periods before especially during the Cold War and I have no doubt that when political will reappears the CD will resume functioning.

In the cluster of deliberative bodies the First Committee of the General Assembly is the forum for disarmament and security issues. It meets annually during the autumn for approximately five weeks to go through an agenda of items. Some of them are 'hardy perennials' that are debated ritualistically and voted upon. Consensus is reached on a few resolutions but the resolutions on nuclear issues are invariably adopted with a division. Voting patterns have changed over the years with most of the former Warsaw Pact countries now voting with NATO while the countries of the Non-Aligned Movement (NAM) are no longer as tightly-knit as during the Cold War. The Security Council's discussion and action on disarmament issues has been confined to proliferation of WMD as in the Summit held in January 1992. It has also addressed country-specific situations as with Iraq.

The UN and its Future in the 21st Century

Another special meeting of the Security Council to discuss WMD proliferation issues is projected for later this year with a view to creating a mechanism analogous to the Counter-Terrorism Committee (CTC) set up in the immediate aftermath of 9/11.

This, I fear, will only re-ignite the concerns of the non-nuclear weapon states that the casteism of the 'haves' and 'have-nots' is being institutionalised at a time when a more inclusive approach is needed. The more specialised disarmament forum – the Disarmament Commission – failed to meet in its 50th year in 2002 and this year concluded its session without consensus on its future agenda. In addition the Working Group set up by a resolution of the General Assembly to agree on an agenda for a fourth special session of the General Assembly on Disarmament (SSOD IV) failed to reach consensus.

All these diplomatic failures are of course indicative of a general malaise in the political arena and cannot be blamed on the machinery itself or its individual components. Political will is frequently cited in diplomatic negotiations - the presence or absence of which can make a vast difference. Clearly the political will of key countries is more important than others. The generation of political will depends largely on public opinion in democracies, on pressures brought to bear on countries and on the policies pursued by incumbent governments.

Ultimately it is the worldview of a small group of very powerful countries that determines whether multilateral disarmament will work or not. It could decide to let some aspects of multilateral disarmament work in a sort of '*a la carte*' multilateralist approach. This indeed appears to be present situation where on Small Arms and Light Weapons (SALW) we have a Programme of Action being implemented globally. On antipersonnel landmines, the Mine Ban Convention and the Additional Protocol of the CCW Convention are working on parallel tracks. A change of policy of a superpower like the USA can accelerate progress dramatically as happened when the Clinton Administration decided, against pressures from some vested interests, to begin negotiations on a CTBT bringing many of its allies to the table reluctantly. Today with the rejection of the ratification of the CTBT by the US Senate and the current administration's policy the prospects for the entry into force of the CTBT are bleak.

Finally there is the category of problems arising from prevailing strategic or defence doctrines. It is the pursuit of these doctrines that influence decision-making in key countries and until these doctrines are abandoned or revised the current crisis in multilateral disarmament is unlikely to end. During the Cold War, the doctrine of Mutual Assured Destruction (MAD) was well known. The conventional arms superiority of the former USSR resulted in that country's adoption of the nuclear policy of 'no first use', abandoned after the Cold War when NATO was perceived to have conventional arms superiority. Russian diplomats have told me that they were instructed to mine the statements of US representatives during the Cold War to find arguments in favour of this *volte face*!! Today only China and India have 'no first use' policies. It had also been hoped that with the end of the Cold War there would be less reliance on nuclear weapons in military strategies. However NATO – the only surviving military alliance and with additional members – remains wedded to the use of nuclear weapons, admittedly as a weapon of last resort. The efforts of Germany and Canada to have this reviewed have failed so far and small wonder that Russia therefore shows more reliance on nuclear weapons today.

The US, the largest Nuclear Weapon State, has recently issued its Nuclear Posture Review and National Security Strategy. Both documents represent a fundamental change in post-Cold War trends. Firstly, the threshold for the actual use of weapons is being lowered dangerously as pre-emptive uses are planned even against non-nuclear weapon states. The contradiction of this with the Advisory Opinion of the International Court of Justice in 1996 and the Security Council Resolution 984 of 1995 providing security assurances for non-nuclear weapon states is obvious. Secondly the new policy – subsequently ratified by Congressional budgetary approval – is to begin research and development on 'mini-nukes' or low-yield nuclear weapons for specific purposes such as 'bunker busters' to penetrate hardened and deeply buried targets. The period of notice required for a resumption of nuclear testing has also been shortened, although the Bush Administration has repeatedly stated that there is no intention to resume testing 'for the moment'. The other nuclear weapon states are also reportedly modernising their nuclear weapons and continue research and development with a view to developing new generations of weapons.

The new salience being given to nuclear weapons takes place in a context of resurgent militarism as global military expenditure reaches the heights of the Cold War years with the USA clearly in the lead. The unilateral abrogation of the Anti-Ballistic Missile (ABM) Treaty to clear the way for the development and eventual deployment of ballistic missile defence systems will also involve huge investments for a programme of doubtful value, especially with the asymmetric warfare strategy of terrorist groups and the acknowledged vulnerability of the system. The distinction between offensive and defensive military doctrines is becoming blurred. Doctrines, which involve the pre-emptive use of a weapon of mass destruction, institutionalise violence. The distinction between the civilized world basing its actions on law and reason and the world of the terrorist using indiscriminate violence on the basis that the end justifies the means must be maintained at all times.

Reference
1. International Commission on Intervention and State Security. *The Responsibility to Protect*. Ottawa: International Development Research Centre, 2001.

The UN and its Future in the 21st Century

Erskine Childers (1929-1996)
UN Free-thinker, Critic and Constructive Analyst

Sir Richard Jolly

Erskine Childers was one of the radical thinkers and activist of the UN. Before joining the UN in 1967, he had a career as an independent writer and broadcaster on international political and development affairs, specialising in UN issues, serving for a while as a periodic consultant, including on a special mission to the Congo for the then UN Secretary General U Thant. In 1967, he joined the UN, working with many of the UN organisations at all levels and in all regions, including nine years in Asia and many positions with UNDP. He had a particular interest in problems of co-ordination, development and humanitarian operations and public communication and constituency-building.

He formally retired from the UN in 1989, after 22 years of service. But his lively interest continued, touring widely and lecturing and writing on UN matters as well as taking on a number of consultancies. In 1996, he became Secretary General of WFUNA, the World Federation of the United Nation Associations, dying suddenly five months later, shortly after giving a speech at its 50th anniversary Congress in Luxembourg.

Erskine Childers was the accomplished scion of one of Ireland's most distinguished families. He bore the same name as his father, who was President from 1974 to 1975, and his grandfather, the author of *Riddle of the Sands* and gun runner for the Volunteers, who served as a British navy flying officer in the first World War before being executed by the Free State forces during the Civil War in 1922.

The UN and its Future in the 21st Century

As a young man, Erskine had moved rapidly to an international life. He studied modern languages at Trinity College, Dublin and then politics and international relations at Stanford in California. By the age of 21, he was travelling to many countries as Vice-President of the United States National Students Association.

His passionate commitments to the UN and to internationalism embraced both North and South. Combined with his journalistic skills he honed a fine vituperative style. He wanted smaller, independent minded states like Ireland to stand up against the myopic elite of the larger countries. Irish neutrality, he argued, was absolutely essential to establish a special relationship with Third World countries, and he mourned the way this had been somewhat diminished by membership of the European Community.

One can only imagine the vituperation with which he would have opposed the Iraq War of 2003-4. He pulled no punches in 1991, referring to the 'combination of buying and bullying' which had intimidated many other countries in the UN into supporting military intervention in the Gulf War, pointing out that the military cost of the war had exceeded 12 years of the UN's global budget. 'Never again should our United Nations and our Charter – which are not the property of the major powers – be left so vulnerable to such apocalyptic abuse'. He called for the great majority of the UN members to repair the damage.

In 1994, with Brian Urquhart, Erskine Childers wrote what still stands as one of the most important and broad ranging studies on the actions required for *Renewing the United Nations System*. This study followed and built on an earlier, pioneering report on leadership within the UN, noting major weaknesses in the way governments selected and appointed the UN Secretary-General and other executive heads in the UN system – and how these procedures could be improved.

What makes these two studies impressive and so important is their ability to be hard-headed but not 'too realistic', to make proposals which were eminently sensible and which, at the same time, recaptured the vision of the early years of the UN. Indeed in the introduction, they referred to this period as 'an oasis of reason, intellectual analysis and idealism' which led to the creation, even before the war ended of 'a blueprint for the post-war world and the institutions which were to 'save succeeding generations from the scourge of war.' *Renewing the United Nations System* took a hard look at the UN system as it is and then moved on to analyse the machinery for equity and sustainable development, for operational activities, for human rights and for humanitarian emergency capacities, together with the decision-making machinery, the finance and management and the nature of the international civil service required for its implementation. The report looked to a more democratic United Nations by indicating various ways in which non-governmental organisations could play a bigger part within the UN.

The analysis and the many recommendations of these reports are noteworthy - and still of great relevance - because they look at the whole of the UN system, not merely the secretariat but also UNDP, UNICEF and the other funds, the specialised agencies including ILO, WHO, FAO, UNESCO, the High Commissions for refugees and for human rights, the institutions dealing with emergencies – and the Bretton Woods system, the latter so often forgotten in considering the UN. Though the analysis and recommendations are visionary and challenging, the whole report is infused with the practical insights and examples which could only come from those who had been insiders to the system.

One feature of the report still worth quoting is the way it takes on several of the myths and derisory epithets so often used to dismiss the relevance of the UN; it is a 'a vast and sprawling bureaucracy', 'a gigantic paper-factory', built on 'large and extravagant budgets'. In a now much quoted rebuttal, they pointed out that excluding peacekeeping staff, the World Bank and the IMF (and now also the WTO), 'the entire UN system world-wide, serving the interests of over six million people in 192 countries, employs [about 50,000 persons] no more workers than the civil service in

The UN and its Future in the 21st Century

the American State of Wyoming, population 501,000. Its staff is actually smaller than the number of public service employees of the city of Stockholm in Sweden, population 760,000'.

The whole report deserves to be read, not summarised. Many of its recommendations, even ten years after they were first put forward, are full of relevance – and even after Kofi Annan, the present Secretary General, has implemented a number of them and made reform a major part of his administration.

But as we approach the 60th anniversary of the UN, it is time to recall again the words with which Erskine Childers and his co-worker, Brian Urquhart, ended the penultimate section of their report, immediately before listing their recommendations. They ended:

> The time for warnings is now past. It may well be that the possibility of the extinction of the human species by weapons of mass destruction has receded. There remains, however, the increasing possibility of a slower form of extinction through indifference and by failure to act.
>
> The instruments for such action do not need to be invented. The United Nations system is in place, however much updating and strengthening it may need. The UN system needs the urgent and sustained attention of all governments, They are directly responsible for it, and it is their responsibility to ensure that at long last the warnings are heeded.

The United Nations at the Crossroads of Ideals and Reality

Ramesh Thakur

A wag is said to have remarked that 'The interesting thing about Richard Wagner's music is that it ain't as bad as it sounds'. The same might be said of the United Nations: it is not quite as bad as it is often made out to be. If the organisation is in crisis, it is a crisis of expectations. Its Charter begins with the grand words 'We the peoples of the United Nations'. The reality is that it functions as an organisation of, by and for member states. The great Soviet-era dissident Alexander Solzhenitsyn once remarked that at the UN, the people of the world are served up to the designs of governments. The United Nations needs to achieve a better balance between the wish of the peoples and the will of governments; between the aspirations for a better world and its performance in the real world; between the enduring political reality enveloping and at times threatening to suffocate it and the vision of an uplifting world that has inspired generations of dreamers and idealists to work for the betterment of humanity across cultural, religious and political borders. There is no better example of this than Erskine Childers himself: with few illusions about UN flaws and shortcomings and the need for reforms, he nevertheless remained, to the end, a dedicated servant of the organisation's founding ideals.

The United Nations is at once the symbol of humanity's collective aspirations for a better life in a safer world for all, a forum for negotiating the terms of converting these collective aspirations into a common programme of action, and the principal international instrument for the realisation of the aspirations and the implementation of the plans. The Charter of the United Nations was a triumph of hope and idealism over the experience of two world wars. The flame flickered in the chill winds of the Cold War, but is yet to die out. The global public goods of peace, prosperity, sustainable development and good governance cannot be achieved by any country acting on its own. The United Nations is still the symbol of our dreams for a better world, where weakness can be compensated by justice and fairness, and the law of the jungle replaced by the rule of law, although the lion in the jungle may prefer otherwise. It is helpful to be reminded by Judge Rosalyn Higgins, in the third Erskine Childers Lecture in 1999, of the World Court's role in keeping international peace and security. Three years later, Denis Halliday returned to the theme of a single standard of international law.

In sum, the United Nations has to strike a balance between realism and idealism. In the midst of the swirling tides of change, the UN must strive also for a balance between the desirable and the possible. Its decisions must reflect current realities of military and economic power. It will be incapacitated if it alienates its most important members. In a world in which there is only one universal international organisation but also only one superpower, the UN must tread a fine line so as neither to become irrelevant to the security imperatives of the US as today's supreme power, nor become a mere rubber stamp for US designs. The challenge posed to the international organisation by the unilateralist impulse in Washington is discussed by Caroline Lucas MEP in the 2003 Erskine Childers Lecture. The UN will lose credibility, its very *raison d'être*, if it compromises core values. The United Nations is the repository of international idealism, and Utopia is fundamental to its identity. Even the sense of disenchantment and disillusionment on the part of some cannot be understood other than against this background.

Human Security

One of the UN's early great achievements was to oversee the decolonisation of large parts of the human family. Emerging from colonial

The UN and its Future in the 21st Century

rule in the shadow of the Cold War that was transcendental as well as global, many of the new countries were less interested in the Moscow-Washington security rivalry than in development. Because they dominated the UN membership by sheer weight of numbers, their particular focus meant that the organisation soon acquired two great mandates: peace and security, and growth and development.

In the 2001 lecture, Professor Paul Rogers notes that with the end of the Cold War, the much anticipated peace dividend failed to materialise. Instead there seemed to be a spurt of ethnonational conflicts, complex humanitarian emergencies and even genocide with massive civilian deaths. The intensification of conflict and human vulnerability blurred the Westphalian line between the domestic and international spheres of human activity. In parallel with this, the dominant paradigm of national security, with its narrow focus on territorial integrity, state sovereignty and political independence, began to weaken under assault from the broader concept of human security.

National security puts the individual at the service of the state, including the ultimate acts of killing others and being killed oneself as and when called for duty by one's government. *Human security* puts the individual at the centre of debate, analysis and policy. He or she is paramount; the state is but a collective instrument to protect human life and enhance human welfare. The fundamental components of human security can be put at risk by external aggression, but also by factors within a country, including 'security' forces where the state is too strong and, at the other end of the spectrum, structural anarchy under conditions of state failure. The reformulation of national security into human security is simple, yet has profound consequences for how we see the world, how we organise our political affairs, how we make choices in public and foreign policy, and how we relate to fellow human beings from different countries and civilisations.

The linkage between the two great agendas of security and development became clearer and more widely accepted after the end of the Cold War. 'Peacebuilding' was the conceptual bridge connecting both agendas. It fits far more comfortably under the conceptual umbrella of human than national security, whether it be with regard to eradicating landmines, protecting civilians from atrocities or reducing maternal, infant and HIV/AIDS mortality through improved health care systems and better access to affordable medicine.

The Changing World Context

The world has changed profoundly and fundamentally, in ways both good and bad, since the birth of the United Nations in the ashes of the Second World War. The issues and preoccupations of the new millennium present new and different types of challenges from those that faced the world in 1945. With the new realities and challenges have come corresponding new expectations for action and new standards of conduct in national and international affairs. The revolution in information technology – which makes global communications instantaneous and provides immediate access to information worldwide – has heightened awareness of conflicts and depredation, poverty and hunger wherever they may be occurring, combined with compelling visual images of the resultant suffering.

When the UN was founded, its membership consisted of 51 states. Today it stands at 191. The newer members have typically been developing and ex-colonial countries that brought to the UN their own set of priorities and concerns and thereby altered the balance of the organisation's work agenda. Alongside the growth in the number of states there has occurred the rise of civil society actors who have mediated state-citizen relations and given flesh and blood to the concept of 'We the peoples of the United Nations'. On balance they have been a positive force for the good, for example with respect to the progressive advancement of the human rights agenda, international humanitarian law, gender protection and empowerment and the protection and conservation of the environment. The new actors have

The UN and its Future in the 21st Century

brought a wide range of new voices, perspectives, interests, experiences and aspirations. Together, they have added depth and texture to the increasingly rich tapestry of international society and brought important institutional credibility and practical expertise to the policy debates.

This has been especially valuable in the post-Cold War context with a new emphasis on democratisation, human rights and good governance alongside the persisting reality of internal wars and civil conflicts, often accompanied with ugly political and humanitarian repercussions. Where political institutions are inadequate and political structures insufficiently robust, the transfer of power can be chaotic, disorderly and violent. Populations are vulnerable to manipulation, exploitation and abuse by unscrupulous armed bandits. The weakness of state structures and institutions in many countries has heightened the challenges and risks of nation-building, and sometimes tempted armed groups to try to seize the levers of political power in order to exploit the resources of economic wealth, including 'conflict diamonds'. Internal conflicts are made more complex and lethal by modern technology and communications and in particular by the proliferation of cheap, highly destructive small arms which find their way into the hands of child soldiers. Violence becomes a way of life with catastrophic consequences for civilians caught in the crossfire.

Moreover, few modern conflicts are purely internal. The networks that sustain them can involve a range of ancillary problems like trafficking in arms, drugs and children, terrorism, and refugee flows. Whole regions can be quickly destabilised. Sometimes the rich world is deeply implicated. Civil conflicts are fuelled by arms and monetary transfers that originate in the developed world, and in turn their destabilising effects are felt in the developed world in everything from globally interconnected terrorism to refugee flows the export of drugs and the spread of infectious disease and organised crime.

Yearly we face the paradox of the major challenges remaining constant, while many of the contingencies demanding urgent and immediate action are inherently unanticipated and unpredictable. For example, war is a constant feature of international relations, yet some of the major outbreaks of armed conflict, internal and inter-state, have caught us by surprise with respect to the locales, protagonists and issues. Poverty has remained stubbornly persistent, yet the distribution of pockets of poverty has changed over the course of the UN's lifetime. One of the best examples of this, of course, is East Asia, which has lifted record numbers of people out of poverty in a remarkably short period. At the same time we face today some challenges that were not and could not have been foreseen in 1945, including, for example, global warming and HIV/AIDS. With '9/11' we saw elements of conceptual confusion between traditional security, challenges to state sovereignty and the threats of terrorism from 'rogue' actors, including non-state actors, with access to weapons of mass destruction.

The primary purpose of the United Nations is the maintenance of international peace and security. The strategic logic underpinning multilateral institutions is that of a world united in action on the road to a common destiny. Reflecting the conviction that the use of force under international auspices may sometimes be necessary in the cause of peace, Chapter 7 of the UN Charter spells out many provisions in relation to collective enforcement. Yet one of the lessons of recent times is that the United Nations is not good at waging wars.

By contrast, the organisation has been especially good at a slow, steady and unremitting effort to find political, economic, legal and institutional alternatives to military force as a way of tackling problems of security as well as development, good governance and environmental protection. This ambitious project of international institution building is far from complete. The organising principle of global governance is multilateralism, and the United Nations lies at the very core of the multilateral system of global governance – governance without global government. The system of collective security proved illusory from the start, and the procedures for resolving disputes peacefully have also proven to be generally elusive. The major UN contribution to peace and security during the Cold War took the form of consensual peacekeeping operations. After the Cold War, this expanded to multidimensional peace operations to reflect the more demanding complex humanitarian emergencies.

In the meantime, however, the human rights and human security agenda had greatly expanded and in the 1990s was often expressed in the form of the so-called challenge of humanitarian intervention. Increasing use was made also of sanctions as an instrument of international statecraft. According to several data sets, the number of armed conflicts rose steadily until the end of the Cold War, peaked in the early 1990s, and has declined since then. The UN Security Council was revitalised with the end of the Cold War, with a jump in resolutions (especially under the enforcement chapter 7 of the Charter) peacekeeping missions and sanctions regimes, with an accompanying fall in the use of the veto by the permanent members.[1]

Often, the developing countries found themselves scrambling to resist, typically in UN forums, the fast-changing norms of humanitarian action and compulsory disarmament, even pre-emptive disarmament and regime change. At the same time, the rapid pace of events placed increased strains on the creaking UN system and intensified the urgency of demands for changes in the workings, structures and policy responses of the organisation.

Reforming the United Nations

The topic of UN reforms, so dear to Childers, is addressed by almost all the contributors in this collection. The United Nations has to operate today in a global environment that is vastly more challenging, complex and demanding than the world of 1945. If existing institutions fail to keep pace with the changing world around us and the expectations of citizens, they will fall by the wayside and be replaced by new forms of association. The

The UN and its Future in the 21st Century

price of continued relevance and survival of the United Nations is thus continual change, adaptation and learning by the organisation. Set up to manage the world in the revolutionary conditions prevailing after a major world war, the organisation has had simultaneously to reflect, regulate and respond to the changing circumstances all around it since 1945, and in particular since the end of the Cold War.

To be faithful to the nations and peoples of the world who have kept faith with it for six decades, the UN must persevere in its efforts to consolidate its strengths, fill in the gaps and eliminate wasteful habits and procedures. Under Kofi Annan's stewardship, the United Nations has been receptive rather than resistant to reform, far more so than is commonly realised. In 1997, the newly elected Secretary-General announced major structural changes alongside budget and staff cuts in order to streamline the unwieldy body.[2] In 2002, he unveiled the second stage of his reform programme, calling for a shift away from endless meetings and reports and a greater focus on the things that really matter to the world's people.[3] Internal structural changes have streamlined co-ordination, facilitated information sharing, strengthened cohesion and given greater strategic direction to the work of the world body.

Efforts to emphasise reform as an ongoing process are reflected also in a number of reviews, initiatives and developments outside the Secretariat. The Brahimi Panel looked back on the half-century's experience of peacekeeping in order to bring it into line with the realities of the new century.[4] Its report contained far-reaching recommendations on improving the efficiency and effectiveness of UN peace operations. The report also underlined the importance of structural conflict prevention, and the integral linkage between peacekeeping and peacebuilding. Other reports have underlined the UN's new-found capacity and willingness to engage in serious introspection with regard to some painful episodes in its history and draw the necessary lessons from them. In an externally commissioned report on the genocide in Rwanda,[5] and through a report of the Secretary-General himself on the fall of Srebrenica,[6] the UN offered candid and critical accounts of the shortcomings in UN peacekeeping for public debate and reflection.

The Security Council has been working better, with innovative means of ensuring more openness and transparency in its decision-making and greater consultation with troop-contributing countries as well as other member states. The Council has also been more daring and imaginative in tackling threats to peace and security on a broader front, for example with respect to the trade in conflict diamonds and a special session on HIV/AIDS as a threat to international peace and security. The General Assembly and the Economic and Social Council (ECOSOC) have made efforts to improve their work methods and standing with more focused and practical treatment of strategic agenda items. The Monterrey conference on financing for development was unprecedented in bringing together different parts of the international system, including the international financial institutions.

The net result of the cycle of reforms and reviews has been to enable the UN to act with more unity of purpose, coherence of efforts, and agility in coping with many challenges over the last five years, including Kosovo, East Timor and Sierra Leone. The 2002 *Human Development Report* marked a new milestone in the organisation saying what needs to be said with regard to good governance.

Reform as Work in Progress

This does not mean that the UN can sit back and rest on its laurels. The agenda for internal reform is never complete for any organisation. The United Nations must not change reluctantly, adapting only grudgingly to the pressure of circumstances. Rather, it must anticipate, lead and embrace change. But it can do so only with the will of member states, the commitment of staff and the support of the peoples of the world. It must continue to change the way decisions are made.

The UN and its Future in the 21st Century

The responses to date to calls for UN action have not been as prompt, effective or uniform as they need to become. The gap between the UN's promise and performance remains unacceptably large. Few can be confident that the next group turning to the UN for protection will not be cruelly betrayed because the world body lacks the ability to make critical decisions quickly, or the mandate and resources to act. Dame Margaret Anstee, in her lecture delivered in 2000, noted that the crisis confronting the UN intensified in the 1990s, at the same time as the need for an effective UN became more urgent.

For most people, the mention of UN reform conjures up either one of two scenarios: reforming the structure, composition and procedures of the Security Council; or eliminating waste, inefficiency, bureaucratic rigidity, costliness and so on associated with the world organisation. With governments in many Western countries, and with ordinary people in many developing countries, the UN is often seen as a bloated, high-cost, junket-loving irrelevance to their real needs and concerns – little more than a talk-fest.

To deliver on the core missions of the organisation, the capacity of the United Nations in general – and of the Security Council, the General Assembly and ECOSOC in particular – have to be strengthened. Structural reforms in the Security Council remain stalemated and most countries see it as having been captured by the major powers. As Razali Ismail and Patricia McKenna noted in the 1997 and 1998 Erskine Childers Lectures, the Security Council is neither democratic nor representative. The structural flaws and procedural bottlenecks in the Council reflect power imbalances and conflicting claims on values and interests along the North-South axis.

The main donors are frustrated with the protracted, wasteful and counter-productive posturing in the General Assembly. The smaller states in particular find the present processes too complex, protracted, demanding and altogether too formidable to be genuine participants and not merely

The UN and its Future in the 21st Century

ringside spectators. We need simplified structures and streamlined processes, with roles and responsibilities clearly delineated, which will restore their sense of ownership and empowerment. The frequent policy paralysis in the two major political organs, the Security Council and the General Assembly, also places a premium on the political role of the Secretary-General. Summit conferences become battlegrounds for vested groups to carry on ideological trench warfare by other means.

But the burden of changing all this rests with governments, not the organisation. Dame Margaret notes how the reform of the organisation is vital, but root-and-branch reform has been held hostage to the vested interests of member states.

The philosophy underpinning Kofi Annan's 2002 report, *Strengthening the United Nations: an Agenda for Further Change*,[3] can be summed up in a few words: clarify, simplify, rationalise, streamline and evaluate. There were five principal messages.

First, the UN must be clear on what to do before it can learn how to do it well. There is a need to shed some accumulated responsibilities that are no longer relevant in today's world, in order to devote more focussed attention on today's urgent issues like terrorism, water scarcity, HIV/AIDS, human rights, ageing, etc. The Secretariat, like any bureau, is a means of structuring political vision into a feasible legislative agenda. The landmark Millennium Summit of September 2000 marked an unprecedented global consensus on the human condition and what to do about it. The motivating spirit behind the sustained attention to UN reforms is how the ambitious template of the Millennium Declaration can best be translated into an achievable agenda of action within a realistic timeframe, through institutional, programmatic and administrative arrangements.

Second, the UN must simplify and rationalise its rules of procedure and processes in order to reduce complexity, cut paperwork and time, and increase efficiency and cost-effectiveness. The organisation cannot become

The UN and its Future in the 21st Century

captive to the tyranny of trivia. So much of the UN's work takes the form of providing documentation and facilities (including interpretation and translation) for debates and decisions by the governments of the world that the efficiency and effectiveness of these services need continual improvement and modernisation. At present there is too much paperwork which is too complex and full of jargon, too long and often produced too late. The organisation needs fewer meetings, simpler processes and shorter documents written in clear and crisp language.

Third, the UN system is dispersed across the world, comprising a number of different units often working together with partners from government, civil society and the private sector. This places a premium on co-ordination. UN agencies, funds and programmes working in each country should be able to pool their resources and undertake joint programming; and establish common databases and knowledge networks.

To achieve its goals, the UN involves all stakeholders and forges new partnerships with governments, the private sector and non-governmental organisations (NGOs), a trend welcomed by most contributors in this volume. The UN works closely with civil society organisations to combat disease, poverty, humanitarian disasters, and to build, consolidate and monitor norms. The relationship with civil society has been examined by a panel of experts who, having consulted broadly, submitted their recommendations in 2004 on how to strengthen the UN-civil society partnership.

Another Annan achievement has been to make the UN much more welcoming towards the private sector. In 1999 the Secretary-General urged global business leaders to make globalisation work for all the people of the world. They responded to this challenge, and the resulting Global Compact provides the UN with a framework of ten core principles, drawn from human rights, labour and environmental standards, for involving the private sector in its various development goals. The Global Compact has the potential to be an important instrument for instilling civic virtue in the

The UN and its Future in the 21st Century

global marketplace.

Fourth, there is a serious disconnection between the establishment of programme priorities and the allocation of resources to achieve common goals. There is little coherence between the disparate planning and budgeting exercises and decisions on institutional priorities are made in isolation from decisions on the use of scarce resources. Long timelines, excessive micro-management, limited budgetary flexibility and arbitrary resource constraints are not helpful to efficiency and efficacy. The planning and budgeting cycle must be simplified, rationalised and made more efficient.

Finally, and this would have been of particular interest to Erskine Childers, the report looked at how to attract and keep the best people as UN staff by offering them a rewarding career as international civil servants. The reforms were never meant to be a cost-cutting exercise. Rather, the goal is to have the right people in the right jobs, with the appropriate structures in place to let them get on with their jobs and be rewarded or sanctioned for their performance. The UN has to be lean, but must not be mean. Nor must cost-cutting be driven by ideological extremism to the point where relentless shedding of 'excess' fat turns the organisation into 'UN Lite'. At the same time, the work ethos of the organisation must be transformed from a culture of entitlements and automatic increments to a culture of results-based performance and rewards.

Conclusion

Shakespeare's aphorism is as applicable to organisations as to individuals: 'the evil that men do lives after them, the good is oft interred with their bones'. Let it not be so with the United Nations. Rather, let us recall with pride its many accomplishments. Razali Ismail gives us a good summary: decolonisation, elimination of apartheid, human rights promotion, refugee protection, peacekeeping and peacemaking missions, international law

The UN and its Future in the 21st Century

expansion and extension, non-proliferation, environmental conservation, and other common problems requiring collective action.

The United Nations was established to provide predictability and order in a world in constant flux. Charged with the stewardship of the world's collective destiny, the UN is both the symbol of a common future for the betterment of all humanity, and the institutional means of bringing about such a better future for all of humanity. The debate over Iraq in 2002–04 demonstrated the true test of UN relevance: both as a brake on an unjustified and unilateral resort to war, and as a forum for legitimising the collective decision to enforce community demands on outlaw regimes.

Dr Jenny Tonge commented in her 2004 lecture that we live in a time when multilateralism is under unprecedented challenge, from arms control to climate change, international criminal justice and the use of military force overseas. At such a time, it becomes especially important to reaffirm, as Paul Rogers did in his 2001 lecture, the role of the United Nations as the principal embodiment of the principle of multilateralism, and the main forum for its pursuit. As Razali already noted in 1997, the causes and consequences of public policy challenges and decisions are international, but the authority for addressing them is still vested in states. The UN's mandates are global, while its staffing and financial resources are less than that of major municipal authorities. Hence the dilemma confronting the United Nations of doing too little and too late, or being over-committed and over-stretched.

Member states are entitled to demand value for money, to insist that the funds they provide should be spent as efficiently as possible, with the emphasis on results and outcomes rather than process. If the organisation fails to accommodate its structures, processes and agendas to the transformations sweeping the world, it will risk atrophy and fade into irrelevance. But equally, if the United Nations does deliver on its side of the bargain, member governments will have to consider ways of funding it better for achieving agreed priorities. They too must be prepared to pay

The UN and its Future in the 21st Century

money for value.

If we want multilateralism to be the preferred route, then strengthening the UN and making it more effective and relevant is imperative. For its performance has been patchy and variable. It has been neither uniform in its response nor consistent in the quality of services provided. The urgency for structural reform of the intergovernmental organs – the Security Council, the General Assembly and ECOSOC – is now extreme, and the work of the high-level panel plus the dynamics of the international political environment have created a window of opportunity that, once closed, may not open again for some considerable time. If the UN is to respond positively to the rising tide of demands and expectations against a steady-state base of resources, it must lift the overall quality and professionalism of its decision-making. Internal reforms initiated by the Secretary-General are an effort to redesign and rededicate the organisation so that in its structure and by its operations, it helps to bring about a world where fear is changed to hope, want gives way to dignity, and apprehensions are turned into aspirations.

References

1. Wallensteen P, Johansson P. Security Council Decisions in Perspective. In: Malone DM, ed. *The UN Security Council: from the Cold War to the 21st Century.* Boulder, Co: Lynne Rienner, 2004: 17-33.
2. *Renewing the United Nations: a Program for Reform.* Report of the Secretary-General. New York: United Nations doc. A/51/950, 14 July 1997.
3. *Strengthening of the United Nations: an Agenda for Further Change.* Report of the Secretary-General. New York: United Nations doc. A/57/387, 23 September 2002.
4. *Report of the Panel on United Nations Peace Operations.* New York: United Nations doc. A/55/305-S/2000/809, 21 August 2000.
5. *Report of the Independent Inquiry into the Actions of the United Nations during the 1994 Genocide in Rwanda.* New York: United Nations, 15 December 1999.

The UN and its Future in the 21st Century

6. *Report of the Secretary-General Pursuant to General Assembly Resolution 53/35 (1998).* New York: United Nations Secretariat, November 1999.

The United Nations in the Twenty-First Century: Prospects for Reform

Razali Ismail

The United Nations is in urgent need of reform, but there is no agreement on what should be done or how this can be achieved, particularly between the developed and developing countries, but also within the UN itself. In particular, the five permanent members and the developing countries differ over the future of the Security Council and the role of the veto. UN peacekeeping is over-stretched, and the member states need to reassess what it can and cannot be expected to do. The UN must work more closely with non-governmental organisations, as in the eradication of poverty and achieving sustainability.

I am honoured to be asked to deliver the first Erskine Childers memorial lecture. Erskine Childers was a true multilateralist who never detracted from attempting to bring about a United Nations committed to a 'world community living in peace, under the laws of justice'. There were others similarly committed, and there are compatriots now who at every milestone in the development of the UN, try to give effect to these aspirations. As an insider, if I may call myself one, often frustrated and jaded by the mundane manner in which business in the UN is usually conducted, I cannot but be impressed by the tenacity of such committed globalists and multilateralists.

The UN and its Future in the 21st Century

The Need for Reform

Many who have observed the operations of the UN have concluded that the world organisation is in need of reform. Proposals for revamping the UN have proliferated in recent years. Some say that almost everything about UN peacekeeping in the post-Cold War environment needs to be reconsidered and reconstructed. Others contend that the Security Council needs to be refashioned to rectify long-standing imbalances; that the UN's development activates need to be streamlined and redirected, the Economic and Social Council needs to be recast, the organisation's finances and accounting practices have to be improved, the international civil service needs to be reduced in size, and the UN needs to be depoliticised and pruned, primed and prodded, toward greater efficiency. The case for better efficiency, co-ordination, and streamlining of the UN Secretariat and its principal organs and specialised agencies is incontrovertible.

The system has, however, proved impervious to change. The complex and diffuse nature of Secretariat operations, run often in semi-independent fashion by various agency chiefs, with competing or duplicating mandates, frustrates purposeful and effective direction. Successive Secretaries-General have been unable or unwilling to impose authority, sometimes for fear of offending a major power. The fault lies on both sides of the house, especially when member states pursue equivocal policies, asking for new mandates and therefore resources for the organisation.

Listening to all this discourse, there is considerable *déjà vu* in today's penchant for UN reform. Talk of reform has been continuous for almost 45 years, although in differing degrees. What is striking is that little by way of reform has actually been accomplished, beyond creeping incremental adjustments. Resistance, inertia and lack of consensus for change have time and again prevailed, and reform has remained much more of an aspiration than a fact. If the UN is to adjust to reflect the twenty-first century and to cope with new demands, it is important that all should share a common premise of what constitutes reform in order to lend the requisite authority to

The UN and its Future in the 21st Century

the UN as a multilateral system, to extend its legitimacy and to strengthen its promotion and compliance with international law. For this purpose it is necessary to assess and come to terms with the UN's inception and history.

The Past

The current politics and structure of the UN continue to bear a strong imprint of its foundation. The establishment of the UN arose from a post-world war situation, with the ideas and institutional force originating from either side of the Atlantic. The ideals and values expressed in the UN Charter were, and remain, the ideals and values of the group of victor nations of the Second World War led by the United States. The headquarters of all the principal agencies and the parent institution itself, stand grouped on either side of the Atlantic, shaping the UN political culture. Of the first four UN Secretaries-General, three came from Western Europe. Only one of the five permanent Security Council members (the P-5) came from outside that frame of reference.

The Cold War also reflected the inter-play of politics of the Atlantic. The two superpowers purposefully chose not to repose the conduct of their vital national security interests in the UN. The collective security that the UN system could theoretically provide was not considered in any way adequate to the protection of essential superpower concerns. Regional military alliances, which underpinned their respective leadership of opposing blocs, were preferred over the uncertain and increasingly disparate framework of the UN. For example, when some measure of nuclear arms control was finally judged to be in mutual superpower interest, it was done so by bilateral means and not within the UN framework.

In the context of the UN reform process at the moment, it is evident that the founder members of the UN place a high premium on the fact that reform should not in any way or manner affect their rights, prerogatives and status. Major powers also fear that they may lose access to senior positions in the

The UN and its Future in the 21st Century

UN Secretariat, where common practice assures key jobs for P-5 nationals. In the UN vocabulary, the extended rights and privileges of the P-5 are called the 'cascade effect', and even extend to permanent representation on the International Court of Justice. The Secretary-General has the power, if he is willing to use it, to change these practices.

Values and Practicalities

As the twenty-first century draws nearer we are witnessing an era where foreign policy and international relations are increasingly values-driven. The United States and other major countries form the vanguard of what amounts to a universal crusade to spread doctrines and practice of their version of good governance and democracy, in tandem with wider acceptance of liberal market economic policy as the pathway to modernisation. But a profound paradox emerges here. As the world grows more democratic, so the UN becomes less democratic - or at least mired in ways of governance reflecting its formative period, which fail to mirror today's world and relative global influence. Realists argue that there is no correlation between a more democratic world and a more democratic multilateral system; that no intrinsic linkages exist. That is an argument that rests upon the distribution of power and those that want to maintain their built-in advantage. The signs are that the fundamental logic of such an argument will be put to the test sooner rather than later in the century ahead.

Critical reflection drives us to the conclusion that despite urgency and obvious need, the UN is probably not going to be reformed in a meaningful way. Differences among member states stemming from power-political rivalries and 'ideological' antagonisms have been fundamental obstacles to UN reform. These differences continue today. Even as the debate between East and West lapsed into obsolescence, the debate between North and South continues, with emphasis on conflicting claims on fundamental values and perspectives. The UN remains a stake and a prize in this

The UN and its Future in the 21st Century

escalating debate. Every proposal for change in the organisation is assessed in the light of advantages bestowed upon one or the other side, and every recommendation for reform offered by one is predictably resisted by the other. Such a situation has tended to cause political gridlock everywhere.

The developing countries of the South regard the UN as a place of last recourse, not having the Group of 7 (G-7) or the Organization for Economic Co-operation and Development, and having to bend to the conditionalities imposed by the Bretton Woods institutions (the World Bank and the International Monetary Fund). These countries believe in the centrality of the UN being a universal house, where they plead their case every September at the General Assembly (GA). They have not accepted the so-called 'division of labour' between the UN and other multilateral bodies like the World Bank, IMF, and the World Trade Organization, where the World Bank is accorded primacy in finance and development, the IMF in structural adjustment, and the WTO in trade and investment regimes. The UN is only allowed to articulate the normative description of 'soft issues' such as sustainable development, population and refugees, human rights and humanitarian issues.

The frailty of such a role for the UN is most recently evident in the outcome of the GA special session in June 1997, which reviewed implementation of Agenda 21 and the commitments of the Earth Summit. The outcome reflected the inability of the UN to grapple with failure of governments to meet commitments and its weakness in being able to catalyse the means and resources to operationalise sustainable development. The UN has precious little to translate words into real action.

Enthusiasm for reform is also unevenly distributed within the UN itself. For many of those Secretariat officials who have been busy 'reforming' for the last 15 years, the possibility of genuine change is greeted with cynicism. For others in the bureaucracy, the prospect of change is threatening, and the tendency to delay or derail reform via resistance from the inside is quite real.

Peacekeeping and the Security Council

The one huge task accorded to the UN is the maintenance of international peace and security. But this is within the parish and exclusive control of the Security Council, which is very much an elitist structure that the developing countries see in need of urgent reform in order to level the playing field and to broaden the decision-making process. If the UN was created by states to serve the interests of states, the states of the South are now insisting on their rights to be counted in the name of sovereign equality. Every aspect of UN reform has to factor in this consideration.

The Working Group on the reform of the Security Council is an amphitheatre for the above. It is not merely about the addition of permanent members to those that can pay for Council seats. The developing countries have waited four decades to become permanent members, and this has been made possible by Germany and Japan making their own justifiable claims to become permanent members, and the concurrent interest of the present permanent members to gain wider support for reducing their financial contributions to both the regular and peacekeeping budgets. This working group must wrestle with the question of the veto - the most intractable issue of reform which personifies the inherent inequality of the majority of members, who would like to see its scope limited and eventually eliminated. The reform of the Security Council hangs on the ability of the P-5 to make the necessary adjustments, at least by voluntary constraint, not to abuse use of the veto as they have done since 1945 for their own imperatives.

An important aspect of the reform of the Security Council has to do with the concerns of a dozen or so important countries who have traditionally supported the multilateral thrust and philosophy of the UN in all its aspects, but who themselves will not profit from an expansion of the Security Council and particularly the addition of new permanent members. I refer

The UN and its Future in the 21st Century

here to countries like Canada, New Zealand, Italy, Spain, Mexico and others in the developing world who aspire to be permanent members but who may well lose in the race. Their position ensures further division within the UN when Security Council reform is instituted.

All aspects of UN reform have to relate to the overall backdrop of the international scene today. It must be recognised that the gap between the legal and political sovereignty of states and their ability to give that sovereignty concrete shape has never been larger than at present, for example, the transboundary nature of environmental pollution, refugee flows across national borders, transnational crime, illicit flow of arms and drugs and global communication webs that defy national controls. Even as this gap widens, there is no corresponding international machinery to do the job. The UN, standing for that international machinery, is not up to the challenge, whether the global problems relate to the traditional peace and security area or to the economic and social fields. Regional machinery such as the Association of South-East Asian Nations, Mercusor and the European Union fare much better, pointing the directions for future linkages between the UN and these bodies.

Despite structural difficulties, the UN has performed well and has an impressive record of past achievements. The UN has rendered many services of incalculable value to its members and to the world community such as overseeing de-colonisation, eliminating *apartheid*, action in peacekeeping and peacemaking efforts, defending human rights, providing assistance to refugees, ensuring the development and extension of international law, and the promotion of collective action on such common problems as resource depletion, demographic strain, and so on. But how well has the UN done in managing today's problems?

The UN appears to suffer from two fundamental problems: the ambiguity of its role in the world and its inability to adapt as the world changes. While the causes and effects of most major challenges facing governments are international, the authority for dealing with such problems remains vested in states. Furthermore, the UN was established to prevent acts of international aggression, but it is now being asked to solve deep-seated, often seemingly intractable internal problems of vulnerable states and their implosion. Today's wars are often wars within a particular state, civil wars fuelled by easy access to cheap weaponry sold mostly by the major powers, where conflicts make no distinction in the death and misery they bring, making humanitarian needs greater now than before.

The UN is currently over-stretched in areas of peacekeeping and enforcement operations more than it has ever been in its entire history, though this only adds up to about 20 per cent of the UN's total activity. In addition the UN is now suffocated by criticism and doubt, derived in part by internal discontent, but also because it is mired in a variety of conflicts for which there are no easy or obvious solutions, for example, Cyprus, Western Sahara, Bosnia and Haiti. The UN's collective security apparatus has been compelled to improvise in these situations. As a result it has frequently found itself confined to the margins of dangerous conflict, unable to even fulfil the more modest tasks of mediation or peacekeeping. It is also clear that national sovereignty and the principle of non-interference can no longer be used as a mask for actions that violate universal values. This means that states and peoples need to readjust their views of what the UN can and cannot do in relation to internal conflicts. The debate at the UN on the reform process, in the context of the working group on an Agenda for Peace, blows strong and hard with proponents of inviolability and sovereignty frustrating consensus in the name of the 'principle of consent' in preventive diplomacy.

The UN was established to provide a co-ordinating core for international activity, but it has a staff no larger than that of major municipal authorities. All the problems on the UN's agenda today require enormous military, financial, physical and staff resources, but these have to be fought for because member states do not have, or are unwilling to place them, at the

The UN and its Future in the 21st Century

disposal of the Secretary-General or the Security Council. At the same time member states are not yet accustomed to thinking that multilateral initiatives are the key to world peace and security, and not just an optional extra.

The challenge facing the UN in being able to deal with today's problems is not necessarily one of scope, but of knowing how to steer a course between inaction and over-commitment. It is about procedures for responding to and managing crises while laying the foundations for preventing such crises in the future. It is also about developing new ways of doing international politics so that potential problems are surfaced and solved. This requires an acknowledgement that the great bulk of the UN's work is not in crisis management, the restoration of peace or peacekeeping, but in the less acknowledged work in the areas of development, disarmament, human rights, humanitarian and refugee relief, and environmental protection.

It is not clear how strongly countries really want UN reform. The sort of reform being addressed, important as it is, is not intended to shape the UN to reflect the world as it is, nor to strengthen the rule of international law. Neither is its purpose to equip the UN to sanction countries that fall to meet international treaty obligations - whether they be enforcement of human rights, trade in nuclear fissile material or mandatory financial payments to the UN itself. This is attributed to the selectivity and power politics applied by permanent members of the Security Council over, for example, Chechnya and Cuba. Neither do the major states accept the International Court of Justice as a principal buttress for the rule of law in international affairs. In fact the reforms which are now the subject of inter-governmental debate in the UN (except for Security Council reform), are not intended to make the UN more democratic, but cost-effective, leaner, more efficient and co-ordinated. The present reform objectives have in some ways diverted attention from the UN's real function and responsibilities, and for some, that is their precise purpose.

The UN Charter embodies universal values but the promotion of such values borders on its politicisation. This is further sharpened to the extent that liberal global values are now promoted to include not only human rights, but also democratic governance and orthodox free market economics. The claim that such a blend of comprehensive and interrelated values provide coherent answers to all the problems of humankind is a notion over which many, and not just those in Asia, will harbour deep reservations. While the equivalence of all human rights is a consensual principle, the primacy accorded to civil and political rights at the expense of social and economic rights would, however, carry with it complex repercussions for industrialised economies at a time when environmental protection and sustainable development have risen to the top of the international economic agenda; when the 'polluter pays' principle is more assertively proclaimed; and when the poverty gap between the rich and the least developed is widening. The facts speak for themselves: 1.4 billion people now live in absolute poverty, 40 per cent more than 15 years ago. When these facts are added to increasing insecurity about basic needs such as access to food and clean water supplies, it is clear that combining the economic and social agenda with the political and civil is no longer an option but a necessity.

Sovereignty: More or Less?

Future historians may come to view the last years of the 1990s as an age of paradox, in which international politics has been dominated by two contradictory facts - increasing nationalism and decreasing national power. The time would seem ripe for adapting international equipment to meet the challenge of such a paradox. But is this possible given the multiplicity of factors involved in composing a solution? And would such a composition place the UN at the centre of the solution?

Over the last several years the UN has been increasingly incapacitated by an identity crisis which prevents it from articulating a coherent vision of its role in today's world, that is at once compelling and attractive to a balanced

The UN and its Future in the 21st Century

majority of its members. It is a crisis rooted in the evolution of the UN's political ethos over 50 years. Uncertainty about what a practical UN role should be has prevented member states from developing and refining the UN's central structure. Even if there were stronger agreement about the UN's specific role, the UN would be poorly equipped to exercise it without a change in its core structure and approach.

The United Nations has always been both less and more than what was hoped for. Proponents lament its inability to persevere and be more effective in the face of persistent conflict, oppression and inequalities. For them it is a failed, or at best, failing opportunity for a better world order. Critics lament its over-extended involvement in international affairs, its regulatory policies and practices. For them the UN is a borderline world government with too much power and too few ideas for its own good and for the good of others. Both views overstate their case and provide too many misguided assessments of the actual and the potential role of this institution.

Any accurate appraisal of the UN must start with the recognition that it is an institution run by 185 directors, five more equal than others, all with little in common except that they all possess sovereign statehood and a recognised right to participate in the UN. Any discussion of UN reform must proceed from recognition of the very real political and economic constraints under which the organisation must operate. The UN and the global community face a set of problems that were neither anticipated nor planned when the UN was established 51 years ago. Only with a clear idea of the source of difficulties that have confronted the UN will it be able to meet the challenges of the future.

The UN remains the rock upon which to build the most encompassing structure of governance; its global reach remains indispensable. Certainly, the UN faces some serious problems in the areas of finances, legitimacy and effectiveness, yet in many areas the most significant reform must take place in the capitals of member states, where the vital ingredients of

The UN and its Future in the 21st Century

political and material support for the UN and multilateralism requires unambiguous governmental and public commitment. No amount of institutional reform will guarantee that the UN will continue to receive these in the future.

The UN will have to transform itself from an organisation serving the interests of states to an organisation serving the interests of people living in an interdependent and global society. It will have to provide opportunities for the articulation of grievances and some kind of participation of non-state actors. It could and should serve as a clearing house for a network of Non-Governmental Organisations and stakeholders, whose work and interests are directed towards achieving greater understanding of the complexities of inter-group conflict and developing concrete solutions for the eradication of poverty, for the building of social equity and ensuring sustainability.

Eventually it is essential that supportive member states work together with NGOs to generate the political pressure necessary to convince reluctant and belligerent governments of the need to maintain the UN, recognising that it is the most viable opportunity for the articulation and management of global co-operation. Greater public interest in international affairs is required, particularly amongst the publics of major countries. This would allow for a resurgent voice for multilateralism, so that the voice of the vocal minority who publicly malign the UN is no longer heard unchallenged.

I sincerely hope that my statement is not out of line with the aspirations and vision of Erskine Childers. I have had the honour of knowing him to some extent, catching a glimpse of his convictions and quest, seeing the man un-Colossus-like but tenacious, an Irishman who drew perhaps from his own wellsprings an empathy for the cause of the South, the weak and the marginalised.

(Delivered 30 June 1997)

Who Rules? The United Nations: Democratic and Representative?

Patricia McKenna

The United Nations as presently constituted is undemocratic, unrepresentative and under-funded, and reform is urgently needed. All countries, not least the United States which owes half the UN debt, must pay their dues, but other sources of funding such as a levy on currency trading should be explored. Reform of the Security Council, though important, will be difficult to achieve, and the immediate priority must be to tackle the social and economic problems and abuses of human rights that underlie most conflict. The International Monetary Fund and the World Bank must be returned to UN control and the influence of transnational corporations curbed. The increasing role of Non-Governmental Organisations is welcome, and a People's Assembly parallel to the General Assembly should be encouraged. The role of the UN in conflict resolution should not be taken over by bodies such as the European Union or NATO; preventive diplomacy under Chapters VI and VIII of the UN Charter should be given priority over peace enforcement under Chapter VII.

Introduction

The name Erskine Childers is a very renowned one in Ireland: we have been blest in this century with not one but three Erskine Childers - father, son, and grandson - who have all distinguished themselves in public service and each, in his own way, died in the pursuit of that service. The first Erskine Childers, a negotiator with Michael Collins of the Treaty with Britain but later to be on the Anti-Treaty side in the Civil War, was executed by firing squad by the Irish Free State Government in 1922 - by his former colleagues. But even in the face of death, he preached reconciliation, and in a famous cell scene in Portobello Barracks in Dublin, Childers pleaded with his son to forgive his executioners, the Government ministers who were responsible, and if the son were ever to enter politics, he must never publicly mention the execution. The Childers name, said the father, was to be a 'healing memory'. The son - also Erskine Childers - did enter Irish politics, served with distinction in a number of ministries, and in the 1970s became a very popular and unifying President of Ireland. Unfortunately, the years of service had taken their toll and he died in office, serving little over a year, at the age of 69, from a heart attack while delivering a speech.

This lecture is in memory of the third Erskine Childers, grandson of the executed Childers, son of the President. This Erskine Childers, initially a broadcaster and journalist, served for twenty-two years as a United Nations civil servant and used his remarkable skills to promote the UN. He wrote in 1993: 'I advocate reform of the UN to improve on the already extraordinary; to strengthen a system that has already recorded breathtaking advances on the great canvas of world history'.[1] Erskine Childers was fully aware of the UN's weaknesses. He wrote extensively on how to correct them. Yet he felt the UN was 'extraordinary', and when he died in 1996, aged 68 - at a UNA meeting in Luxembourg (like his father, of a heart attack after delivering a speech) - he was still passionately championing the UN vision. The UN Charter's 'We the Peoples' was a focus for him: the UN must be more democratic and more representative. That is the focus of my talk.

The UN and its Future in the 21st Century

Is the UN Democratic and Representative?

The short and obvious answer is 'No'. Like the European Union, the UN has a democratic deficit, a deficit institutionalised from the very start in the UN Charter. The Charter, which begins with 'We the Peoples... 'and then sets out some of the finest principles and goals for humanity, then proceeds to invest control and veto power in an unrepresentative and undemocratic Security Council. Nor does the General Assembly represent 'We the Peoples': it represents our Governments - which do not always represent us. Not every state in this world is a democracy. Even those that nominally are can have electoral systems that skew electoral results in an unrepresentative fashion (if it were not for Proportional Representation we would not have two Green Party MEPs and two Green Party TDs in Ireland!) and political systems which under-represent half of humanity: women.

The General Assembly system of one-State one vote is a very necessary one in a world assembly but is not in theory representative of the world's 'peoples'. That is why Erskine Childers' idea of a People's Assembly alongside the General Assembly is so important. (Childers pointed out however that the proportion of votes of North and South in the General Assembly almost exactly matches their respective share of the world population.) Aside from the UN's own workings, it is also faced with the reality of economic globalisation, which has wrested democratic power from the nation-states themselves, let alone the UN which represents them. This is a major challenge.

Nevertheless, the UN is clearly the most 'representative' organisation in the world, the greatest world forum we have. This is the UN's great strength and its legitimacy. It is a reason I am so wary of the European Union moving into areas like peacekeeping, crisis management, and even armed intervention which should be done solely under the auspices of the UN – (see below).

The UN and its Future in the 21st Century

There is a clear need for great reforms at all levels of the UN, as is seen in the large number of studies and proposals coming out from various think tanks, Non-Governmental Organisations, the EU, and from the UN itself. To begin with, the organisation was never intended to cope with 185 independent states (it began with fifty-one and the UN architects were told to plan for seventy at most). There are plans to improve the UN's efficiency. Kofi Annan's proposals for reform will help to eliminate duplication, provide clearer lines of leadership, and shift some resources from administration to development work. But both Erskine Childers and Kofi Annan have cautioned against concentrating too much on housekeeping operations in the UN. Problems here have been exaggerated. Attacks on a bloated bureaucracy (about 50,000 civil servants) forget that nearly 6,000 million people are being served. The McDonalds workforce is nearly five times that just to serve hamburgers!

Funding

The work of the UN is being seriously undermined by lack of money. The constant wrangles about money owed to the UN go to the very heart of democracy and equity. Programmes for the organisation are being run on a bargain basement basis. The UN's annual budget (for all agencies and funds) is about $10 billion, less than $2 for every person in the world. The total cost of all UN peacekeeping activities in 1996 was $1.4 billion, or less than 0.2 per cent of worldwide military spending. Funds such as UNICEF and the UNDP working for economic and social development, for children, agriculture and food distribution, can only spend something like 80 cents per human being, while in 1994, the world's governments found they were able to spend $134 per human being for their militaries. Killing machines are worth more than life support systems! Yet the UN is broke.

In 1997, it was owed $2.3 billion. As is well known, the main culprit in not paying dues is the US government, which owes over half the UN debt: £1.4 billion - the equivalent of one stealth bomber. The payment of UN dues and

The UN and its Future in the 21st Century

peacekeeping assessments is binding on member-states. (We know this because the US sought an advisory opinion over thirty years ago from the International Court of Justice on this very issue: at that time the baddies were the Russians!) In order to keep afloat, the UN has been 'borrowing' money from its peacekeeping funds – so that it has been unable to reimburse states (including my own) for participating in peacekeeping operations: and early last year, over 70 countries were owed $800m.

The United States has been using its non-payment as a form of political leverage, to exert pressure on the workings and proposed reforms of the UN system. Erskine Childers was always very strong in arguing, not just against the bully-boy tactics displayed in this case, but against the consequent violation of democracy. The budget of the UN is based on a fundamental tenet of democracy: the ability to pay. Rich and poor are to be equally represented, despite the difference in their financial contribution - the principle upon which 'equality of political voice in governance and policy formation is grounded' (Childers).

In a speech in September 1995 to a 'Colloquium on The UN at Fifty: Whither the next Fifty Years?' at the European Parliament in Brussels, Erskine Childers passionately attacked the so-called 'realists' who continue to argue that 'he who pays the piper calls the tune' (or, in this case, 'he who is supposed to pay the piper...'!). He said that discussions on reforming and strengthening the UN had been 'grotesquely' distorted by such 'realism':

> One of its most insidious influences is the dictum that the governments that 'contribute most' to the UN's budgets should naturally have special influence in its policies and even in the composition of its organs - the Security Council, the Economic and Social Council, the General Assembly, everywhere throughout the UN system. The capacity to pay is the root principle of democratic revenue-raising and governance in the very countries that demand special influence in the UN on grounds of their contributing the largest money amounts. It is the principle that it is as great a burden for the poorer citizen to find his or her smaller money

amount of taxes as it is for the richer to find their larger money amount.

Accordingly, since there is equity of burden, no one should have special influence in governance; no rich person and no corporation is entitled to special posts in or influence on the policies - or reforms - of public-service institutions. The citizens of Europe had to struggle for a long time to overcome precisely this undemocratic premise in their own countries; they would abandon democratic national governance to modern plutocrats and corporations if they now accepted it at home.

A way around this stranglehold on UN finances is to explore other means of funding, not as an alternative to dues, which should still be assessed and paid, but as an additional source of income. Not only would this (partly) relieve the UN from 'undue influence', enhance the control of 'We the Peoples' and ensure the UN's continued existence, but it would allow the UN to tackle its enormous global agenda for the fostering of peace and sustainable development. For example, annual currency trading is ten times the global GNP and a tax of just one half of one per cent of trading income would generate over $1.5 trillion a year - a big boost to the current UN annual budget of $ 10 billion.

A global carbon tax on the consumption of fossil fuels could raise nearly $1 trillion a year. Such monies would not only vastly improve the world's environment, foster sustainable development and help to fulfil the global commitments of Rio's Agenda 21, but they could be ploughed back into the 80 per cent of the UN's work that is devoted to helping developing countries, promoting and protecting democracy and human rights, saving children from starvation and disease, providing relief assistance to refugees and disaster victims, countering global crime, drugs and disease, and assisting countries devastated by war. The UN estimates it needs a budget of about $50 billion to seriously tackle poverty globally.

The UN and its Future in the 21st Century

The Security Council

But before turning to the one quarter of the human race who are living in 'almost unimaginable suffering and want' (UNICEF), who are supposedly represented in the UN and are to be assisted primarily by the UN's Economic and Social Council (ECOSOC) - the body under the General Assembly established to deal with the economic and social causes of conflict - I consider the Security Council.

Much attention has been focussed on reforming the totally undemocratic Security Council. Despite all the proposals - increasing overall numbers, increasing the number of permanent members, with or without vetoes and the like - there seems little hope of change here. Childers himself referred to the Security Council as having 'fascist flaws', thrust 'into the otherwise noble, principled architecture of the UN Charter':

Had not the powers in 1945 just led a world war against systems of governance in which a minority faction would:

- Create permanent, unelected seats for itself.
- Arrogate to itself the power to block admissions of others to the institution of governance.
- Wield the police power in the community.
- Hold the power to block nominations to the chief public-service post.
- Have the power to block any amendments to the constitution giving themselves these special privileges?

'When I was doing my studies, this was indeed called fascism'. (Colloquium on 'The UN at Fifty,' European Parliament, 8 Sept 1995).

I see no sense in extending this undemocratic veto to even more states and would also be totally opposed to the often-floated idea of creating an EU seat - permanent or otherwise - on the Security Council. It would solidify the dominion of the North over the South even more forcefully and I do not want Ireland represented by a block EU vote. Over the past decade, the Green Party in Ireland has campaigned strenuously against the evolving EU Common Foreign and Security Policy, appealing for a 'no' vote in referenda on the Single European Act, the Maastricht Treaty, and last May, on the Amsterdam Treaty. The Greens are opposing not only what we see as a movement towards an EU nuclear military bloc, but we are also concerned that Ireland's independent voice and contribution to international affairs, particularly its disarmament and peacekeeping work at the United Nations, would be severely compromised and silenced under some sort of EU mantle.

Our Minister for Foreign Affairs, Mr. Andrews, has recently spearheaded a major disarmament initiative, joined by Sweden, Brazil, Egypt, Mexico, New Zealand, Slovenia and South Africa, (the New Agenda Coalition).[2] This initiative attacks the nuclear 'logic' now maintaining vast nuclear arsenals, a 'logic' which has inspired India and Pakistan to get 'logical' as well. At the launch of this initiative, Mr Andrews attacked the 'complacency' of the nuclear weapons states, highlighted the case at the International Court of Justice on the illegality of nuclear weapons, and pointed out that Ireland was the only EU state to actively support that case. Forty years ago, in 1958, the then Irish Minister for Foreign Affairs, Frank Aiken, first proposed the Non-Proliferation Treaty at the UN. The point here is that it is widely acknowledged that Mr Andrews did not initiate his disarmament proposals in the EU because he knew they would not be supported there. That is why I do not want the EU representing me - or Ireland - on issues of war and peace at the Security Council.

However, an EU seat is probably not a serious runner at the moment. I cannot imagine Britain or France accepting it. There is no sense 'reforming' the Security Council until the reforms can be meaningful. Childers envisaged a chamber of 23 or 24 states '…entirely elected on the basis of regional representation and rotation, in which most of the big countries will always have seats. There must be no vetoes, but graduated majority voting according to the type and gravity of the decision to be taken'. (European Parliament speech).

This is a goal, but meanwhile, perhaps the best policy is to concentrate on the other institutions of the UN, to ensure that the root causes of conflict - social and economic problems and violations of human rights - are being seriously tackled. The Security Council is only supposed to be called in when things go wrong. We must ensure that more things go right in the first instance.

Globalisation and Human Rights

This is the fiftieth anniversary of the Universal Declaration of Human Rights, which reaffirmed the stirring declarations of the UN Charter itself, of 'promoting and encouraging respect for human rights and fundamental freedoms for all without distinction as to race, sex, language or religion'. It has taken many years to translate some of these rights into legally binding state obligations. We in Ireland are of course very proud of the appointment of our former President, Mary Robinson, to the post of High Commissioner on Human Rights, and are hoping that human rights will be given a higher profile and priority in the workings of the UN. She appears to have embraced the broader human rights agenda of economic and social rights alongside civil and political ones. I am however personally concerned - as are others (notably the *Irish Times*) - that Mrs. Robinson's human rights efforts can be a little selective. Developing countries are concerned that she is more likely to home in on their violations than on abuses in the West. The bombings of Afghanistan and Sudan received no comment from Mrs. Robinson, nor has the US blockade of food and medicines to Cuba, a silence which has earned Mrs. Robinson condemnation from the former UN Assistant Secretary-General, Peter Bourne.

If the UN is to be genuinely democratic and representative, it must do its

The UN and its Future in the 21st Century

best to use its institutions to promote democracy in the international community, and that democracy must entail the achievement those basic human rights aspired to in the Charter and the 1948 Declaration. The UN actively promotes democracy and has successfully, monitored elections in Mozambique, Cambodia, South Africa, the former Yugoslavia and El Salvador. It has an enormous (though inadequately funded) humanitarian and development programme, and there have been successes. UNDP figures show that life expectancy in the developing world has increased by one-third in the last thirty years, infant mortality has halved, more diseases have been eradicated and primary education and children's nutrition have improved.

However, the gap between the richest and poorest has doubled, and the top 20 per cent are now sixty times better off than the poorest 20 per cent. 13,000 children a day still die of preventable diseases, and yet the West has diminished its aid to the developing countries for the fifth year in succession. Dag Hammarskjold used to say that the UN had never meant to take humanity to heaven but to save it from hell. But saving it from hell is not just a matter of reversing the downwards slide in Western aid or even of pumping more money into the UN (although that would certainly help). The growing gap between North and South is largely due to the globalisation of the economy (the 200 largest transnational corporations now account for nearly a third of the world's economy), the lack of political control of this process and the fact that human rights, democracy, and sustainable development are not uppermost in the boardrooms of transnational corporations (TNCs).

Nor have they always been uppermost in some of the UN's own specialised agencies, notably the World Bank and the International Monetary Fund, whose harsh structural adjustment programmes (SAPs) have wreaked havoc in developing countries with, in many instances, total disregard for the wishes of democratically elected governments. Many countries have been forced to privatise public industries, reduce public services and eliminate restrictions on currency exchange and foreign investments.

The UN and its Future in the 21st Century

Schools and hospitals are shut to pay off debts to Western banks. (Ironically, many of the teachers in these schools were trained under UNDP/UNESCO programmes, only to have their jobs taken away by 'structural adjustment' policies!) Africa spends four times as much money repaying interest on its loans as on health care.

In a recent article, Noam Chomsky (*Guardian*, May 15, 1998) attacked the IMF and the World Bank for their role in exacerbating poverty and world debt. Borrowing in developing countries had been actively promoted in the Seventies and Eighties, but the IMF is now seen increasingly as 'the credit community's enforcer'. Both the agencies have reversed their initial Bretton Woods role of regulating and controlling capital movement, to one of assisting the liberalisation of financial flows. In 1970, 90 per cent of transactions were related to the real economy (trade and long-term investment) and the rest were speculative. By 1995, it was estimated that 95 per cent of transactions were speculative, most of them short term (80 per cent with a return time of a week or less). It has long been known that 'liberalisation of capital flow serves as a powerful weapon against social justice and democracy'. The crises and upheavals in Mexico, the Asian economies, Rwanda, Zaire, Somalia and elsewhere are in part testimony to this.

The new proposed Multilateral Agreement on Investment (MAI), called 'the constitution of a single global economy' by the World Trade Organisation, is an additional assault on 'We the Peoples', a one-sided Bill of Rights for the TNCs and rich investors. Our economies will be further removed from democratic control. Foreign investors will be given legal status on a par with nations, allowed to sue governments, and yet be virtually unimpeded by governmental regulations or any social obligations. Workers rights and protection of the environment will all be weakened. Examples of suits already taken under the present GATT and North American Free Trade Area (NAFTA) regimes include the Ethyl Corporation suing the Canadian Government for banning the petrol additive MMT as a public health risk and pollutant, and Metalclad, an

The UN and its Future in the 21st Century

American firm, suing the Mexican Government because of delays in opening a hazardous waste disposal facility. If the MAI is approved, things will get worse.

The strength of multinationals has reached new heights - or depths - when considering the controls which biotechnology firms are developing, not only over food and food production (a fairly fundamental commodity!) but over life itself. The recently approved directive on biological patenting in the European Parliament, passed despite strong opposition from the Green Group, will give these firms the right to patent life and facilitate 'bio-piracy' in developing countries. One of these firms, Monsanto, has a market value of $96 billion, larger than the GNP of most countries, including Ireland. The World Trade Organisation and its food standards body, Codex Alimentarius, could threaten the EU with punitive sanctions if US genetically modified foods were not given access to European markets. In Ireland we have been told – and I think you were similarly informed in Britain last April, when your Government had to reverse a decision to impose a moratorium on genetically modified crops - that EU Directive 90/220 prevents any EU member state from banning crops which have been approved under EU law.

The UN must reassert its role in the economic sphere. The Preamble of the UN Charter says it is 'to employ international machinery for the promotion of economic and social advancement of all peoples'. Article 55 states that 'with a view to the creation of conditions of stability and well-being which are necessary for peaceful and friendly relations among nations based on respect for the principle of equal rights and self-determination of peoples, the United Nations shall promote higher standards of living, full employment and conditions of economic and social progress and development' as well as 'solutions of international economic, social, health and related problems'. Erskine Childers campaigned strongly to have Article 58 of the Charter properly implemented: 'The Organisation shall make recommendations for the co-ordination of the policies and activities of the specialised agencies' - policies, not just activities - and he constantly

The UN and its Future in the 21st Century

highlighted the role of the UN in macro-economic and macro-social strategies to be carried out under the auspices of the Economic and Social Council for the General Assembly.

This has not been allowed to happen. The UN has been disenfranchised. It should now reassert its role in global governance of the economy, with the World Bank and World Trade Organisation brought firmly into the UN policy framework as they are supposed to be. If both the planet and its peoples are to be saved, this framework must be based on Rio's Agenda 21: the pursuit of sustainable development. We must act quickly to ensure that not only are our democratic rights protected, but that life itself does not come under the control of Billion Dollar Man.

The Role of Non-Governmental Organisations

For the UN to reassert itself will require not just will from the top, but, more decisively, will from the bottom. Erskine Childers, in his last speech, stated his common theme: that the UN will only work well when 'ordinary citizens as well as the privileged' are informed and active on its behalf. There is a powerful role here for 'We the Peoples' and representative groupings of civil society, the NGOs.

What more concrete proof of their role do we need than the 1997 Nobel Peace Prize winners, the International Campaign to Ban Landmines? This campaign brought together more than 1300 organisations in over 75 countries. It managed, in the Nobel Committee's words, to change a landmines ban from 'a vision to a feasible reality'. It changed the position of governments, challenged their inaction, shamed major powers, and managed to get a landmines convention drafted, signed and now to become binding international law on 1 March 1999. The World Court Project brought together NGOs from around the world to successfully challenge the legality of nuclear weapons in the International Court of Justice at The Hague.[3]

The UN and its Future in the 21st Century

The important role of NGOs has also been well shown in the various international conferences, on the environment, (Rio and Kyoto), on women, and on development. At the Earth Summit in Rio, the alternative NGO forum of 4000 NGOs from 70 countries managed to negotiate forty-one treaties, and to capture the imagination and broaden the environment agenda much better than the General Assembly. The NGOs already have significant inputs into ECOSOC but not into other UN institutions, in particular not into the General Assembly and its main committees. During 1996, for example, there were five high level General Assembly working groups dealing with various areas of UN reform which NGOs were not allowed to observe or attend, although many of the suggestions under consideration had been adopted at world conferences in which they had been involved. However, there are now suggestions to formalise these inputs and even suggestions of establishing a UN NGO Assembly, or Civil Society Forum, alongside the General Assembly.

Meanwhile, NGO influence at national level is increasing, and this should be reflected at UN level. Influence is also seen at local level where NGOs have, for instance, established alternative banking systems (Zimbabwe) and housing co-operatives (Uruguay), and helped to combat assaults on the environment. Groups like Amnesty International and Greenpeace can set standards, conduct independent research, and effectively lobby on our behalf, not only with Governments but with the UN.

In May 1998 Geneva, an NGO conference (predominately from southern countries) took place on how to combat globalisation. Different approaches emerged: lobbying, non-violent confrontation and the construction of alternative trading systems were all considered. The Manifesto from the conference called for the strengthening of the local market systems 'by developing producer-consumer linkages and co-operatives' and stated that 'direct democratic action' against 'undemocratic' globalisation should be combined with the constructive building of alternative and sustainable lifestyles. This is strong stuff, and examples of civil disobedience mentioned included destroying imported foodstuffs to protect local farmers (India), and the destruction of genetically modified maize in France and beetroot in the UK and Ireland. The conference was split on the use of such direct action. However, the Fair Trade network, and the concept of 'Thinking Globally, Acting Locally' in order to counter globalisation and regain some control of our lives, was strongly backed. Vandana Shiva, the Indian environmentalist, argued that globalisation had forced people, North and South, into 'a common condition of exclusion'. 'It's the first time that Northern citizens have experienced this - it's a situation we have always experienced and we now have grounds for a new solidarity'.

A People's Assembly

Increased NGO influence at the United Nations will make the UN more representative. But to make it more democratic, another reform is advocated, by Erskine Childers amongst others. This is for a People's Assembly, first mooted by Ernest Bevin in 1945, which would give citizens a direct input into the UN. Erskine Childers advocated that this Assembly could be modelled on the European Parliament but I am doubtful of that model - the Parliament's wishes are often ignored. But the power of a UN Peoples Assembly is that it would contribute to the objective of making the UN more powerful by making it more relevant to the ordinary citizen, the very point already cited in Erskine Childers' last speech. To bring the issues of the UN to the level of the ballot box would be a tremendous achievement. It would both influence the UN and those countries who are not very keen on democratic elections or universal franchise, and, increase pressure for the opening up of those societies.

International Peace and Security

If we can bring 'We the Peoples' into the UN Chamber we might be able to recapture the original spirit of the UN Charter. One of the main motivating

The UN and its Future in the 21st Century

forces, in the aftermath of two devastating world wars, was 'to save succeeding generations from the scourge of war', and 'to practice tolerance and live together in peace with one another as good neighbours'. I finally turn to the issue of war and peace, and why the UN must have primacy of control in conflict resolution.

There have been well over 150 wars since the UN Charter was signed and many millions killed, the majority of them civilians. In the 1990s, after the end of the Cold War, another four million have died in wars and one in every two hundred people in the world today is displaced or a refugee.[4] At the end of 1997, there were fifteen UN mandated missions still in existence, involving nearly 15,000 troops, military observers and police drawn from seventy-one countries. We in Ireland are very proud of the UN peacekeeping role of Irish troops since our first days at the United Nations.

When the Berlin Wall came down, many in the world hoped, and felt it possible, that the UN would now come into 'its own', able to at last fulfil the hopes of its Charter free from the tensions of the Cold War. UN activity did increase. There were notable successes (in El Salvador, Mozambique, and seemingly in Cambodia). But we have also witnessed the unhappiest of times for the UN, with the turmoil in such areas as Somalia, Rwanda, the Gulf, and the former Yugoslavia throwing up tremendous challenges to the entire UN system. But, as we know, the UN can only function as web as its members win allow. Some of 'its' failures were due to the UN not being able to carry out its role because that role had been usurped by the United States: this was the case in both Somalia and the Gulf (and in Haiti). Operation Desert Storm was dressed up as a UN operation under Chapter VII, but neither the Security Council nor the UN Secretary General were involved in the conduct of that war.

We are now greeted with the spectre of over one million Iraqi children dead because of sanctions imposed by the United Nations (UNICEF and WHO figures), and kept in place at the insistence of the United States government. The recent bombings of Sudan and Afghanistan were acts of

The UN and its Future in the 21st Century

state terrorism, a direct contravention of the Geneva Convention and a defiance of everything the UN stands for. All those who believe in the rule of law and in the United Nations should have strongly condemned these bombings. At the time, 1 compared them to the actions of the Real IRA in Omagh. I stand by that analogy and see it as hypocritical to condemn one while supporting the other (as Tony Blair did). Both were inexcusable, unlawful, and caused the deaths of innocent civilians. Our world is definitely not a safer, better place as a result.

There is growing concern that the Chapter VII enforcement powers of the UN are being given higher priority than the Chapter VI (Pacific Settlement of Disputes) and Chapter VIII (Regional Arrangements for settling disputes) sections of the Charter. It is also a very unsatisfactory and dangerous development for the UN to be allowing not only the United States, but NATO, to act on its behalf. This flies in the face of the most fundamental values upon which the UN Charter is based, and a superstate or a military bloc - both in this case based on nuclear weapons policies which have been found counter to international humanitarian law by the UN's own World Court – should not be mandated to carry out the UN's will.

Both the European Union and NATO are attempting to undermine the UN's role in peacekeeping and are posing, I believe, very serious threats to world security in the process. The Green Party has opposed this development strenuously. The Amsterdam Treaty has brought NATO's European wing, the Western European Union, further into the EU. The WEU's Petersburg Tasks are now EU 'tasks', and include peacekeeping, humanitarian missions, and crisis management/enforcement missions. The Petersburg Tasks do not require a UN mandate. Irish troops have never acted abroad without a UN mandate. The Amsterdam Treaty leaves it open (through its 'crisis management' tasks) for the EU to become involved in interventions anywhere in the world, facilitated by the WEU and NATO. By what right, on what basis of international law, does the EU take on this world policeman's role?

The EU has earned great respect for bringing together age-old enemies in a co-operative community. Its greatest contribution to world peace would be to continue this contribution to peace-building – co-operation built on non-military means. Instead it is trying to evolve into a militarised nuclear superstate, undermining not only the UN itself but the UN's regional Chapter VIII body in Europe, the Organisation for Security and Co-operation in Europe (OSCE). It is also supporting the continued existence of NATO, a Cold War military bloc that should have followed the Warsaw Pact into oblivion.

NATO's so-called Partnership for Peace is another weakening of the UN's role and another means of perpetuating NATO's existence, and - in NATO's own words - of assisting its 'expansion', (to the delight of the arms manufacturers, as it opens up lucrative arms markets in Eastern Europe, thought to be worth over $30 billion). Neutral Ireland is under great pressure to join the PfP, pressures we have so far thankfully resisted. However, nearly every country in Europe - including Russia - are now members. Part of the myth of the PfP (and of a militarised EU) is that it will be assisting the UN, helping it to respond earlier and better to crises like that in the former Yugoslavia. But a well-resourced supported UN/OSCE is the proper vehicle for doing that. The PfP is not answerable to the UN, its actions do not have to be UN mandated and those that are will be under the control of NATO, not the UN.

When the UN's own World Court finds that the nuclear strategy underpinning NATO is illegal, and nuclear weapons are clearly seen as anathema to the UN system, it is incredible that NATO is allowed to continue and grow in this way. Acceptance of NATO nuclear doctrine prompts India and Pakistan to set off nuclear bombs and undermines the entire Non-Proliferation Treaty process. I hope that the dangers for the UN in allowing a northern nuclear alliance to become its agent can be recognised, and that there will be a re-focus on the primacy of the UN as the guarantor of international peace and security.

The UN and its Future in the 21st Century

Conclusion

When one asks whether the UN is democratic and representative and who rules it, the reply is that the UN at the moment represents a political and economic elite wielding inordinate and undemocratic power. However, as Erskine Childers said, the UN is also an 'extraordinary' forum: flawed, yet the most representative gathering of all the people that the world has ever had. Ultimately 'We the Peoples' can rule; and reform the UN into the body it was meant to be. There are clear and feasible ways to provide the UN with adequate, independent finance, such as a pound on airfares, taxing arms sales or a levy on currency transactions. Enough money in itself would allow a revolution in the workings of the UN, strengthening its ability to fulfil the promise of its Charter.

Raising popular participation in the UN and awareness of its work, a People's Assembly, empowering NGOs and citizens groups will all assist revival of the UN. An international meeting of NGOs is already planned for the Millennium. An International Criminal Court has now been established, despite the opposition of the world's remaining superpower. The present World Court must also be more vigorously supported: it is under-utilised and its jurisdiction is not compulsory (my own country fails to accept it). A major conference, The Hague Appeal For Peace and the Abolition of War,[5] will revitalise and reaffirm the role of international humanitarian law and push for general and complete disarmament. At that conference, the Green Group in the European Parliament will be joining with the Quakers and Peace Brigades International to examine the role that civilian non-violent action can play in conflict areas. Mary Robinson - with the strong support of Kofi Annan – will, I hope, raise human rights awareness, and enforcement, to new levels. And Kofi Annan, earlier this year, dramatically reinstated the role of the UN in the maintenance of international peace when he travelled to Iraq, negotiated, and halted yet another wave of destructive bombing of the Iraqi people.

The UN and its Future in the 21st Century

The oneness of this planet has been brought home increasingly to the world's population this century, with most of the latter half clouded by possible global annihilation from nuclear war. This threat has abated somewhat but the move to General and Complete Disarmament must be more convincingly pursued in the 21st century. The oneness has also been heightened by awareness of the environmental destruction that awaits us if the world's inhabitants, particularly the wealthier and more destructive, do not co-operate in creating a sustainable planet. We are connected in the oneness of common threats. We are also connected, not only in danger but also by the common bond of our humanity, as neighbours and family on one planet. This is the positive side of globalisation, a communications revolution interrelating and inter-linking us as never before. People power has never been so possible or so potent. We must organise and make common cause for our extraordinary common planet.

References

1. Childers E. *In a Time Beyond Warnings. Strengthening the United Nations System*. London: Catholic Institute for International Relations, 1993.
2. Joint Declaration by the Ministries for Foreign Affairs of Brazil, Egypt, Ireland, Mexico, New Zealand, Slovenia, South Africa and Sweden (New Agenda Coalition). *A Nuclear Weapons-free World: the Need for a New Agenda*. Dublin, 9 June 1988.
3. International Court of Justice. *Advisory Opinion: Legality of the Threat or Use of Nuclear Weapons*. UN Document A/51/218. New York: United Nations, 1996.
4. Carnegie Commission on Preventing Deadly Conflict. *Preventing Deadly Conflict: Final Report.*Washington DC: CCPDC, 1997.
5. *Mission Statement: The Hague Appeal for Peace and an End to War. Medicine, Conflict & Survival* 1998; **14**: 260-1.

(Delivered 25 September 1998)

'... To Save Succeeding Generations from the Scourge of War': The Role of the International Court of Justice

Rosalyn Higgins

What the International Court of Justice Is

The International Court of Justice is the judicial arm of the United Nations. It is the institution to which certain organs of the United Nations and certain specialised agencies may turn to seek legal advice. And it is the tribunal to which States may (indeed, according to Article 36 of the Charter, should) refer their legal disputes for resolution.

The Court - which is the successor to the old Permanent Court of International Justice, functioning at the time of the League of Nations - has its seat in The Hague, in the remarkable Peace Palace. The provenance of the Court is both interesting and not widely known. In 1893 the Czar of Russia had proposed, against a background of deteriorating international relations, a Conference on Peace and Disarmament. The invitations went out to Paris, Berlin, London and Washington. He suggested eight agenda items, with the eighth being the development of a uniform system for mediation and arbitration as a means of dispute settlement. In 1898 the first Peace Conference did take place, in The Hague, at the Dutch Royal Palace.

In due course there were established a Permanent Court of Arbitration (which still exists to this day), the Permanent Court of International Justice and then the International Court of Justice. Its founding history, and the place the post-

The UN and its Future in the 21st Century

war ICJ has under the Charter, means that it has always been closely involved with issues of war and peace. Fifteen Judges, representing all the major legal systems, are elected for nine-year terms by simultaneous vote in the Security Council and the General Assembly. The present Bench comes from China, Madagascar, France, Sierra Leone, the Russian Federation, the United Kingdom, Venezuela, the Netherlands, Brazil, Jordan, the United States of America, Egypt, Japan, Germany and Slovakia.

The Court's Role in Keeping International Peace and Security

Chapter VII of the Charter ascribes the primary responsibility for peace and security to the UN Security Council. But the Charter, in its principles and purposes, identifies what must be done to achieve peace - securing of human rights and fundamental freedoms, economic and social development, peaceful settlement of disputes. These tasks are ascribed to different organs of the UN (and other functional bodies have been added over time). The ICJ's contribution to peace and security is not to set itself up as an alternative Security Council; it is to settle legal disputes. How exactly this is to be done is laid out in the Statute of the ICJ (which is attached to the Charter) and in the Rules of Court which the ICJ has drawn up itself (and periodically updates). Article 36 (6) of the Charter says that 'legal disputes should as a general rule be referred by the parties to the ICJ in accordance with the provisions of the Statute of the Court'.

From 1946 to 1966 the International Court of Justice had a moderate but meaningful docket. In the early seventies - for a dozen years in fact - it was hardly used at all. By contrast, it now has a very heavy docket. The end of the Cold War is part of the story of the current heavy use of the International Court, but certainly not all of it. The upturn in recourse to the Court began in the first half of the 1980s, several years before the arrival of *glasnost* and *perestroika*. Many former colonial States who had achieved their independence in the early 1960s had by the 1980s begun to see that international law served their own ends as much as those of the developed countries. But, finally, in the late 1980s, the Marxist doctrine by virtue of which there were no neutral men - and hence no place for impartial judicial recourse - was coming to an end.

The evidence that today the Court's work is drawn from States around the world is not hard to find. The Court's current or very recent docket consists of cases concerning Romania and Ukraine; Mexico and the United States; Germany and the United States; Malaysia and Singapore; Republic of Congo and France; El Salvador and Honduras; Benin and Niger; Democratic Republic of Congo and Uganda and Rwanda; Nicaragua and Colombia; Liechtenstein and Germany; Bosnia-Herzegovina and Yugoslavia; Iran and the United States; Hungary and Slovakia; Cameroon and Nigeria; Indonesia and Malaysia; Guinea and the Democratic Republic of the Congo; and Yugoslavia and various NATO States.

As the developing States have come to recognise that international law secures their interests, as much as that of the First World, and as the old rigidities of the Cold War lose their grip, it is quite clear for all to see that States are 'getting the litigation habit'.

Honesty requires us to acknowledge that the treasured ideal of the early peace movement of this century - that resort to international adjudication would prevent the outbreak of war - is unrealistic. Far from international adjudication generally preventing war, it is peace that lends strength to the settlement of international disputes by adjudication. The Permanent Court of International Justice flourished in the 1920s, in a decade of *détente*, and declined in the 1930s with the rise of the international tensions provoked by the Axis Powers. Since the end of the Cold War, the ICJ has had a heavier docket than ever before.

What the Court Can Do

Its role is to settle disputes between States and also to give advice, when that is requested, to designated UN organs and specialised agencies. Contrary to general supposition, compliance with Judgements or Advisory Opinions is not a significant problem. It is true that, like the Pope, the Court has no divisions. There is provision for recourse to the Security Council for the enforcement of judgements. Given the politics in the Security Council (and especially when the State concerned might have the right of veto), this is not a promising mechanism. But the problem is in fact a very small one. States have to consent to have recourse to the Court (and I shall say more on that shortly). To give that consent is already to accept that it has been given even for circumstances that one might later regret. Accordingly, the Court's judgements are nearly always complied with. Indeed, the Court has now dealt with 105 cases since 1946, and compliance has only been a problem in about five of them.

Examples in the Peace and Security Area

The case law of the Court is replete with disputes that affect international peace and security. Sometimes, of course, two States can be locked in a dispute of the greatest importance to them, and it is desirable for every reason of good sense that the Court resolve them, but even so there is no real risk of military conflict. The bitter conflict in the 1990s between Slovakia and Hungary about the hydroelectricity on the Danube was one such example; the case between Spain and Canada, which concerned fishing off Newfoundland, was another such.

But there are other cases in which the Court's role is not merely to settle disputes that adversely affect international relations, but to contribute to the maintenance or restoration of international peace and security.

The *Corfu Channel* case (*United Kingdom v. Albania*), 1949, arose out of the explosions of mines by which some British warships suffered damage while passing through the Corfu Channel in 1946, in a part of the Albanian waters which had been previously swept. Ships were severely damaged and members of the crew were killed. The United Kingdom accused Albania of having laid or allowed a third State to lay the mines after mine-clearing operations had been carried out by the Allied naval authorities. The Court found that Albania was responsible under international law for damage and loss of life, which had ensued. It did not accept the view that Albania had itself laid the mines or the purported connivance of Albania with a mine-laying operation carried out by the Yugoslav Navy at the request of Albania. On the other hand, it held that the mines could not have been laid without the knowledge of the Albanian Government. Albania accused the UK of having violated Albanian sovereignty by sending warships into Albanian waters after the explosions. The Court found that the UK had exercised the right of innocent passage through international straits. On the other hand, it found that the minesweeping had violated Albanian sovereignty, because it had been carried out against the will of the Albanian Government. In particular, it did not accept the notion of 'self-help' asserted by the United Kingdom to justify its intervention.

The *Hostages* case (*United States v. Iran*), 1981, was brought by the United States following the occupation of its Embassy in Tehran by Iranian militants on 4 November 1979, and the capture and holding as hostages of its diplomatic and consular staff. It pointed out that while, during the events of 4 November 1979, the conduct of militants could not be directly attributed to the Iranian State - for lack of sufficient information - that State had however done nothing to prevent the attack, stop it before it reached its completion or oblige the militants to withdraw from the premises and release the hostages. The Court noted that, after 4 November 1979, certain organs of the Iranian State had endorsed the acts complained of and decided to perpetuate them, so that those acts were transformed into acts of the Iranian State. The Court gave judgement against Iran.

In the *Frontier Dispute* case *(Burkina Faso/Mali)*, 1986, Burkina Faso (then known as Upper Volta) and Mali notified to the Court a Special Agreement referring to a Chamber of the Court the question of the delimitation of part of the land frontier between the two States. Following grave incidents between the armed forces of the two countries at the very end of 1985, both Parties submitted parallel requests to the Chamber for the indication of interim measures of protection (an interim injunction). The Chamber indicated such measures by an Order of 10 January 1986. This dealt with the use of force. And its Judgement on the merits was delivered on 22 December 1986 (this dealt with the territorial entitlement).

The *Military and Paramilitary Activities in and against Nicaragua* case *(Nicaragua v. United States)*, 1986 was of considerable importance. Nicaragua filed an Application instituting proceedings against the United States of America, together with a request for the indication of provisional measures concerning a dispute relating to responsibility for military and paramilitary activities in and against Nicaragua. On 10 May 1984 the Court made an Order indicating provisional measures. One of these measures required the United States immediately to cease and refrain from any action restricting access to Nicaraguan ports, and in particular the laying of mines. The Court also indicated that the right to sovereignty and to political independence possessed by Nicaragua, like any other State, should be fully respected and should not be jeopardised by activities contrary to the principle prohibiting the threat or use of force and to the principle of non-intervention within the domestic jurisdiction of a State. On 27 June 1986, the Court delivered its Judgement on the merits. The findings included a rejection of the justification of collective self-defence advanced by the United States concerning the military or paramilitary activities in or against Nicaragua in part because no evidence was shown of a request for such assistance. It decided that the United States was under a duty immediately to cease and to refrain from all acts constituting breaches of its legal obligations, and that it must make reparation for all injury caused to Nicaragua by the breaches of obligations under customary international law and the 1956 Treaty.

In the *Territorial Dispute* case *(Chad/Libya)*, 1994, Chad filed an Application instituting proceedings against the Libyan Arab Jamahiriya. The Court delivered its Judgement on 3 February 1994. It proceeded by embarking upon a detailed study of the instruments relevant to the case. The Court then described the line resulting from those relevant international instruments. Considering the attitudes adopted subsequently by the Parties with regard to their frontiers, it reached the conclusion that the existence of a settled frontier had been accepted and acted upon by the Parties. Lastly, referring to the provision of the 1955 Treaty according to which it was concluded for a period of 20 years and could be terminated unilaterally, the Court indicated that that Treaty had to be taken to have determined a permanent frontier, and observed that, when a boundary has been the subject of agreement, its continued existence is not dependent upon the continuing life of the Treaty under which that boundary was agreed.

On 8 July 1991, Qatar filed an Application instituting proceedings against Bahrain with respect to sovereignty over certain islands and shoals and the delimitation of maritime areas. This was the *Maritime Delimitation and Territorial Questions* case (*Qatar v. Bahrain*), 2001. Although there was no fighting, there were great tensions between the two States. In its Judgement of 16 March 2001, the Court divided the disputed territory between Qatar and Bahrain and indicated a single maritime boundary. Both parties fully accepted the Judgement and declared the following day a national holiday to celebrate the end of the dispute and better relations between the two countries.

The *Oil Platforms* case (*Iran v. USA*), 1997, started on 2 November 1992, when the Islamic Republic of Iran filed in the Registry of the Court an Application instituting proceedings against the United States of America with respect to the destruction of Iranian oil platforms. In its application, Iran alleged that the destruction caused by several warships of the United States Navy, in October 1987 and April 1988, of three offshore oil production complexes, owned and operated for commercial purposes by the National Iranian Oil Company, constituted a fundamental breach of various provisions of the Treaty of Amity and of international law. The United States submitted counter-claims alleging aerial attacks on ships flying its flags and other illegalities. On 6 November 2003, the Court delivered its Judgement on the merits. It found the attacks by the United States did not violate a 1955 commerce treaty between the United States and Iran since the attacks did not adversely affect freedom of commerce between the territories of the parties. The Court also rejected the United States' counter-claims. At the same time, the military action of the United States could not be justified under a clause in the Treaty exempting certain actions from obligations contained in the Treaty. The Judgement confirmed the applicability of the international law criteria of necessity and proportionality in relation to the use of force in alleged self-defence.

The *Genocide* case (*Bosnia & Herzegovina v. Yugoslavia*): On 20 March 1993, the Republic of Bosnia and Herzegovina instituted proceedings against the Federal Republic of Yugoslavia in respect of a dispute concerning alleged violations of the Convention on the Prevention and Punishment of the Crime of Genocide. The Court concluded that there was a legal dispute, and that it did indeed fall within the provisions of Article IX of the Convention. It found, *inter alia*, that it followed from the object and purpose of the Convention that the rights and obligations enshrined by it were rights and obligations *erga omnes*. During 1993, the Court issued and then confirmed provisional measures requiring Yugoslavia to take all measures within its power to prevent commission of the crime of genocide. In 1997, the Court admitted Yugoslav counter-claims charging that Bosnia and Herzegovina had breached its obligations under the Genocide Convention through actions principally against Bosnian Serbs. These counter-claims were later withdrawn by Yugoslavia in 2001. The *Genocide* case is now awaiting a hearing on the merits.

The *Cameroon v. Nigeria* case, 2002: On 29 March 1994, Cameroon filed an Application instituting proceedings against Nigeria with respect to the question of sovereignty over the Bakassi Peninsula. On 12 February 1996, Cameroon, referring to the 'grave incidents which [had] taken place between the ... forces ... in the Bakassi Peninsula since ... 3 February 1996' asked the Court to indicate provisional measures. By an Order dated 15 March 1996, the Court indicated a number of provisional measures aimed principally at putting an end to the hostilities. Nigeria raised preliminary objections challenging the jurisdiction of the Court and the admissibility of Cameroon's claims, but the Court found it had jurisdiction to deal with the merits of the case. In its

The UN and its Future in the 21st Century

Judgement of 10 October 2002, the Court determined the boundary between Cameroon and Nigeria from Lake Chad to the sea, decided that the Bakassi Peninsula belonged to Cameroon, and requested both parties to withdraw their military, police, and administration from the affected areas 'expeditiously and without condition'. At the request of the Presidents of both countries, the United Nations set up the Nigeria/Cameroon Joint Border Commission to facilitate the implementation of the Judgement. It has been moving step by step to do this.

There are many other cases in which past conflict forms the background to the Court's task, or which, should they be allowed to fester on, have the potential for conflict. I will simply briefly mention the *Western Sahara* case; the *Aegean Sea* case and the *Namibia* case.

Limits to the Court's Contribution to Peace and Security

Need for Consent to Jurisdiction
The Court is available for sovereign States to settle their disputes; but they cannot be compelled to use it. It may seem desirable to make reference to the Court of legal disputes a mandatory obligation. But the Court itself has no power to achieve this. So, for the moment, the consent of States is required. But there are several ways in which that consent can be expressed. Two States may have reached the end of the road in trying to settle a dispute diplomatically. They may decide to let the Court resolve the matter: We have such examples in the litigation between Slovakia and Hungary over the dam project on the Danube; and between Namibia and Botswana over their frontier. The States concerned may have been urged by a regional organisation to have a mutually agreed recourse to the Court. It was upon the insistence of the OAU that Libya and Chad finally came to the Court with the problem of the famous Aouzou Strip. The consent-based jurisdiction of the Court may be founded in another way - by becoming party to a treaty which contains a clause whereby it is agreed that, if there is a dispute as to the application or interpretation of any of the provisions of the treaty, recourse

shall be had to the Court. Jurisdiction for the case brought by the United States against Iran over the hostages taken at the Tehran Embassy, was based on the Vienna Convention on Diplomatic Relations, to which both States were party. And the case which Bosnia and Herzegovina is bringing against Serbia and Montenegro is based upon an ICJ clause in the Genocide Convention.

There is a further method of expression of consent to the Court's jurisdiction, known to international lawyers as 'the Optional Clause' under the Statute. This consists, essentially, of formally notifying agreement to be taken to Court by any other State accepting the same commitment. This has had a special significance in the recent Kosovo cases, which I return to below.

Of course, wherever consent is not given directly, there will be room for denying that the consent given in the treaty, or under the Optional Clause, applies in the particular case. The combination of the need for consent in a world of sovereign States, and the potential for controversy as to the meaning and scope of any consent given in advance, means that a sizeable part of the Court's case law is directed to the determination of its own jurisdiction. In that context, the growing tendency for *ad hoc* agreed references to the Court, which go straight to the merits, is very welcome. The Court should ideally be contributing to world peace by resolving the substance of cases, rather than having to satisfy itself that sovereign States have given their consent to it settling their disputes, one way or another.

The recent cases concerning Kosovo illustrate the point exactly. The dreadful columns of refugees who were expelled after the NATO bombing began are so sharply and distressingly in our minds that we are perhaps apt to forget what had gone on before - what indeed had led to the attempts to improve matters through peaceful means at Rambouillet. I refer to the atrocities by Serb military and paramilitaries against the ethnic Albanians, which had already gone on for all too long. They were being killed and pushed out of their villages long before the NATO action. But with the NATO action a new variation on the horror began - not only killings and destruction, without care as to where the Kosovars should go, but now their positive expulsion from

The UN and its Future in the 21st Century

Kosovo, and the destruction of their identity papers so that they should never return.

The NATO States eventually decided the situation could only be dealt with by force. Whereas it had previously been NATO's firm policy to act as the military arm of the UN, when the Security Council called upon it (as in Bosnia), it now decided that the stance of the Russian Federation and of China meant that the Security Council would never make that call. There *were* resolutions deploring events in Kosovo, but the position of certain States in the Security Council meant that there would never *be* a resolution calling for military action to stop the atrocities. NATO therefore decided that it would act alone, without UN authorisation. I do not want to offer any public pronouncement on the legality of this action, because that matter is still technically before the Court. I simply quote the phrase used by the International Court in its ten Orders of 2 June 1999: 'the use of force in Kosovo raises very serious issues of international law'.

Yugoslavia's main concern was to get the bombing stopped. It asked the Court for 'provisional measures' - that is to say, an international injunction. But, in the International Court, as in any court of law, you can't come and ask for an Order that a State or States desist from certain action unless there is a case, a litigation, that demand attaches to. Otherwise a court can have no idea whether or not to issue an injunction. In all courts - and the International Court is no exception - injunctions are ordered when there is a real risk that the subject matter of the dispute will otherwise physically disappear, or that events will occur which will make any eventual judgements pointless.

So Yugoslavia brought a case, claiming first, that the bombing by ten named NATO States was unlawful, both in terms of lack of Security Council authorisation and in terms of types of bombs being used, and the fact that some civilian targets were being hit. Second, Yugoslavia claimed that each of the defendant States (USA, UK, France, Netherlands, Portugal, Canada, Belgium, Spain, Italy and Germany) was committing genocide of the Serb people.

When it receives a case the Court cannot immediately decide the merits - that requires a certain time for carefully prepared legal argument, both written and oral. The point of asking for provisional measures (an injunction) is not to wait for the substance of the case to be decided, but rather to get your 'stop' order at once, and the Court will only give this if it feels that it may have jurisdiction, in due course, to go on and decide the merits of the case.

The Court thought it unlikely that there would be a legal basis for genocide claims against the NATO respondents. As for the jurisdiction over the claims alleging illegal use of force, Yugoslavia's *own* acceptance of the court's jurisdiction (which it had made three days earlier on 25 April 1999, specifically to bring this case) presented considerable problems. This was because (and here I must be a little technical) Yugoslavia had specified that it would agree to litigation before the Court of 'disputes arising' and 'events occurring' after 25 April. It clearly did not want the Court to pronounce upon its own earlier actions in Kosovo. But although the bombing continued, and there were indeed relevant 'events occurring' after 25 April, the dispute had surely arisen before 25 April. The bombing had been going on for over a month, and the dispute between NATO and Yugoslavia about the rights and wrongs of it had been fully argued out by all concerned in the Security Council on 24 and 26 March.

So the Court found that, *prima facie*, it did not seem to have been given the jurisdiction by Yugoslavia to hear the issues on their merits and therefore could not consider whether to order an injunction on the bombing. In two cases in particular (those concerning the United States and Spain) there were technical legal considerations which made it clear beyond all doubt that the cases simply could not proceed. In the other eight cases (including that against the UK), Yugoslavia still remains at liberty to try to show that the Court really *does*, after all, have jurisdiction to determine the merits of that case. These eight cases are now back before the Court, which is currently deciding on the preliminary objections to jurisdiction and admissibility advanced by the NATO States and on other technical matters, which Yugoslavia (now

Serbia and Montenegro) has raised.

Should the Court find that it has the necessary jurisdiction, then the Court will make its contribution to peace and security by clarifying this complex interface between the restraints of Chapter VII of the Charter on the use of force and the moral imperative not to ignore systematic slaughter and displacement of ethnic or religious groups.

The Question of Lacunae

Can it be the case that the International Court is thwarted in its wish to contribute to international peace and security by another factor, namely, the non-existence of an answer in international law? The question of whether or not there are 'gaps' in the substance of international law is known to international lawyers as the question of *'lacunae'*. There are many aspects to this interesting problem.

To some international lawyers, international law is a body of rules, which over the years have become more and more developed and dense. Nonetheless, in the view of these lawyers, there are not yet legal rules to govern every legal situation or problem. In such a circumstance, they argue, the judge should state so, and declare a *non liquet* - that is, pronounce that international law does not yet provide an answer.

There is a good example of this in the position taken by Judge Vereshchetin (the Russian judge) in the ICJ's case on *Legality of the Use of Nuclear Weapons*. Looking at the key question of whether it could ever be lawful to use nuclear weapons, if the very existence of a State or its peoples was in issue, he stated that international law did not yet provide an answer and that a *non liquet* was the honest response.

There is, however, a totally different way of looking at this issue, and it is the way I prefer. First, law is not really 'rules'. It is rather a *process* by which authorised decision-makers (judges of the ICJ and other international tribunals, legal advisers of foreign offices, UN legal officials) make normative decisions. This view of international law rejects the classic idea of law as being 'neutral'. The decisions to be taken are unashamedly for the realisation of values. The values of the international law system include such matters as peace, stability and the realisation of human dignity regardless of race, sex, creed, gender, or colour. The decision maker, faced with a very difficult question, looks at the available legal authority (past cases, treaties) and applies them to the new problematic circumstances in the way most consistent with the attainment of these values or policy objectives.

I have to say that I do not, in any event, understand the *lacunae* argument as it is said by some to apply to the question of nuclear weapons. One cannot expect a specific 'rule' to deal with every single unthought of question any more than one can in domestic law. All one needs are relevant norms - that is, guides to lawful behaviour - that one can then apply to the circumstances to which a court has not *yet* been called to apply them. As the Court made clear in its Advisory Opinion on the use of Nuclear Weapons, the relevant law is on the one hand the law of the Charter (which governs when force may be resorted to) and on the other, humanitarian law (which governs how force may be used, that is, with what effects, with what protected targets, and so on). It seems exactly the judge's role to apply these governing principles of law to the question of nuclear weapons. I see no *lacunae* in the law.

Relations with the Security Council

I would like to explore briefly the question of whether the Court's contribution to international peace and security is constrained in any way by the work of the Security Council. The Court's relationship with the UN generally is a delicate one. It must be independent and non-political. Yet, as a main organ of the United Nations, it too must have the objects and purposes of the UN always in view. Nor, in the real world, can the Court be unaware of the political context to which the litigation is brought, or an advisory opinion sought.

The UN and its Future in the 21st Century

The Court has insisted, in various cases (e.g. the *Aegean Sea* dispute between Greece and Turkey; and the 'Contras' dispute between Nicaragua and the United States) that the fact that a matter is before the Security Council does not preclude the Court simultaneously dealing with the legal aspects of the matter. The Court is aware that the political organs have, under the Charter, *their* job to do. The ideal outcome is for the Court to be able to contribute, on a parallel track, to the same Charter ends as all UN organs must seek to realise. There are many examples of such mutually reinforcing action. The crisis that surrounded the taking of hostages at the US Embassy in Iran by the revolutionary guards was one such - the political work in the Security Council and the legal adjudication on the issue in the Court occurred side by side. The same phenomenon has been at work on matters relating to Bosnia. And the Security Council established an observer group to oversee compliance with the Court's Judgement in *Chad v. Libya*, with very successful results, as Libya withdrew its army from Chad within four months of the Judgement.

Today, though, we live in a unipolar world, where predominant power lies with one of the Permanent Members of the Security Council. Although nothing whatever has changed in the voting rules of the Security Council, and the same majorities are still required for action to be agreed upon, there are some who feel that power nonetheless has its silent effect. They argue that, accordingly, action by the Security Council is not always lawful and that the ICJ must be the ultimate guarantor of the legality of acts by the UN, including the Security Council.

This issue came very much into focus with the *Lockerbie* affair. After the atrocity of the explosion on Pan Am 103, which killed so many people and caused devastation in the village of Lockerbie, a meticulous forensic investigation was carried on over months by a team of scientists. They came to the conclusion that two persons, said to be the agents of the Libyan security service, had placed a bomb on the plane at a stop it had made in Frankfurt. Under international law, a country where a crime has been committed has jurisdiction over those charged with the crime. If a plane or a ship is destroyed, the flag country of that plane or ship also is entitled to carry out a trial. Both the UK and the US therefore asked Libya to release the named suspects to them for trial. When there was no response they invoked the support of the Security Council, placing before it the scientific report that led them to believe these persons were responsible. The Security Council (which had an existing long-term interest in the question of terrorism and international peace) passed a resolution calling for the persons to be released for trial in either the USA or Scotland. When there was no response, the Security Council passed a second resolution, ordering the release for trial upon penalty of sanctions. Sanctions were then put in place.

Libya brought an action in the ICJ against the USA and the UK. It claimed that these countries were violating its (Libya's) rights to try any alleged air terrorist, itself, in its own country. It invoked a particular air piracy treaty, the *Montreal Convention*, in support of its position.

Its argument necessarily put in question the legality of the Security Council resolutions, because it was not the USA and the UK alone who wanted trial on one of those countries, but the entire Security Council. In the initial phase of the case the UK argued that it was enough for the Court to know that the Security Council had passed a binding resolution under Chapter VII of the Charter. That was, for the Court, the beginning and end of the matter, and, said the UK, the Court should dismiss the case.

The Court declined to dismiss Libya's claim. It said it would decide the merits of the argument and the UK's arguments could be reviewed later as part of that process. It was not clear whether this would entail what national lawyers call 'judicial review' - a review by a judicial body of the legality of acts of the executive. The problems are complex.

The Court probably has the authority to decide if decisions by UN bodies are constitutional, in the sense of taken within the bounds of procedural regularity. Some take the view that the Court must also be able to determine if decisions of the Security Council (or any other UN organ) are compatible with the objects and purposes of the UN and with international law more generally.

But are there categories of decisions that simply may *not* be reviewed by the Court - *exactly because* the Charter, in its stated distribution of powers, intended otherwise? Put differently, are the decisions of the Security Council in the area of peace and security (a role specifically given to that body) definitive? Can the Court ever challenge a finding by the Security Council that the actions of a State have caused a threat to international peace? And, even if not, can it examine the measures taken by the Security Council, to ensure their proportionality to the wrong done or their compatibility with other legal obligations?

The answer to these difficult questions, so relevant to the Court's role in the area of peace and security, will have to wait for another case. I put it that way because, the two named suspects were eventually, with the active assistance of the Secretary-General of the UN, brought into custody for trial by a Scottish Court - not in Scotland, but, under special arrangements, a Scottish Court sitting in the Netherlands. That, of course, was a criminal trial in which the individuals were the accused; it is different from the inter-State case in which the UK and the USA are the defendants. The latter case was removed from the Court's List at the joint request of the Parties on 9 September 2003. Libya, which has acknowledged responsibility for the bombing, has also agreed to pay compensation to families of the victims.

Two recent decisions of the International Court have shown further ways of contributing to peace and security. First, in the *Palestine Wall* Advisory Opinion in 2004, the Court found that the 'wall' or 'security barrier' built by Israel violated various international obligations, that the wall must be dismantled immediately, and that Israel must make reparation for any damage caused to Palestinian property. Although advisory opinions are in principle non-binding, this non-binding character does not mean that such opinions are without legal effect. The *Palestine Wall* Opinion contained important legal reasoning on international humanitarian law, was accepted by an overwhelming vote of the General Assembly, and contributes to the framework for peace in the Middle East. Second, a pending case - the

The UN and its Future in the 21st Century

Armed Activities on the territory of the Congo (Congo v. Uganda) – is also of significance for peace and security. The case involves a claim by the Democratic Republic of the Congo against Uganda alleging aggression and massive breaches of humanitarian and human rights law. The hearing was postponed because of negotiations between the Parties, but the case is likely to come back to the Court before long. The issues are of the greatest contemporary importance, as they touch on the interface of the contemporary law of intervention and violations of human rights and humanitarian law.

Concluding Remarks

We live in an era of decentralisation of international judicial authority. The International Court of Justice no longer stands alone: there are human rights courts, a new Law of the Sea Tribunal in Hamburg, the World Trade Organization Panel, and International Criminal Courts.

Some topics that the International Court can deal with are now dealt with elsewhere, but it is busier than ever. It alone is the Court that can deal with issues directly affecting peace and security. The Court is very conscious of the fact that it is the main judicial organ of the United Nations and will continue to make its contribution to saving succeeding generations from the scourge of war.

(Delivered 18 June 1999)

The UN in Crisis?

Margaret Joan Anstee

It is fashionable to suggest that the United Nations is in crisis. But the UN has been in almost perpetual crisis since its creation – the Cold war erupted almost immediately afterwards. And crisis – and its resolution – are the UN's *raison d'etre*. There is no doubt, though, that its situation has become more serious in the 1990s, for a variety of reasons. Its chronic financial insolvency has reached a new nadir. Some dramatic failures in peacekeeping have overshadowed successes. It has been the subject of constant public criticism, particularly in the USA, and has lacked support from key member states. Is it, however, terminally ill?

The UN is beset by a series of paradoxes. The first is that it staggers from one crisis to the next at a time when the demand and the need for an effective international organisation are daily becoming greater. Globalisation and the shrinking world, brought about by the development of technology and communications, have unleashed forces that undermine the already declining ability of governments to control their own territories and policies. Meanwhile the power wielded by the largest transnational corporations, some of which are larger than many UN member states, increases all the time. Large corporations go into crisis – and out of business – when demand for their products falls. The UN is in exactly the reverse position.

The second paradox is that while globalisation increases apace and the world's problems, such as international crime, drug trafficking, terrorism, pollution, and the threat of global warming and climate change, transcend state frontiers, the concept of sovereignty is still very much alive and

The UN and its Future in the 21st Century

jealously guarded, although increasingly irrelevant.

Secretary-General Kofi Annan's suggestion to the General Assembly last year that UN humanitarian intervention could be justified in certain cases met with a negative reaction from some developing countries, who interpreted it as a cloak for American or Western neo-colonialism. The developed countries are no more enthusiastic to relinquish sovereignty. Senator Jesse Helms gave a warning – or threat? – to the Security Council: 'a UN that seeks to impose its presumed authority on the American people, without their consent, begs for confrontation... and eventual American withdrawal.' Sir Brian Urquhart commented recently that 'he did not say whether this doctrine should apply to other sovereign countries – Iraq or Serbia, for example'.

In these circumstances, prospects for a strong and effective UN, as opposed to the present institutional arrangements – which may be called on if convenient, and which are unpredictable and slow to act – do not seem hopeful in the foreseeable future.

How has the Crisis Manifested Itself?

The crisis has many inter-related aspects and elements but I will deal with only a few: political, economic and social, financial, organisational structures and reform.

Political
The days of clamour for a New International Economic Order and of the North-South dialogue that marked the 1960s and 70s are over. But tensions between developed and developing countries are as strong, if not stronger, than ever, and the gap between them is increasing, especially in the case of the poorest countries, exacerbated by the differential effects of globalisation and the spread of the market economy. Yet the UN itself seems to be a less effective channel for addressing the concerns of

The UN and its Future in the 21st Century

developing countries, and a less effective forum for debating them than before, for example in the heyday of the UN Conference on Trade and Development (UNCTAD) – another paradox!

The political weakness of the UN has also been demonstrated in a series of peacekeeping setbacks. Post-Cold War euphoria led to a great explosion of peacekeeping operations in the early 90s, but soon evaporated in a series of debacles, notably in Angola, Bosnia, Rwanda and Somalia. The UN (in the narrow sense of its own secretariat) became an all too easy scapegoat and whipping boy for the media and anti-UN campaigners, and is blamed by member states for shortcomings often of their own making. Successes in peacekeeping, such as Namibia, Mozambique, Central America and (relatively) Cambodia are often forgotten, while member States' responsibility for failures, such as lack of political will, as tragically in Rwanda, and their reluctance and delay in providing the necessary money, equipment and personnel, are overlooked.

The Security Council itself is not geared to strong and decisive action, being essentially a body of compromise, reconciling different political interests. As a result, some of its resolutions are Delphic in their obscurity and the mandates and resources it authorises for complex operations are inadequate for the task in hand. UNAVEM II, in Angola, in 1991 – 3, is a tragic case in point.

Given the many condemnatory resolutions passed by the Council but unsupported by decisive action it is understandable that unscrupulous warlords may come to regard it as a toothless tiger. I am convinced that Jonas Savimbi, fighting in the Angolan bush in late 1993 in defiance of the Council's demands that he accept the results of the elections, was well aware of the simultaneous inefficacy of UN actions against Radovan Karadzic and Ratko Mladic in Bosnia. A dangerous 'copy cat' syndrome of 'cocking a snook' with impunity at the UN has gained momentum.

Sanctions, when imposed, are often too little, too late, and ineffectively implemented. When they do bite, sanctions can be a blunt instrument, hitting the wrong target. A notably encouraging development, however, is the recent hard-hitting Fowler report and concomitant action to give teeth to the Council's mandated sanctions against UNITA in Angola.

Other problems stem from different responses by the Security Council, leading to accusations of double standards – for example, the discrepancy between the resources accorded to Namibia, Cambodia and Bosnia and those assigned to Angola in 1991. Many thousands of troops were sent to Kuwait, but only hundreds elsewhere. Today we see similar differences of scale between Kosovo and East Timor. As I watched the East Timor tragedy evolve it seemed to me at first to be horrifyingly like 'Angola all over again' – the operation successful but the patient dies. Fortunately, in the case of East Timor, the patient was rushed into intensive care at the last moment.

Economic and Social
The eye-catching features of the UN are its political aspects and particularly its peacekeeping work. But in concentrating on these, it is often forgotten that the Preamble to the UN's Charter includes among its main purposes 'to promote social progress and better standards of life in larger freedom'. The UN has had many quiet successes in the economic and social field; nevertheless, it does not seem to play the same leadership role as in its early days. Where are the current eminent and visionary UN thinkers to match Myrdal, Tinbergen, Lewis, Prebisch and Singer? The post of Director General for Development and International Co-operation, first proposed in the Capacity Study (the 'Jackson Report') in 1969 and tardily (and poorly) implemented in 1975, was abolished in 1992, while Brian Urquhart and Erskine Childers' proposal for a Deputy Secretary-General for International Economic Co-operation and Sustainable Development in their 1994 book [1] was never implemented.

In the absence of strong economic and social leadership in the UN, major issues of economic and indirectly, social, policy have increasingly passed to the International Monetary Fund and the World Bank. These, with their weighted voting, are unrepresentative, and as Specialised Agencies are not on the same level as the UN proper. The World Trade Organization has also become a powerful player.

Meanwhile, there has been a vertiginous decline in development aid from the developed to the developing world and this has seriously affected the UN Development Programme. The 1969 Pearson Commission recommendation that developed countries should allocate 0.7% of their GNP for development assistance has still been achieved by only a few countries. In some, including the UK during the Thatcher years, the percentage has declined. In the UK it is rising to 0.33% as a result of the recent Comprehensive Spending Review under the present government, but still has a long way to go. In 1999 the UN budget for peacekeeping increased by over 300% while that for development fell by almost 50%, a matter not only of serious economic concern for many developing countries, but also a political issue.

Humanitarian and disaster relief is also escalating exponentially; governments, under public pressure, are much more willing to contribute to these than to development aid. Another paradox arises here. Humanitarian relief can only be a palliative, while development assistance attempts to address the basic causes of conflict and contribute to long-term stability. It would be simplistic to argue that economic and social factors are the *main* cause of all conflicts but they almost always play a large role: poverty; availability of land, as in El Salvador; access to resources, as in Angola and Sierra Leone; and skewed distribution of wealth.

The UN's over-arching aim, to maintain international peace and security, was originally rather narrowly interpreted. But it is now increasingly appreciated that peace and security mean much more than the absence of war and a new concept is emerging of security, which can no longer be measured merely in terms of military expenditure or defence budgets. There cannot be social or political stability where there is discrimination, widespread poverty, or vast differences in income and economic opportunities. Security, in this broader sense, is also adversely affected by the social effects of programmes of structural adjustment and economic stabilisation, and in the transition from a centrally planned to a market economy, as evidenced in the former Soviet Union. A corollary to all this is that sustainable peace cannot be achieved by peacekeeping operations alone, no matter how successful these may be.

Hence we have the current emphasis on post-conflict peace building and conflict prevention through preventive diplomacy. The two are intimately linked but the simpler umbrella term 'peace-building' cannot be used because of political sensitivities about perceived intervention – the ogre of national sovereignty again. Post-conflict peace building is itself a misnomer, since peace-building must often start before conflict has totally died down.

Post-conflict peace building requires concurrent and integrated action on many fronts at once, involving a plethora of actors. These include reconstruction, restoring productive processes, vocational training and job creation for ex-combatants to re-integrate them in society. Good governance should be developed through democratic processes and institutions, sound judicial systems with honest and effective administration, the protection of human rights, and fair economic and social development. Investment in education, especially for women, together with health and social services, is vital.

The present organisational structures and *modus operandi* of the UN system are not geared to this integrated approach. For example, in New York the inter-related activities of peacekeeping and post-conflict peace building are divided between two departments. The UN system of Specialised Agencies and organisations is built up largely on sectoral lines, so that the response to increasing inter-relationship between problems, instead of closer articulation and inter-action, takes the form of everyone trying to get on the band-wagon, expanding their mandates, and vying for the lead role. The result is even more duplication and inter-Agency rivalry than before – another paradox: emergence of the need for more integrated action is met by increased fragmentation.

The traditional solution to such situations in the UN system – fatal in my view – is to set up still more co-ordinating machinery leading to layers of 'co-ordinators of co-ordinators'. Instead, more modest and pragmatic solutions are needed and are eminently feasible, provided common sense and a genuine commitment to co-operation prevail.

Financial

As it confronts ever-increasing demands, the UN flounders in constant financial crisis. For many years, zero growth has been imposed on its regular budget. Peacekeeping assessments have also been cut to the bone, with much reliance on 'mixed financing' as in Kosovo and East Timor. Crippling arrears in paying even agreed assessments compound the problem of inadequate budgets with a chronic cash flow crisis.

The most desperate point was reached in 1995, when the US paid only 48% of its regular budget dues and 40% of its peacekeeping assessment. The situation at the end of 1999 was marginally better. The US has paid in more but subject to conditions, and overall unpaid assessments on both the regular and peace-keeping budgets are still considerable with the US still the main debtor. Yet we are not talking of astronomical sums. The total regular core budget of the UN is $1,250 million per annum (covering the New York, Geneva, Vienna, and Nairobi offices and the Regional Commissions). In comparison, this is about 4% of New York City's annual budget, and $1 billion less than that of Tokyo's fire department.

Mixed financing makes already complex operations even more difficult to manage, especially when – as again in Kosovo and East Timor - arrears also mount up over voluntary donations. As Kofi Annan comments in his Millennium Report: 'Our resources are simply not commensurate with our global tasks'. How can anyone manage effectively, plan ahead and be

The UN and its Future in the 21st Century

visionary if one doesn't know how the next day's bills are to be met?

Organisational Structures and Reform

It is abundantly clear that the UN's present organisational structures are inadequate for its task. However, the prospects for the far-reaching reforms required are bleak. What needs to be done is evident and logical, and has been rehearsed in a multiplicity of reform proposals from the Capacity Study in the 1960s and the Group of 18 proposals of the 1980s to *Renewing the United Nations System*[1] and many others beside. All these bear a striking resemblance to one another; why then, have these ideas not been implemented?

A basic problem is that the UN is not a logical organisation. Member states, even like-minded ones who constantly clamour for reform, find it difficult to agree – especially when their own interests are involved. There are myriad examples. Our recommendations in 1987, in implementing the Group of 18 report, for a small unit to collect information on impending crises as an early warning tool for the Secretary General, led to cries in Washington that we were setting up a KGB, and in Moscow that we were creating a CIA! In that particular reform process the United States got everything it wanted – staff reductions, a new, more controlled budgetary process, and a zero growth budget, but still did not pay up.

Even when member states do agree on a desirable course of action, they often cannot agree on the modalities, as with the revision of the budgetary assessments system and reform of the Security Council. Again, member states criticise slow deployment of peace-keeping missions, due to the cumbersome procedures involved in soliciting troops and police from individual countries, but most refuse to allow the UN to have its own rapid reaction force, even if staffed by volunteers. In these circumstances progress on effective reform is hard to achieve. More seriously, when one reform process disappoints, another is instituted. These constant upheavals and staff reductions – with the threat of more to come – have devastated staff morale, and undermined efficiency, defeating the object of the exercise.

Where Do We Go From Here?

Yet the story is not all gloom and doom. There has been some real progress towards making the world a better place. War Crimes Tribunals on former Yugoslavia and Rwanda are in place, the International Criminal Court has at least been created, if not yet fully operational. Lessons *have* been learned from mistakes in past peacekeeping. The courage of men and women still prepared to risk their lives in bringing peace to conflict-riven areas of the world must be saluted. There has been an alarming rise in their death toll: aid workers are now more at risk than military peacekeepers. Had Childers and Urquhart's proposal for an Humanitarian Emergency Police ('White Helmets') to protect aid workers, their transport, and their supplies, been adopted, many lives would have been saved and much material wastage avoided.

Nevertheless, it is quite evident that progress, such as it is, is far too slow. The only long-term hope for humankind and the world is a strong and adequately funded United Nations, with the resources and the authority to carry out the tasks assigned to it. At the moment, the radical change needed to bring this about is a pipe dream, in a world in which one super-power calls the shots, and given the continuing fixation with sovereignty in most member states.

The UN is not terminally ill. It is unlikely to die or be subjected to euthanasia, but that could mean that an even worse sickness may be in store. Prolonged crisis and weakness due to continued under-funding and the lack of political will to strengthen the organisation could lead to continuing accusations of ineffectiveness, which then become a self-fulfilling prophecy. How can a better intermediate resolution of the crisis be found?

The UN and its Future in the 21st Century

It is impossible to continue to believe in across-the-board reforms, as proposed in the Capacity Study or *Renewing the United Nations System*, no matter how logical. Key ideas, so often endorsed but not acted upon, must be kept alive in a different way, and applied on an *ad hoc* basis as circumstances permit. The way forward, in my view, is through significant individual changes that will have a multiplier effect. Major steps, such as drastic changes in the method of selecting the Secretary-General and Heads of Agencies, instead of the political horse-trading that goes on now, combined with a single, longer term in post for these top officials, and a consolidated budget for the UN system, would at one fell swoop solve many problems of co-ordination.

Above all, intense public and media pressure must be stimulated to bring about the required change – 'We the Peoples of the United Nations…' must become a reality. This will be very difficult; because of prevailing indifference and ignorance. Action for UN Renewal, United Nations Associations, and similar non-governmental organisations have a key role to play but the net must be cast much wider and the younger generation must be engaged.

The Internet has recently been used successfully to mobilise widespread demonstrations *against* organisations such as the World Trade Organization and the International Monetary Fund. Could it not be massively incorporated into a universal campaign *for* the renewal of the UN? This idea would surely appeal to Erskine Childers' rebellious Irish spirit and his genius for imaginative communication. The best way we can commemorate that spirit and genius is by keeping his ideas alive in such ways.

Reference
1. Childers E, Urquhart B. *Renewing the United Nations System*. Uppsala: Dag Hammarskjöld Foundation, 1994.

(Delivered 27 June 2000)

The UN and its Future in the 21st Century

Addendum

The four years since I gave this lecture have, sadly, confirmed my thesis that the United Nations seems doomed to exist in a perpetual state of crisis. This is perhaps inevitable in a world in which multilateralism and unilateralism remain in conflict and national sovereignty, however limited in real terms in a vertiginously shrinking world, continues to dominate so many international and national politics.

The paradoxes and inter-related elements of the crisis that I identified in 2000 are still evident, especially in the political and economic and social fields. The backlog in financial contributions to the United Nations has eased somewhat, but the budget is pathetically inadequate for an international organisation called upon to resolve huge and multifarious global challenges that threaten the survival of humanity. There have been new attempts at structural reform. The Brahimi report of 2000 produced useful recommendations for making the vital area of peacekeeping more effective, a number of which have been implemented. In September 2004, a new high-level group with broader remit is expected to make recommendations designed to adapt the structures and functioning of the organisation to the fresh and emerging challenges of the 21st century. It will be interesting to see whether they can come up with viable ideas for the strengthening and expansion of the Security Council and even more interesting to observe member states' reactions to their proposals.

A new and alarming paradox has been thrown up by the upsurge in terrorism and the cataclysmic attack of 11 September 2001. Events so clearly demonstrating the global nature of the threat and the consequent need to combat it multilaterally through the United Nations have, instead, led to divisions in the Security Council and the increase of unilateralism. In the run-up to the invasion of Iraq the UN came to be considered by the United States as at best irrelevant and at worse an obstacle to the attainment of its policies.

Yet at the end of 2000, when the UN appeared to be at its nadir, public interest in the organisation, to the importance of which I gave special emphasis at the end of my lecture, and public pressure for its involvement, grew enormously, at least in this country. In pubs and at dinner tables people who had never paid much attention to the Security Council, much less known how it functioned, could be heard clamouring for a second resolution.

As has invariably happened in the past, when the post-conflict problems in Iraq became intractable the UN was called in, tardily, and with an inadequate mandate and resources. It became a target, and the tragic culmination of this botched process of international negotiation was the brutal murder of Sergio Vieira de Mello, and other friends and colleagues devoted to the cause of peace, in August 2003. The need for peace building after conflict, and for the involvement of the whole UN system in this highly complex and multidisciplinary activity, has never been more graphically shown the Iraq.

No weapons of mass destruction were found there but the possibility of their falling into the hands of a nihilistic terrorist whose single, fanatical aim is to overturn the existing order, overhangs humanity with the threat of ultimate doom. Yet most of the major powers in the world seem intent on addressing the symptoms of the terrorist disease, rather then its roots in poverty, marginalisation and exclusion, the conditions that breed ready recruits for organisations led by fanatical terrorist leaders.

Any thinking person who seriously ponders the future of the world must conclude that the United Nations, with all its shortcomings - and there is no lack of vociferous critics who proclaim them daily, drowning out the voices of those who think otherwise – is even more indispensable in the twenty-first century. The overwhelming challenge is how to harness political and public pressure to make possible the necessary reforms and the proper use

The UN and its Future in the 21st Century

of the organisation as a bulwark for collective security rather a last reluctantly turned to when disaster looms. That will require revised definitions by member states of sovereignty, of where their true self-interest - and survival - lies. It will demand political leadership of the highest order. At this time of writing there are few encouraging signs of such radical change.

(August 2004)

The United Nations and the Promotion of Peace

Paul Rogers

Despite the end of the Cold War, many other conflicts persisted in the 1990s. The hope that a peace dividend would help to alleviate poverty was replaced by doubts regarding the effects of free market globalisation and environmental constraints. Future concerns include the continuing aftermath of the Cold War, the increased destructiveness of modern warfare despite, the increased sophistication of modern weaponry, the widening poverty gap between a wealthy elite and the majority of the world's population, and developing global economic and environmental threats. The response to all this should be economic co-operation for sustainable development, including trade reform, and radical change in the environmental impact of the industrialised countries.

Yet it appears that the response of the US, and to a lesser extent Europe, is to maintain the *status quo* in its own interests by military means, an attitude that seems to have been reinforced by the events of 11 September 2001. Nevertheless, these developments are opposed by citizen groups in the developed world and by analysts in the South. The United Nations and its agencies have been at the forefront of analysis and proposals for action in many of these fields. Its role is likely to increase in the next thirty years, and it must be made as effective a global body as possible.

The ending of the Cold War 12 years ago was expected to lead to a more peaceful and stable world. [1] With the greatest source of potential conflict removed, and the possibility of diverting the billions of dollars of the peace dividend into social programmes, there were real hopes that progress would

The UN and its Future in the 21st Century

be made in the alleviation of poverty. Even the immediate horror of the Gulf War did not diminish that prospect. Indeed, many saw the development of a broad international coalition against Iraq's belligerence as proof that a new world order was well under way.

By the end of the century, people were less sanguine. Two of the most enduring conflicts, between the Israelis and Palestinians and between India and Pakistan, showed no sign of easing, former Yugoslavia was plunged into war for much of the 1990s, there were bitter conflicts in the Caucasus and protracted violence in Colombia, Mexico, Algeria, Somalia, Sri Lanka, Spain, Indonesia and many other countries. Only in Northern Ireland, Peru and a few other conflict-zones did there appear to be prospects for curbing conflict.

Moreover, by the turn of the century, grave doubts were emerging over the effects of free market globalisation. Public movements in the South against the perceived excesses of the free market had spread to Northern countries, as unlikely coalitions of interest groups staged mass demonstrations in Seattle, Washington, Prague and Genoa. While these movements eased their actions in the immediate aftermath of 11 September 2001, there remained an unease at the lack of progress towards a fairer world economy. Even the cuts in military spending had largely ceased by the end of the old century, and one effect of the attacks on 11 September was an immediate increase in United States defence spending, to be followed almost certainly by some other western countries.

Within this uncertain world, the United Nations remained as the prime intergovernmental organisation, working in many of the relevant fields through its specialised agencies, attempting to promote arms control and disarmament for conventional as well as mass destruction weapons, and seeking to promote peace-keeping and conflict prevention through a range of channels.

The UN and its Future in the 21st Century

Future Conflicts

Looking to the future, we need to address four issues: what are the likely 'drivers' or parameters of future conflict, what are their probable effects in terms of types of conflicts that are likely to be prevalent, how can we best avoid such conflicts, and what is the role of the United Nations in doing so?

Of the potential drivers of conflict, one is certainly the enduring effects of the Cold War. That 45-year period left a legacy of weapons developments and proliferation that remains a feature of the world scene. While some control of nuclear and chemical excesses is in place, there remains a problem of proliferation of both classes of weapon. The potential for biological weapons has been demonstrated by the US domestic experience in late 2001, and the cascade of light arms from conflict-prone regions at the end of the Cold War has greatly added to violence in many parts of the world, most notably much of Africa and South West Asia.

Moreover, there have been marked developments in the field of conventional warfare. While most attention has been focused on precision-guided weapons, including cruise missiles and laser-guided bombs, a parallel development has been the increasing sophistication of area-impact weapons systems designed specifically to cause maximum damage over a large area. They include cluster bombs, fuel-air explosives and, in particular, multiple-launch rocket systems that deliver anti-personnel sub-munitions. Some of these, when fired as a barrage, are as destructive as small nuclear weapons.

These developments are a reminder of the destructiveness of modern conflict, but beyond the processes of weapons proliferation lie two further parameters of conflict. One is the root problem of the widening gap between an increasingly wealthy elite and the majority of the world's population. Spread across the world but located mainly in countries of the North Atlantic community and some in the West Pacific, an elite of around one billion people has surged ahead of the rest. On figures from the UN

The UN and its Future in the 21st Century

Commission on Trade and Development, [2] the richest fifth of the world's population had 69 per cent of the world's wealth in 1965 but 81 per cent by 1990, with inequalities increasing through the 1990s. The poorer sectors of the world's population may not have got poorer, but well over two billion people continue to have to manage on the equivalent of two dollars a day.

What has been called economic *apartheid*, with a minority of the world's people surging ahead of the rest, seems set to continue in the coming decades, aided by relatively higher population increases in poorer regions. Birth rates have certainly declined markedly but the demographic transition is a fifty-year process, not least as billions of people born over the past thirty years grow up and have children of their own.

More generally, there is a strong argument that the increasingly globalised free market is delivering patchy economic growth but is consistently failing to deliver economic justice. But this is against a background of decades of determined efforts in southern countries to promote development, many of them focused on improvements in primary education, literacy and communications.

The results have been impressive, but one of the largely unrecognised effects has been that the marginalised majority of the world's people are becoming far more aware of their own marginalisation. As a consequence, a potential revolution of frustrated expectations is beginning to make itself felt, not least in the evolution of anti-elite insurgencies and a more general anti-elite and anti-western mood in many countries of the South.

These may be expressed locally or globally and they may, in more extreme cases, involve the development of radical social movements that focus on religious, ethnic, nationalist or political identities. The 'Shining Path' rebellion in Peru had a brutal quasi-Maoist base, whereas the Zapatistas in Mexico draw support for a more tolerant socialist agenda primarily from indigenous peoples. In many parts of North Africa and the Middle East, Islamic movements are at the core of revolt, whereas in South Asia, Hindu

The UN and its Future in the 21st Century

nationalism is significant. Ethnicity remains central in many parts of South-East Asia, not least Indonesia, and a complex mix of ethnic, religious and cultural identities has been central to conflicts in the Balkans and Caucasus.

What is frequently the case, though, is that perceptions of marginalisation, elite control and even external control are primary issues in the development of discontent and radical response. Nor is this confined to local responses - the attacks of 11 September followed a decade of attempted actions against western interests. While previous attempts at mass-casualty terrorism had failed in New York, Paris and elsewhere, their significance was there to be seen, if all too often ignored. [3]

Environmental Constraints

The final parameter of potential conflict is the developing phenomenon of global environmental constraints. This has long been predicted, certainly back to the *Limits to Growth* debate of thirty years ago, [4] but is now much more clearly apparent, as is the realisation that it has profound security implications.

There are two broad areas of concern. One is the potential for increased conflict over resources, especially those of a strategic significance that have a small location base. Some of these are resources of specialised use, such as the cobalt and tantalum reserves of central Africa that have a played a major role in recent conflict, and the rock phosphate reserves of Western Sahara, important fertiliser components in world agriculture, that lie behind much of the conflict between the Polisario Front and Morocco.

Most significant of all is the location of world oil reserves, with some two-thirds of all known reserves in the Persian Gulf region. Moreover, most of the most easily obtainable reserves are located there, new reserves are being discovered at a faster rate than production, and the reserves are amongst the cheapest in the world. The Gulf War itself was fought primarily over the control of Gulf oil, and much of the anti-American mood from which the al-Qaida network and others have drawn their support comes from a perception of US control of the Gulf and support for a neo-feudal Saudi elite.

The second area of environmental concern lies with global human impacts. An early marker was the impact of chlorofluorocarbon (CFC) pollutants on the ozone layer, a problem appreciated in the early 1980s, not least because of the activities of the UN Environment Programme (UNEP). By focusing on the potential impact of CFCs, UNEP helped prepare the ground for action in the late 1980s that led to some quite effective international co-operation to phase out the pollutants. While the problem of ozone depletion remains significant, the international response does show that, in some circumstances, there is a real possibility of global co-operation.

Even so, of much greater long-term significance is the phenomenon of climate change, caused primarily by the emission of 'greenhouse' gases, especially carbon dioxide, from the burning of fossil fuels. Since the use of fossil fuels is an integral part of urban industrial societies, the control of such greenhouse gases is likely to prove very much more difficult than responding to ozone depletion.

Until about five years ago, most forms of climate change were expected to have their main effects on temperate latitudes, regions of relative wealth that might be able to cope. In the longer term, sea level changes would affect many tropical countries, including rich alluvial delta lowlands that support many millions of people, but in the shorter term it was anticipated that the northern and southern temperate latitudes would experience the major effects, mainly in the form of temperature increases and changes in rainfall patterns. These regions were, for the most part, composed of wealthy countries that might be able to make the necessary adaptations.

More recently, there has developed a view within climatology that the tropics will also be affected, both in terms of violent weather events causing great harm to impoverished communities, and a more general tendency for changes in rainfall distribution. The latter aspect is by far the most significant, with huge implications not just for social well-being but for international security.

There are indications that, over the next half century, the tropical regions of the world will experience substantial shifts in the distribution of rainfall, with more rain tending to fall on the oceans and in the polar regions and progressively less rain falling over the tropical land masses. The likely effects include the partial drying-out of some of the most fertile regions of the tropics, leading to a substantial decrease in the ecological carrying-capacity of the land, resulting in decreases in food production.

These are the areas that support a very substantial part of the human population, much of it by subsistence agriculture. Many of the communities are very poor, and form part of impoverished states that have very little capacity to respond to such fundamental changes. As a result, the likelihood of persistent food shortages and even famines become much greater, leading to increased human suffering, social unrest and a greatly increased pressure on migration.

Taking these factors together, we can envisage, at least on present trends, the interaction of increasing socio-economic divisions with the effects of environmental constraints in a world that has a wide range of advanced and highly destructive military capabilities. On present trends, we run the risk of what the conservationist Edwin Brooks called 'a crowded, glowering planet of massive inequalities of wealth, buttressed by stark force yet endlessly threatened by desperate people in the global ghettos.' [5]

Among the forms of conflict that are most likely, anti-elite insurgencies will be particularly common, with paramilitary action directed not just against local elites but against their transnational supporters, whether these be states or corporations. There will also be substantial security implications stemming from greatly increased migratory pressures.

Migration is already a major political issue in Europe, with anti-immigrant political parties quick to utilise the vulnerabilities present in the poorest sectors of societies that are receiving immigrants. If migratory pressures increase tenfold or more, as is a likely consequence of climate change, then harsh military responses that in turn lead to 'militant migration' are likely. Environmental conflict is also increasingly likely, not least over the control of the Persian Gulf oil supplies, a range of strategic minerals and, in particular, water resources.

The Response

To avoid the development of 'a crowded, glowering planet' requires progressive and often radical action on a number of fronts. Perhaps most important of all is the need for persistent progress towards economic co-operation for sustainable development. Economic co-operation requires action on three fronts - debt, trade and aid. The debt burden on many less developed countries remains the biggest single obstacle to development, and the much-lauded progress of the last three years has, in reality, achieved little so far. There is therefore an urgent need for a sustained and extensive programme of debt cancellation, with immediate action aimed at the most heavily indebted countries.

In parallel with this, there remains an essential requirement for trade reform, given that the post-colonial trading system was so unbalanced as to give industrialised states a near-permanent trading advantage. A sustained integrated commodities programme coupled with generalised tariff preferences would transform the trading position of most southern states, providing an immense boost to development prospects. While less significant, development assistance remains important, especially in the form of multilateral assistance for gendered programmes of sustainable development aimed at the poorest communities.

Even if there were to be the necessary transformation of debt relief, trade

The UN and its Future in the 21st Century

reform and aid strategies, it would not have the necessary global impact without radical changes in the environmental impact of the advanced industrialised countries. This requires rapid progress towards sustainable economies, especially in relation to curbing current rates of resource use. Perhaps most important of all is the need radically to scale down the emission of greenhouse gases, a process that will require a combination of energy conservation measures with the taking up of a wide range of renewable energy strategies.

While the Kyoto accords begin the process of moving towards low carbon economies, they represent no more than a tentative initial step. Expert opinion indicates that urban industrial states need to decrease their greenhouse gas emission by around 60 per cent - far more than is anticipated at present.

If it was possible to move towards a global system in which there is sustained action on issues of the socio-economic divide and environmental constraints, then it would be possible to envisage a genuine easing of the tensions that are currently developing in an increasingly fractured world. They would need to be accompanied by a wide range of measures intended to curb excesses of militarisation and weapons development, as well as international co-operation on issues of conflict prevention, peace-keeping and post-conflict peace-building. How, though, do they compare with actual trends?

The Western Perspective

In contrast to what is required, the current international security paradigm, dominated by the United States and its western allies, is much more a matter of maintaining the *status quo*. It was characterised aptly by James Woolsey, head of the US Central Intelligence Agency in the early 1990s, when he described the transition to the post-Cold War world as the west having slain the dragon (of the Soviet threat) but now living in a jungle full

The UN and its Future in the 21st Century

of poisonous snakes. [6]

What is most commonly seen from a western security perspective is a volatile world of many threats to western interests and therefore to international peace and stability. This view is especially strong in the United States, not least since the election of George W. Bush. Conservative circles within the Bush administration see the United States as having an historical role, as the world's only superpower, to preach the gospel of the globalised free market, with the United States the guarantor of stability, in its own image. This was a view memorably expressed by Charles Krauthammer [7] when describing the need for the United States to pursue its own security needs in a unilateral manner:

> Multipolarity, yes, when there is no alternative. But not when there is. Not when we have the unique imbalance of power that we enjoy today - and that has given the international system a stability and essential tranquillity it had not know for at least a century. …The international environment is far more likely to enjoy peace under a single hegemon. Moreover, we are not just any hegemon. We run a uniquely benign imperium.

The instruments of this benign imperium have involved a transformation of the armed forces of the United States and, to an extent, its allies. Instead of the massive tank armies and other features of the Cold War, we now have much more emphasis on long range force projection, whether by aircraft carriers, sea-launched cruise missiles or strategic bombers. There is a heavy emphasis on amphibious operations and special operations forces, a far greater concern with space-based reconnaissance and the use of drones, all subsumed in a belief of the need to be able to fight wars in far-off places in pursuit of security interests. There is a particular concern with the support of local elites and commercial interests - the US currently has counter-insurgency training missions in some 55 countries.

Overall, there is a deep-seated belief that control can be maintained and that the lid can be kept on the pot of discontent and opposition to the *status quo*

The UN and its Future in the 21st Century

- liddism rules OK.[1] Moreover, it is a view that has been reinforced by the tragic events of 11 September. There seems to have been a profound failure to recognise the implications of those atrocities, and the manner in which they require us to rethink our security attitudes. Instead there was a three-month war in which an intensive air campaign aided participants in the Afghanistan civil war to unseat the Taliban regime.

Bombing one of the poorest countries on earth certainly helped lead to the destruction of an appalling regime, but those replacing it included groups with a record on human rights that was every bit as bad and, in the process, many thousands of people were killed, including over 3,000 civilians. In the 'war on terrorism', there was a persistent concentration on the presumed perpetrators of the atrocities, but little or no attempt to recognise the depth of their support in the Middle East and South West Asia, nor its connection with western military forces in the Persian Gulf.

More generally, and especially in the case of the Bush administration, there has been a wider tendency to pursue individualistic rather than global policies. This has included the refusal to ratify the Comprehensive Test Ban Treaty, opposition to the strengthening of the Biological and Toxin Weapons Convention (BTWC), withdrawal from the Anti-Ballistic Missile treaty, and criticisms of the anti-personnel land mine treaty and aspects of the UN's proposals on the control of light arms. There has been a reluctance to co-operate on many other issues, not least the proposed International Criminal Court, conventions on terrorism and, most notably, the Kyoto accords.

In some areas, European governments have adopted a more progressive stance, especially on Kyoto and on regional issues relating to East Asia and the Middle East. There has also been a greater concern with debt relief and a few aspects of trade reform. In other areas, it is the western attitude as a whole that is problematic rather than that of the US alone. Thus, there is very little willingness in Europe to entertain the major issues of North-South trade reform or questions of intellectual property rights. Only a few countries are seeking to improve their official development assistance programmes, and even support for the Kyoto protocols rarely recognises that these are no more than a beginning.

At the same time, there is a concern that the response to 11 September 2001 is essentially military while being politically superficial, with a private acceptance among a number of European governments that a failure to address the root causes of these problems is against long-term common security interests. [3] Furthermore, there is evidence of much public concern with the wider global problems that are in process of development. Arguments for debt relief have come primarily from citizen groups, issues of environmental constraints retain a strong public profile and there is a developing recognition that the global wealth-poverty divide is both ethically unacceptable and a potential source of deep instability.

Moreover, it is also becoming apparent that the views on global security that are peculiar to western states are not those of the majority world. Analysts in the South see the world in an entirely different way, most commonly arguing that it is dominated by a largely western-orientated elite that is producing greater and greater divisions. Such analysts are slowly getting a voice in the west, and they add powerfully to those in western states that are working for a more just and peaceful world.

A Role for the United Nations

In such circumstances, and recognising that there is a potential coalition between campaigners, non-government organisations and elements of government, how significant is the potential role of the United Nations? Can it play a major part in the transformation of global systems, or is it largely the prisoner of a few of the more powerful states?

One of the most notable features of the process of responding positively to the problems facing the global community is that the UN and a number of its agencies have frequently been at the forefront of analysis and proposals for action. Even though there are formidable problems of bureaucracy and inefficiency, the examples are legion. On the matter of CFC pollution and ozone depletion, UNEP did much to help establish an international regime to bring the problem under control. On health issues, the World Health Organization has been instrumental in key areas of disease control and public health.

On the wider issues of poverty and the rich-poor gap, the UN Development Programme has recently been particularly effective in providing evidence for current trends. Over a much longer term, and especially in the 1960s and 1970s, the UN Conference on Trade and Development was persistent in its attempt to focus attention on the fundamental linkage between the nature of the world trading system and problems of underdevelopment. The UN's concern with human rights has frequently resulted in criticism of some of its work, yet the UN Commission on Human Rights has persistently tried to point to the problems of human rights abuses, doing so in a way that involves valid criticisms of member states.

The UN has also been active in significant areas of arms control and disarmament, whether this be in relation to weapons of mass destruction or to problems of light arms transfers. In the areas of conflict prevention, peacekeeping and post-conflict peace-building, there is a considerable body of experience that has accumulated, especially in the past decade. For all its problems, the UN endeavours to put that experience to effective use, in spite of the problems of trying to work with diverse governments, each with their own particular interests and concerns.

Perhaps the real significance of the current global predicament is that it involves diverse sets of problems that are progressively interacting. The core elements are the socio-economic divide, environmental constraints and weapons proliferation, and they require responses that are both broadly based and global. As such, there is little alternative to promoting and making more effective the work of the UN. In a very real sense, the next thirty years may require us to rely much more on the UN than we have done in the past fifty years. If this is the case then it is in everyone's interest to make it as effective a global body as is possible.

References

1. Rogers P. *Losing Control: Global Security in the 21st Century*. London: Pluto Press, 2000.
2. UN Commission on Trade and Development. *Trade and Development Report 1997*. Geneva: UNCTAD, 1997.
3. Rogers P, Elworthy S. *The United States, Europe and the Majority World after 11 September*. Oxford: Oxford Research Group (51 Plantation Road, Oxford OX2 6JE), 2001.
4. Meadows DH, Meadows DL, Randers J, Behrens III WW. *Limits to Growth*. London: Earth Island, 1972.
5. Brooks E. The implications of ecological limits to growth in terms of expectations and aspirations in developed and less developed countries. In: Vann A, Rogers P, eds. *Human Ecology and Development*. London: Plenum, 1973: 125-39.
6. Woolsey J. Testimony to Senate Hearings. Washington DC, February 1993.
7. Krauthammer C. The Bush doctrine: ABM, Kyoto and the new American unilateralism. *The Weekly Standard*, Washington DC, 4 June 2001.

(Delivered 12 June 2001)

Addendum

Following the termination of the Taliban regime in Afghanistan at the end of 2001, the Bush administration widened the 'war on terror' to include an 'axis of evil' of three countries, Iran, Iraq and North Korea, and also embarked on a global campaign to track down and detain or kill the leadership of al-Qaida and its affiliates. During the course of 2002, more than a thousand people were detained without trial, many of them at Camp X-Ray at the Guantanamo US base in Cuba.

There were early expectations of progress towards stability in Afghanistan, although UN and other officials pointed repeatedly to the need for substantial civil aid backed up by a peace-keeping and stabilisation force of up to 30,000 troops. The Bush administration also anticipated success in its war against al-Qaida, expecting to detain or kill Osama bin Laden and the Taliban leader, Mullah Omar.

In practice, there were many further operations by al-Qaida and its affiliates during 2002 and 2003, including major attacks in Indonesia, Kenya, Turkey, Morocco, Saudi Arabia and Pakistan, culminating in a devastating series of attacks in Madrid early in 2004. Furthermore, progress in Afghanistan was extraordinarily slow, with rampant insecurity, the re-emergence of warlords and a massive increase in opium poppy cultivation. There was also a resurgence of Taliban activity that, by mid-2004, was tying down a force of some 20,000 US troops.

In spite of these developments, the Bush administration had determined to start the process of defeating the 'axis of evil', and the regime of Saddam Hussein was terminated in a brief but intense conflict in March/April 2003, leading on to a protracted insurgency that, even 15 months later, was involving around 140,000 US troops and over 20,000 from other countries including Britain.

By mid-2004, over 11,000 Iraqi civilians had been killed and more than 20,000 seriously injured. While most of the casualties were caused in the first three weeks of the war, the developing insurgency is, at the time of writing (August 2004), exacting a continuing toll. Although the United States is no longer the formal occupying power, it is operating through a client regime, expects to maintain current troop levels for several years and is embarking on the building of a number of permanent bases. Against the expectations of the Bush administration, a long-term insurgency in Iraq looks highly probable.

At a more global level, clear divisions have developed between the United States and some Western European countries, and, across the world, there has been an upsurge in anti-Americanism. Much of this is unrecognised within the United States, but there is still an acceptance that problems are developing with the achieving the goal of a New American Century.

Key issues addressed in the lecture, including global socio-economic divisions and environmental constraints, have only partially been marginalised by the 'war on terror'. Moreover, the very problems being experienced by the United States in Iraq and Afghanistan make it increasingly likely that creative and less military alternatives to current approaches may be considered.

In this context, the United Nations was largely sidelined in the run-up to the war in Iraq, but wise counsel emanating from within the organisation is now being considered to an extent that seemed unlikely a year ago. It is also the case that issues such as climate change and socio-economic divisions are become more prominent in the agenda of international affairs, even if still largely discounted in Washington.

It follows that there is a considerable opportunity for framing the international agenda in a progressive manner, not just in terms of responding to political violence but especially in addressing the longer-term

The UN and its Future in the 21st Century

issues. In this context the role of the United Nations will be greatly significant, and the more that current militaristic responses to political violence are shown to be unworkable, the more the role of the United Nations should come to the fore.

(22 August 2004)

The United Nations: the Embarrassment of International Law

Denis J. Halliday

The United Nations should be working towards an international community living in peace under the aegis of international law. Although progress was made in its early years, notably in de-colonisation, with its membership increased from 50 to 189, major inequalities remain between its nations and their peoples. The Security Council, and in particular its five permanent members, has been guilty of double standards in enforcing international law. Investment should create prosperity and not increase demand for arms. Independent oversight of the UN, and particularly the SC, by civil society is needed. If the legitimacy of the UN is to be restored, the SC should become more representative, the power of the General Assembly restored, and the role of the International Court of Justice increased. All members of the UN, especially the P5, must respect international law as enshrined in the UN Charter and Conventions.

Many years ago, Secretary-General Dag Hammarskjöld said that he saw the United Nations as 'a venture in progress towards an international community living in peace under laws of justice'. I suspect that he would be disappointed at the progress the UN has made since. He might well note that the 'laws of justice' – international laws - are indeed in place, but sadly rejected, violated with impunity, or simply neglected, by many member states. Failure by the Security Council to respect the provisions of international law, flowing from the Charter itself, now sadly serves to embarrass the UN and its member states. Conspicuous is the absence of balanced application - domestically, internationally and most damagingly via decisions of the Security Council.

The UN and its Future in the 21st Century

Nevertheless the UN remains the most essential instrument for world peace and security. Global interdependence is an integral reality of the same. International law and its proper application by member states of the UN are essential to the product of inter-dependence – peace and security. The Security Council is charged with the responsibility for the maintenance of that global well-being for all in both North and South.

Inequalities amongst nations and their peoples are only too apparent inside the United Nations, inside the Council, and throughout the world. We are all too familiar with the terrible impact of, among others, North- driven globalisation; ethnic strife; genocide; the internally displaced; refugees; military coalitions; aggression in several forms; modern warfare with its high level bombing of civilians; exploitation of the environment; abuse of non-renewable natural resources; and the application of double standards in foreign policy and the work of the Security Council.

In short, and it is bizarre in the year 2002, the ancient notion of 'might being right' is alive and well, and perceived by some to be acceptable! Speaking from my layman's viewpoint, and from my own experience serving the United Nations - and recognising that 34 years does not an expert make – in particular in respect of the workings of the Security Council, this is where I focus. It is international law and its proper application that must drive the work of the United Nations - not the 'might' and national interests of some, the most powerful, member states.

A sole hyper-power is dangerous. Rejection of international law is both arrogant and irresponsible. Despite the inherent weaknesses of the Charter, the peoples of the world need the UN to function, not as intended in 1945, but more in the best interests of all peoples and all states around the world.

This is not a 'feel-good' lecture on the UN, yet I am the first to underline the good work that is being accomplished everyday by agencies and bodies within the UN Family. Instead – still a believer in United Nations value-

The UN and its Future in the 21st Century

added - I want to share some personal thoughts on the UN and its application of international law. I examine the reality of that application today, some of the consequences and what we might want to consider doing about creating positive change. Or can we indefinitely ignore the corruption of the Charter, already imperfect, by the five Permanent Members of the Security Council? I do not believe we can.

However, first let me say that one of the reasons I was pleased to accept the invitation to deliver the Erskine Childers lecture for 2002 is that over many years I had the pleasure to work with Erskine himself. I first met him in Bangkok, Thailand when he headed up an innovative project of his own making funded by the United Nations Development Programme to demonstrate the importance of communications and information in the successful implementation of development assistance projects. He showed most effectively that flows of information within-country between the parties, concerned such as government, community and individual, were invaluable for success.

Later, in the UNDP headquarters in New York, I again had the pleasure of working with Erskine when, as Head of UNDP information Services, he brought fresh creativity to information in support of development activities within the UN system of organisations itself. And finally, when I was Assistant Secretary-General for UN Human Resources Management, I met with Erskine as he collaborated with Sir Brian Urquhart on a number of think pieces. I was tapping his brain, not he mine!

In this lecture, I make use of some ideas that he and Brian Urquhart developed in their 1999 book.[1] This publication addresses various means to enhance the effectiveness of the UN, including the concept of a one term Secretary-General selected in a thorough and rational manner on the basis of identifiable criteria. This is of course the kind of revolutionary change we have yet to see, and we sadly have to acknowledge that most member states, certainly the powerful veto-holders, do not appear to want an independent and strong Secretary-General who just might take initiatives, or use his power under Article 99 of the Charter to publicly admonish and demand compliance with the obligations of membership.

I think that Erskine would agree with me that global well-being in the broadest sense, demands that we, and the member states, must learn to perceive internationally. This includes awareness of, and commitment to, the obligations that the United Nations imposes, and the importance of strength, authority, integrity and effectiveness. And a future of global peace and security for all, without a legally functioning, morally strong and fully participatory UN, is unlikely and perhaps impossible.

We need to remember that the UN is the only legitimate world body intended to legislate, promote and demand respect for human rights and the well being of all men and women, North and South, without regard to race, sex, language, or religion, as set out in Article 1 of the Charter. These are goals that I imagine all of us in this room share. But the UN and its ability to serve those ends is in great danger.

Recently we have witnessed the humiliation of the Secretary-General and the Security Council by outright rejection of the resolution to have an investigation of the tragedy of Jenin in the occupied territories of Palestine. We should not forget the deliberate bypassing of the UN in the form of the NATO attacks on Kosovo. We see Iraq having little choice but to refuse re-entry of UN disarmament inspections, given American intentions to attack militarily once again, Washington legislation calling for the overthrow of its head of state, and the disgraceful record of UNSCOM functioning as an intelligence source. Can we ignore the illegal aggression on the people of Afghanistan undertaken without any discussion by the Security Council under Chapter VII of the Charter, a prerequisite for any such military action, and in violation of the defensive-only constraints set out in Article 51?

This lecture is in part intended to unsettle your thinking and to have you consider the necessity of reform in respect of the UN, in particular the

The UN and its Future in the 21st Century

Security Council - and then do something about it. I am hopeful that some of you are in positions, or will be in positions one day, to do just that.

One of my own failures, of which my daughter Fransisca frequently reminds me, is that my generation has neglected many aspects of the global environment. I am sure you are all sensitive to the need for environmental protection and monitoring. Today, we are also guilty of neglecting the UN to the extent that we now have evidence of an urgent requirement for oversight. I refer to active monitoring of the most important and fundamental work of the organisation, namely peace and security - the unique mandate of the Security Council. Just as we neglect the corruption of the global environment, we are also neglecting the corruption and proper functioning of the Security Council. Certain member states are treating the mandate of the Council and its proper application of international law as carelessly as many of us treat the environment and the earth's scarce natural resources.

The history of the UN and its origins in 1945 after the appalling horrors of World War II are well known. The victors of that war established the UN to tackle worthy goals. Unfortunately, they also determined to protect their own national interests and desire for control. Another League of Nations, of which the United States was not a member, was to be avoided. This was done among other things through the establishment of veto power and permanent membership of the Security Council for the chosen few, that is, the victorious nations of the war. It was founded with the participation of only some 50 independent states. Happily, thanks to the end of most colonial regimes, today's UN has 189 member states, with the recent addition of Switzerland. Whether these member states are truly independent or not, I leave my listeners and readers to decide. It is difficult to define independence in the context of economic and military domination by a few powers that are wedded to the 'might is right' concept.

Despite the hidden - and not so hidden - agendas of 1945, enlightened work was accomplished in San Francisco when the Charter was adopted and again in 1948 when the Universal Declaration of Human Rights was established. In addition, throughout the 1950s and 1960s the General Assembly played a key role as the venue and the instrument for the global process of de-colonisation. However, the unmonitored and unrepresentative power of the Security Council today is undermining much of that hopeful and participatory beginning.

Over the years the role and the core importance of the fully representative GA has been diminished. This is also true of the International Court of Justice - the World Court. The important work of the Economic and Social Council has been neglected as development assistance and co-operation has been consistently under-funded. Instead, billions of US dollars are invested in military research and development and arms manufacture and sales, mainly by the same five Permanent Members of the Security Council who are entrusted with maintaining peace and security! At the same time, the most basic human rights of billions are neglected - the rights to development, food, health-care, education, employment and housing. Even the right to live, and have hope, cannot be taken for granted in our sorry world.

Obviously all this must be changed. Remarkably, the head of the World Bank acknowledges that poverty, which undermines these same human rights, is the root cause of terrorism. Why did the SC fail to discuss that reality after 11 September 2001? Why do major member states think that more violence such as we have seen in Afghanistan and Palestine will bring an end to terror? Why is it that the vulnerability the North now suddenly feels, does not lead to a new understanding - that billions throughout the South feel the same life-threatening vulnerability every day? Yet we are surprised by the violent cry for recognition and attention that terrorism represents.

Perhaps the permanent members of the Security Council, the largest arms traders, have not learned the importance of investing in live people and vital communities? That seems incredible. It should be obvious that they need to spend generously on conflict prevention in its various forms, instead of billions of dollars on war, aggressive interventions and often belated peace-keeping - which, by definition, represents a failure of the UN to anticipate and assist in resolution of differences before they grow out of control. The UN must invest in people before the damage is done, before ethnic strife has killed, before genocide, and before the refugees and displaced persons have been wrenched from their homes and livelihoods. Is that so difficult?

Member states with global and exploitative ambitions must be convinced by their friends and Northern allies to accept an organisation capable and primed to intervene non-violently, even though this would hurt their profitable arms trade. They need to allow the UN to use its moral authority to establish respect for civil, political and other human rights and to draw down on the benefits of cultural, religious and social differences, in keeping with the spirit of the Charter.

Investment must be used to create prosperity and provide hope. Investment is poorly used when intended to increase demand for arms manufacture and sales; to open opportunities to test new and dreadful weapons, including so-called smart bombs and depleted uranium; to facilitate conditions of irreparable damage to the environment and in exploiting cheap labour, thereby set aside the economic and social rights of others. Investment should better be used to encourage and enhance social, political and economic improvements consistent with the Universal Declaration of Human Rights. For example, money should be put into education. Do we doubt that such an investment would reap extraordinary rewards for us all? Aggression under the guise of humanitarian intervention, or the American 'war on terror', the terrible consequences of which we have witnessed recently in Afghanistan and in Palestine, is not a productive investment for any country.

The neglect of Chapter VI and abuse of Chapter VII of the UN Charter by the five permanent members of the SC has become increasingly questionable. And 'questionable' is too gentle a word – I should say that it has become increasingly frightening for the smaller member states. And we should all be frightened for example, by the deadly military reaction – via State terrorism – to crises that should be addressed non-violently by the international community under Chapter VI. We cannot afford to forget that the vast majority of member states represented in the General Assembly have no involvement in Security Council decisions that affect their world stability, and often tragically create situations that lead to greater human chaos and suffering.

Structurally and in reality, there is no higher authority in or outside the UN to monitor the SC and interpret proper application of the Charter. The World Court has no established role in this regard. Many of us believe that some independent civil society oversight body is required urgently, a body with a North/South mix to oversee Council decisions and their implementation and impact on civilians in particular. Simple international publicity, exposing consequences, double standards and commission of crimes against humanity, might suffice to diminish and ultimately end the corruption of the Charter. Public international embarrassment might curb the excesses of the Permanent Members.

For example, currently we see every day double standards of application in the Middle East resulting from the vested interests of one or more Permanent Members. Some 'friends' can reject UN resolutions with impunity whilst other member states do so at dreadful cost to their innocent civilian populations, punished by the UN through neglect, sanctions and often warfare - I need not name names.

We have seen the terrible results of the failure of UN member states to acknowledge genocide – as determined by the Convention - in the case of Rwanda. The UN did no better for the thousands killed in Sebrenica. We have seen the terrible consequences of prolonged economic sanctions – almost twelve years of a uniquely comprehensive and punitive UN embargo - for the children and adults of Iraq. We have witnessed Security

The UN and its Future in the 21st Century

Council delay in respect of stopping the killing in Timor, and we have heard silence for the people of Chechnya. We have witnessed the careless high level bombing attacks on Afghanistan, by 15,000 feet heroes, with loss of civilian life - an attack never considered nor approved by the Security Council under Chapter VII of the Charter.

Most recently we have seen America prevent the UN from protecting the people of Palestine from state terrorism and military invasion of Palestinian space. We watch as massive destruction of human rights take place before our television eyes. We have UN member states that seem unwilling to comprehend the root causes of suicide bombing- the desperation of the weak, marginalised and forgotten - and thereby end the deaths of innocent Israeli civilians. Instead we see the continuation of military aggression and use of sophisticated weapons against an almost unarmed populace, for whose safety the UN is responsible. As mentioned already, we have witnessed the almost unbelievable rejection by Israel, supported by the US, of a SC resolution calling for an examination of the tragedy of Jenin.

I hardly need to recall the failure of the UN to stop, or even address, the crimes against humanity committed by the UN-backed American coalition during the Gulf War. Are we to understand that the illegal invasion of Kuwait is justification for the Basra road massacre, or the employment of depleted uranium? Nor do I need to recall the UN failure to intervene in the invasion of Lebanon, in refugee-camp massacres, and the 22-year-long illegal occupation of southern Lebanon combined with repeated punitive air attacks on civilian infrastructure in breach of the Geneva Conventions and Protocols.

The common factor in these neglectful cover-up situations is the involvement and vested self-interest of Permanent Members of the Security Council, the same member states entrusted to defend the word and spirit of the Charter, not diminish it, and certainly not to actively corrupt it.

These cases of double standards and national self-interest in Council decision-making emphasise the dangers in the future. If we are in the coming decades, to have a United Nations that protects the best interests of the majority of people throughout the world, North and South, as opposed to protecting the vested interests of the Northern powers, reform has to be undertaken.

Reform in itself will not suffice unless there is a significant change of attitude on the part of member states, particularly the veto-wielding five. I am not advocating world government. I *am* calling for recognition that no one country is above, or immune to the requirements and obligations of international law. Respect for such law ultimately best serves, and protects, all member states, despite the need for periodic compromise and adjustment of domestic law. When we have rejection of such law by the P5, and in particular by the US, we have a situation that undermines the efforts and moral authority of the UN to have other less powerful member states comply.

This crisis of rejection applies to such fundamental provisions of international law as the Convention on the Rights of the Child; the Convention on Land Mines; the Kyoto Accords; the Biological and Toxin Weapons Convention; the Law of the Sea; and the International Criminal Court, to mention a few. You will appreciate that not only is American leadership undermined by its unwillingness to be part of such global legal provisions, but, more importantly, the credibility of the UN itself is undermined. It is threatening and embarrassing for the world body to have its most powerful member state not endorse such important international legal provisions.

Congressional rejection of UN provisions and international conventions, and its willingness to disregard Security Council resolutions, is most damaging. The situation is not helped by having an unfriendly host country (an issue Erskine Childers addressed) openly criticise and threaten the organisation and certain member states wishing to appear at UN headquarters, and at the same time, while failing to pay financial

The UN and its Future in the 21st Century

assessments, endlessly hammering the UN for its bureaucracy and undermining – and effectively removing - its Secretary-General when dissatisfied.

The voices of the South must be heard in the SC, and the power of the more representative General Assembly needs to be restored. The World Court needs a greater role, with its decisions binding on member states. The weakening of the independence of the UN has led to a crisis of confidence in the organisation today that is very apparent as one travels and speaks with people in Europe, the Middle East and throughout much of the South.

If we are to enhance the credibility of the UN, the Security Council cannot remain unrepresentative. It cannot continue to be manipulated by a few and must be restructured. It must have full and effective representation of all the countries of the world, North and South. The majority of people, including the great and small countries of the world, must have rotational permanent and equal presence on the Council. In my view, we must have permanent seats for elected regional representation, that is, for the member states of Central and South America, Southern and South East Asia and of course, proper permanent representation of Sub-Sahara Africa and the Middle East.

We must change the Old Boys' Club of Five into a non-veto holding chamber, where the voices of the South will be permanently present, and more importantly, heard and respected. That will change decision-making, provide added strength and wisdom to the Council and bring viewpoints to bear that remain largely unheard today. We must demand only one standard of application for all, including the veto-powers, with respect for the intent and spirit of the Charter, the Universal Declaration of Human Rights and other aspects of international law.

These changes need to be combined with an oversight authority to monitor the performance of the Council, the quality of its decisions, their compatibility with the Charter itself and other international legal provisions.

If we do not move the UN in this direction, much of the world will continue to question its very legitimacy and its decisions, which impact so widely, and sometimes so dangerously, on countries that have no access to the decision making process. Without such legitimacy, the role of the Security Council and the UN itself is undermined. This will take the UN to a situation more untenable than we have today – where the failure of Permanent Members and other states to respect international law not only causes great embarrassment, but damages the importance, credibility and authority of the UN.

Those of you associated with the United Nations, who want to see an organisation that is respected and whose decisions are compatible with the Charter, must recognise the responsibility that each one of us has for the restoration of credibility. We must all do our part to bring the UN back from the brink - which is where it is today. We need to work for a membership of states and participation of civil society that revitalises and enhances the organisation, and accepts the obligations of the Charter and other aspects of international law. The resolutions of the SC and the GA must be compatible with the spirit and intent of the Charter, and so must the consequences of these decisions as they apply to member states and their peoples.

We must work towards remaking the United Nations in the spirit of the preamble to the Charter to reaffirm '....faith in fundamental human rights, in the dignity and worth of the human person, in equal rights of men and women and of nations large and small......'.

Reference
1. Childers E, Urquhart B. *A World in Need of Leadership: Tomorrow's United Nations.* Uppsala: Dag Hammarskjöld Foundation, 1996.

(Delivered 6 June 2002)

Crisis in the UN, NATO and the EU

Caroline Lucas

Introduction

I am very honoured to have received the invitation to deliver the 2003 Erskine Childers lecture on *Crisis in the UN, NATO and the EU* – an ambitious title if ever there was one. And what better time to be delivering such a speech - despite the end of the Cold War *we still live in a hugely dangerous and insecure world.* Launching Amnesty International's 2003 Annual Report, its Secretary General, Irene Khan, said that the American government's response to the 11 September 2001 attacks 'far from making the world a safer place, has made it more dangerous by curtailing human rights and undermining the rule of international law'.[1] One of the key critiques of the Iraq war was that it would make global terrorism more likely, not less, and recent developments seem to be bearing out that verdict.

We are, quite clearly, currently entering a new phase in the international system. The geopolitical shift that has taken place since the end of the cold war has been monumental - a shift that has culminated in George W Bush and his neo-conservative backers taking control of the United States Presidency. The world is currently facing an American government with a more unilateral approach to foreign policy than at any time in recent history. This has led many to question how the international system should be run.

It has even raised the most fundamental question of all: *should there, indeed, be an international system at all, or would we do better simply with*

The UN and its Future in the 21st Century

variable geographies of 'coalitions of the willing'? In the *Spectator* a few weeks ago, an article appeared by Richard Perle, a key architect behind the US driven war on Iraq, and chair of its defence policy board, an advisory panel to the Pentagon, which the *Guardian* reported under the headline 'Thank God for the death of the UN. Its abject failure gave us only anarchy. The world needs order'. It starts:

> Saddam Hussein's reign of terror is about to end. He will go quickly, but not alone: he will take the UN down with him....What will die is the fantasy of the UN as the foundation of a new world order. As we sift the debris, it will be important to preserve, the better to understand, the intellectual wreckage of the liberal conceit of safety through international law administered by international institutions.[2]

I think it says something about the tone of the article that I had to check that it was not a spoof. Certainly for myself, and I'm sure for many others, *security through international law administered through international institutions* is a noble aim that we aspire to. To see it so blatantly attacked, pilloried and ridiculed comes as something of a shock. I examine how it is that this aspiration has become so debased by so many, in the US administration in particular, and what needs to be done to revitalise our international institutions to enable them to fulfil the aim of global security more effectively and credibly.

Multilateralism *versus* Unilateralism

It would indeed be difficult to deny that many of our international institutions are indeed in crisis, and are in urgent need of reform. But I suspect this is not the principal reason why the elements in the US administration are so dismissive of them. On the contrary, I would argue that it is precisely because they *could* be very effective that the US is refusing to join them. Take the International Criminal Court: the US is furious with European leaders, because they have tried to stop the UN

The UN and its Future in the 21st Century

Security Council voting to renew the exemption of the US from prosecution by the new war crimes tribunal.

In an extraordinarily bitter attack, the Bush administration has accused the European Union of 'actively undermining' American efforts to protect its peacekeepers from prosecution, and that 'Europe's objections will undercut all our efforts to repair and rebuild the transatlantic relationship just as we are taking a turn for the better after a number of difficult months.'[3]

In the case of the Kyoto Protocol on climate change, the US is reluctant to sign because its provisions might just affect the way American corporations do business.

The US is withdrawing from international institutions not because they do not work - although many of them could work a lot better, as I shall discuss - but because they do not allow the US to follow its unilateral desires. When it came to Iraq, the United Nations failed, in US terms, because it refused to do what the US wanted. For many of the rest of us, that signalled a success, not a failure.

Why, then, does the US advocate a unilateral approach? To understand this we need to look at what drives US foreign policy. There are, I believe, two driving forces:

- firstly, the desire to be the world's unchallenged economic and political force. To do this the US must protect its domestic economy from foreign companies while at the same time opening up foreign markets to its own companies. Crucially, this necessitates control of energy supplies and their transport routes, otherwise the US economy would be fundamentally unstable and a hostage to those who control the energy supplies and routes;
- secondly, a desire to be the world's unchallenged military power. This is primarily directed against China, Russia and the European

Union, the only powers anywhere near capable of challenging the US militarily in the foreseeable future.

But to what extent is this unilateral intent new? It has been argued that what Bush did in Iraq was not something completely new; President Clinton used military force at least three times without Security Council authority:

- in Bosnia in 1995;
- in bombing Baghdad for four days in December 1998;
- in attacking Yugoslavia over Kosovo in 1999.

But Bush's behaviour can be seen as different in several ways:

- His drive for war on Iraq was prompted by the new doctrine of pre-emption – a frightening *carte blanche* for interventions almost anywhere;
- Bush was explicitly trying to achieve regime change, whereas Clinton's unsanctioned use of force had more limited objectives;
- And, critically, Bush was issuing a direct challenge to the UN. Prior to Clinton's intervention over Kosovo, it was already clear that Russia and China would veto any action, and so the US never drafted a resolution calling for force. Bush's speech, by contrast, bluntly demanded that the UN show its 'relevance': 'All the world faces a test, and the UN is facing a difficult and defining moment. Will it serve the purpose of its founding, or will it be irrelevant?' He might just as well have said: 'Will it serve the purpose of its founding, or will it serve the political interests of the United States?'[4]

We now, therefore, stand at a moment of enormous political significance. Not only do we face a devastated Iraq, where large components of the population are calling not just for 'No to Saddam Hussein', but 'No to the US' as well; and a humiliated and enraged Arab world, along with a shattered system of alliances. We are also seeing mounting international

The UN and its Future in the 21st Century

opposition that includes an emerging global people's movement saying not only 'No to Washington's War', but also 'No to Washington's Empire'.

The war on Iraq was not only an oil-grab, important though that aspect of the war undoubtedly was. It was also part of a broader attempt to reshape global power relations as part of a relentless drive for power and empire. The US administration has used 11 September 2001 as an opportunity, justifying its unilateralist position, to advance its foreign policy goals and promote US interests. Intervention in Afghanistan, whilst failing in its public justification of making Afghanistan a place where terrorists could not operate, has given the US control over central Asia - Turkmenistan, Kazakhstan, and Azerbaijan. It now has military bases in those countries for use *vis-a-vis* China, Iran and Russia, and has also secured the vast new oil and gas producing areas of central Asia. Whilst providing security of supply to the US, control over these energy reserves will also give the US further leverage over the EU and China.

If this sounds too extreme, or you are in any doubt about it, take a look at the publications of the Project for a New American Century. They are shocking in their blatant claim for US world domination.[5]

The US seeks domination of space as well. The website for US Space Command shows that the US is seeking to turn space into a war zone. That is not my interpretation – they proudly admit it. The US wants to 'control space' and from space to 'dominate' the Earth below. The cover of its 'Vision for 2020' report shows a laser weapon shooting a beam down from space zapping a target below, with the words: 'The globalisation of the world economy will continue – with a widening between haves and have-nots'. The implication is clear: from space, the US would keep those 'have-nots' in line.[6]

The UN and its Future in the 21st Century

NATO

But, continuing the assessment of international institutions, and the US response to them, what of NATO? I would make the case that NATO was created primarily to enable the US to maintain its control over Western Europe. Ostensibly, of course, its public rationale was to provide protection from a Soviet invasion, an invasion we now know was never considered as a serious option by the Soviet Union. Crucially for the Americans, NATO also forestalled European autonomy on defence and security matters whilst the apparent Soviet threat remained. A Europe that was dependent on America for its security was a Europe that would not threaten US key foreign policy goals.

With the demise of the Soviet Union, the US's main lever for exerting control over Western Europe disappeared - the end of the Cold War liberated Western Europe from its dependence on the US. With NATO in limbo for the last ten years, some member states of the European Union have begun to develop their own Common Foreign and Security Policy.

However, the US is not in retreat in Europe - indeed, it is fighting a strong offensive rearguard action. Whilst the US is clearly of the mind that NATO is militarily redundant, it still considers NATO to be a crucial *political* alliance. It sees the role of a post-cold-war NATO as preventing the EU from developing too strong a common foreign and defence policy, which could co-ordinate military and political policy without reference to US interests. This could also explain why the US is so keen on enlargement of the EU. Not only does an enlarged EU offer the US a larger single (and stable) market for US companies, for genetically modified crops for instance, but it also presents more opportunities to keep the EU politically divided over foreign policy. A politically divided EU, with France, Germany and others wanting an independent EU foreign policy, but the UK, Poland and others prioritising the transatlantic alliance, the thinking must be that the EU will be less of a challenge to the US on a global level.

The UN and its Future in the 21st Century

Given such a transatlantic rift, the demise of NATO is probably inevitable, since it no longer has a *raison d'être* for independent minded European states. This is to be welcomed, but I would caution against replacing NATO with a militarised Common Foreign and Security Policy for the EU. The costs of seeking to match the US as a military competitor would, in my view, be far too high in its effects on other spending on social and public services, health and the environment.

I believe that the Organisation for Security and Co-operation in Europe (OSCE), which is the organisation most inclusive of all European countries, could be best placed to replace NATO. It uses consensus decision-making and is not dominated by the larger countries. It refrains from unwanted interference in the internal affairs of member countries and works in co-operation with non-governmental organisations.

I welcome the OSCE's broader view of the concept of common security, which in many ways is similar to the Green concept. The aim of the OSCE, in principle, at least, is to prevent and solve conflicts, both in the short and the long run, by addressing underlying causes such as human rights abuses, economic inequalities, and ethnic tensions.

The use of consensus decision making in the OSCE means that action takes time to agree and compromises have to be made, but the decisions made have strong support. Crucially, I also support its emphasis on arms control and disarmament and the provision of mutual rights of inspection into other countries' security affairs, demonstrating the value of openness and transparency in building mutual confidence. The OSCE must be substantially developed to render it more effective in achieving these aims. But it offers the building blocks, at least, for strengthening peace across Europe.

The UN and its Future in the 21st Century
Role of the European Union

I have said very little so far about the role of the EU. Can it, and should it, aspire to be the counterweight, politically, economically and militarily, to US strength? The question is not as straightforward as it sounds.

Militarily
A respected political analyst wrote recently that the main problem with the EU is that 'it doesn't do war'.[5] In my view, nor should it, and it was never supposed to: half a century ago, the European Union's founders decided to 'pool' some national sovereignty in order to bind themselves together so that conflict between them would become impossible.

Robert Kagan, the conservative American thinker, argues that while US 'warriors' will fight wars in the 'post 9/11 Hobbesian jungle', self-satisfied and risk-averse Europeans are capable 'only of doing the dishes' (quoted in ref. 7). Kagan is being deliberately provocative, but his taunt may usefully encourage us to work out where our comparative advantage as members of the EU lies. The 'softer' powers of development, nation-building, and democratisation should not be undervalued: to the contrary, they should be developed. As one irritated Eurocrat recently snapped, 'war is for wimps.'

Economically
In some ways, it is even harder to imagine the EU as a counterweight economically. As a member of the European Parliament's Trade Committee, I have watched the EU pursue the agenda of ever greater economic globalisation every bit as vigorously as Washington.

There is indeed a paradox at the heart of the EU, summed up in two recent European Summit objectives. At Lisbon, the EU adopted a major new objective – to become the most *competitive* economy in the world. Just a short time later, under pressure from Greens and others, it adopted a further objective – to become the most *sustainable* economy in the world.

The UN and its Future in the 21st Century

Unless the quality and direction of the EU's economic activity changes, these two objectives are not reconcilable. The EU has some of the best environmental policy-making in the world, but it often fails to achieve the environmental standards it sets itself. This is primarily because whenever there is a potential collision between economic competitiveness and environmental sustainability, the economic priorities tend to win. The proposals for an EU energy tax, which could be one of the single most effective ways of internalising environmental costs and shifting towards sustainability have been blocked for years, on the grounds that such a tax could damage the competitiveness of European industry.

Politically
There is certainly the potential for the EU to act as a political counterweight, but only if it first achieves the pre-condition of legitimacy.

I would make the case that the EU currently faces a crisis of legitimacy:

- the derisory turn-out in the last European elections;
- anger and frustration from civil society movements which often attends EU summits. At Gothenburg, this spilled over into major street protests, as people claimed that the EU now ranks as part of the 'problem', along with the World Bank and IMF, rather than as part of the 'solution';
- Ireland's original 'No' vote to the Nice Treaty (which I would argue was only changed to a Yes in the second referendum because the question was changed to for or against enlargement).

The ongoing Convention process was intended to bring EU institutions closer to the people. But it would be very hard to say that this has achieved: the process has still been very remote, very top-down.

Our verdict here must, then, be that the EU has the potential at least to play the role of counterweight – if it is fundamentally reformed.

The UN and its Future in the 21st Century

Democratically
You will not be surprised to hear me as an MEP arguing for more powers for the European Parliament; it needs a new 'Big Idea'. Fifty years ago, its aim was clear – to bring peace to Europe by binding countries together in an ambitious free trade project. Now that project risks being an end in itself, and people are no longer clear what the EU is *for*. A new Big Idea could be about genuine attempts to achieve sustainability in all its facets. The EU could be a leader in renewable energies, in learning to live more lightly on the planet, and in pioneering different economic models – but it needs to resolve its internal contradictions first.

Reform of the United Nations

To return to my starting point: how could the UN itself better achieve global security?

The UN system needs fundamental transformation. The current structure of the UN Security Council, with permanent seats for France, the UK, the US, Russia and China, is not only undemocratic but also quite unworkable because of the right of veto. There should be no permanent seats and no veto.

Under a reformed UN, the most important decisions, such as going to war, would require an overwhelming majority of the assembly's weighted votes. Powerful governments wishing to recruit reluctant nations to their cause would be forced to bribe or blackmail not just three or four other members of a Security Council, but rather most of the rest of the world, in order to obtain the results they wanted.

What should be the weight of each of those votes? How can it possibly be right that the 10,000 people of the Pacific Island of Tuvalu possess the same representation as the one billion people of India? [8] Each inhabitant of Tuvalu, in other words, carries 100,000 times as much weight as each

The UN and its Future in the 21st Century

Indian. Countries should be represented in proportion to their populations, and decisions should be made by a weighted absolute, or two-thirds, majority.

But these kind of institutional reforms are not enough on their own. There are at least two further challenges:

- Dominque Moisi, deputy director of France's Institute for International Relations, believes Iraq only brought long-festering problems to the surface. According to him, 'the old concepts of legality and legitimacy have split. The UN stands for legality but not for legitimacy' (cited in ref.4). The implication is that there must be more thoroughgoing democratisation of UN institutions, such as exploring the possibility of sending elected politicians or people's assemblies to represent our interests there.
- The second challenge is to define more clearly what we mean by 'security'. Security must be more than just military security. We will only have a more peaceful world when we tackle the root causes of conflict – and that means tackling the poverty and inequality that makes the growth of conflict more likely.

As Thomas Jefferson remarked, 'as new discoveries are made, new truths discovered…institutions must advance also to keep pace with the times.' [9] One of today's new truths is that freedom is about much more than the right to vote, once every few years, for one of a few increasingly identical groups of politicians. Freedom is also about the right to decide your economic destiny – and that is precisely what globalisation – the global spread of neo-liberal capitalism – is taking away from people the world over, impoverishing them in the process.

We therefore need major changes in our global financial system and regulation – and the UN has a key role to play. As Erskine Childers himself recognised, it is still entirely appropriate to envisage the strategies for the International Monetary Fund and World Trade Organisation being

The UN and its Future in the 21st Century

negotiated and agreed at the UN. Unless we address the vast and increasing inequalities between rich and poor, global insecurity can only grow.

That means fundamental changes in the rules and processes of the WTO and a shift away from ever-greater international competitiveness, with every nation trying to out-compete the other, leading to a downward spiral of social and environmental standards. In its place, there must be a greater stress on building local and regional economies over which people can have greater control. And it means an end to the dominance of the EU and US at world trade talks.

Reform proposals are all very well, but what will make them happen? If they have not happened yet, what grounds for hope do we have that they might in the future? I will end on a positive note, because - contrary to much that is said and written about the UN today - I do not share Richard Perle's belief that it will die and good riddance.

There may be no country or group of countries capable of launching a military challenge to Washington's power drive, but there is, perhaps for the first time since the end of the Cold War, a serious competitor challenging the US empire for influence and authority. This is global public opinion, including a mobilised international civil society joined by key governments as well as the United Nations itself. None of these on their own might be enough. But together:

> All of those forces together make up the astonishing movement towards a new internationalism that today forms the global challenge to the empire. And the United Nations, while not the only sector, is at the centre.[10]

The combination of events in mid-February 2003 - the unprecedented Security Council response to France's Foreign Minister Dominique De Villepin's call to defend the UN as an instrument of peace and not a tool for war and the resulting refusal of the Council and its members to accede to US demands, the outpourings of millions across the globe on 15 February

The UN and its Future in the 21st Century

2003 when 'the World says no to war', and the amazing reaction to those demonstrations, provide even clearer evidence that we are at a critical historical juncture. An analysis in the *New York Times* defined this as a moment proving that once again there are two superpowers in the world 'the United States, and global public opinion'.[11] And if we can harness that global public opinion to reform our institutions, we will be well on the way to a more secure world.

To quote George Monbiot again:

> ...the US seems to be ripping up the global rulebook. As it does so, those of us who have campaigned against the grotesque injustices of the existing world order will quickly discover that a world with no institutions is even nastier than a world run by the wrong ones. Multilateralism, however inequitable it may be, requires certain concessions to other nations. Unilateralism means piracy: the armed robbery of the poor by the rich.[8]

The challenge we face, then, is not just to write different rules. That has been done a hundred times over by NGOs, progressive think-tanks and governments. The challenge is to mobilise public opinion into believing that those changes are urgent and necessary – and to build the political will. I believe we are seeing an emerging global movement, for example – the 2002 World Social Forum at Porto Alegre, Brazil, and on the 15 February 2003 marches – that might just prove the catalyst to achieve it.

References

1. Khan I. Security for whom? A human rights response. In: *Annual Report*. London: Amnesty International, 2003. At: http://web.amnesty.org/report2003/message-eng
2. Perle R. United they fall. *Spectator*, 22 March 2003: 22, 26.
3. War crime vote fuels US anger at Europe. *Guardian*, 11 June 2003. At: http://www.guardian.co.uk/international/story/0,3604,974891,00.html

4. Steele J. Disunited nations. *Guardian*, 20 May 2003.
5. Project for a New American Century. At: www.newamericancentury.org
6. US Space Command. *Long Range Plan*. At: www.spacecom.af.mi./usspace
7. Black I. Postwar world. *Guardian*, 24 May 2003.
8. Monbiot G. How to stop America. *New Statesman*, 9 June 2003: 16-18.
9. Jefferson Memorial, Washington, Panel Four. At: http://www.monticello.org/report/quotes/memorial.html
10. Bennis P. Going global: building a movement against empire. *TransNational Institute*, 15 May 2003. At: www.tni.org/acts/fm/paper/htm
11. Tyler P. *New York Times,* 17 February 2003.

(Delivered 12 June 2003)

After Kosovo, Afghanistan and Iraq- What is the future for the UN?

Jenny Tonge

As a child my father often quoted Samuel Johnson: 'Patriotism is the last resort of the scoundrel'.[1] Today he would probably say that religion takes pride of place – but he tried to instil in us that nations were like football teams, moving up and down the Premier League in the case of the United Kingdom, or struggling along in the Fourth Division with no backers and no good players in the case of many Third World countries.

Sometimes a really good team, highly respected by other teams, can go through a terrible patch with a bad manager, or, as in poor Beckham's case, by a captain who makes the fatal mistake of kicking his penalty over the bar.

How Like the United States and the UK Today.

The United States has been slipping in world opinion for some time, but I think the UK until recently has been respected for fair play and the quality of its foreign policy decisions. Some of us may disagree, but on the whole I think this is a fair statement. I well remember Robin Cook's now famous speech in the Locarno Room of the Foreign and Commonwealth Office, spelling out the new government's foreign policy with an ethical dimension. I was there, a new MP, enthralled by the new dawn, the decency, the honesty and the sheer common sense of it all. 'Oh, how are the mighty fallen!'

Over the last fifteen years there has been a huge upheaval in world order. What now seem the safe and predictable days of the cold war are over. In a speech at Chatham House in March 2004, Lord Hannay of Chiswick, UK

The UN and its Future in the 21st Century

Permanent Representative to the United Nations from 1990 to 1995, described how everything changed:

> For the UN a whole range of things, previously unthinkable or impossible, suddenly became politically possible. An old style aggression by Iraq against Kuwait was halted and reversed under UN authority. A considerable number of third world proxy wars were brought to an end and the wounds gradually healed under the UN's auspices – in Namibia, Cambodia, El Salvador, and Mozambique. The evil of *apartheid* was peacefully transformed into a democratic South Africa. But it soon became clear that this was not 'Paradise Regained'; no new world order emerged, merely the symptoms of a new disorder. The UN itself, as ever the victim of excessive expectations revealed some fundamental weaknesses. At first the weaknesses were those of execution and effectiveness. In Somalia, in Bosnia and in Rwanda, the UN simply failed to muster the resources and the determination, in one case to put a state back on its feet after its comprehensive failure, in another to manage peacefully the break-up of a state and in the third to counter a genocide. In each case the members of the UN willed the ends but they did not will the means. When the going got rough, they stood back and left the UN to take the blame for failure. Then, in more recent years, another, more fundamental, weakness emerged, an inability to agree on the conditions for a collective action and the use of force – first in Kosovo and then in Iraq – even when the UN's own mandatory resolutions were at stake.[2]

Kosovo

As a novice spokesman on International Development in 1999, and an obedient member of our Foreign Affairs team, I supported the action in Kosovo. We could not stand by and allow the worst ethnic cleansing since World War II to go on in Europe's backyard. We saw it as a European problem and also a NATO problem. There was no UN resolution.

Our then leader insisted that troops should be on the ground, whilst bombing of strategic targets from 15,000 feet was achieved. It did not happen and we all know the consequences. I confess I am unsure now about that action, though Europe and NATO have stayed there, helping to reconstruct the Balkan States rather more successfully than in Afghanistan and Iraq. The Kosovo Liberation Army provoked that war, but the refugee

The UN and its Future in the 21st Century

crisis started when we started bombing.

Afghanistan

The next great world event was the flying of hijacked commercial airliners into the Twin Towers in New York and the Pentagon in Washington. Thousands of civilians were killed and the US began to understand, or some Americans began to understand, the terror and mayhem caused by blanket bombing and modern warfare. To civilians, many of them women and children, it does not matter whether suicide bombers or high level state-sponsored bombers carry out the destruction of their lives – the effect is the same.

Tragically for the world, George Bush and his masters were in charge of the White House and 9/11 gave them just what they wanted – an opportunity to seek out *Al Qaida* and Osama Bin Laden, Islamic fundamentalists generally, and of course Saddam Hussein in Iraq. Many of us held our heads in horror as George W Bush used the word 'crusade'.[3] It was also a way of securing oil supplies for the consumers in the US.

After a few weeks when one dared hope that the US and its allies might reconsider the best way of dealing with terrorism on such a scale, the bombing of Afghanistan commenced 'targeting', we were told, the caves and hideouts of *Al Qaida*; a resolution was passed at the UN for action. I got into trouble with my party over this, and also received daily ridicule from Labour and Tory MPs in the House of Commons. I argued that if the US wanted to find a needle in a haystack, it would not bomb the haystack. I also argued that Afghanistan was a failed state, oppressed by the Taliban who had given shelter to Bin Laden when he was expelled from Sudan, a failed state whose people were starving, desperate and would be subject to the cruelty of warlords if the Taliban were to release its grip.

Some of you may remember that I suggested whimsically that we '…should bomb Afghanistan with food and aid, and deal with the suffering of the people whilst our intelligence forces sought out Bin Laden'. Sadly, some limited action was taken by the US to bomb with food – in similar packaging to explosive mines.

Afghanistan, despite international conferences and pledges of aid, has now reverted to near anarchy outside Kabul. The pledges have not been delivered, and President Karzai is struggling to keep even Kabul peaceful. There has been minimal progress for women and more opium poppies are being grown than ever before, despite efforts by the Department for International Development and others to discourage this. As we all know, opium provides money for warlords, who buy arms from illegal arms dealers – another nearly failed policy from the Blair government. Do you remember the Export Control Bill? I do, I was on the committee.

And after all this Bin Laden is still with us. *Al Qaida* grows like a multi-headed hydra. Their 'successes', if we can so call the terror and mayhem caused by suicide bombers, are increasingly seen by the Arab and Muslim world as, like Robin Hood and his merry men, fighting for justice for the poor.

Iraq

Let us briefly remind ourselves how Tony Blair and George Bush tried to persuade us, the 'coalition of the willing', why we should go to war with Iraq.

- Saddam Hussein had weapons of mass destruction.
- Saddam Hussein defied existing UN resolutions.
- Saddam Hussein abused the human rights of his people.
- Saddam Hussein has links with terrorism and *Al Qaida*.

I do not have time to rehearse the arguments – we have all done so. I would only point out that other countries, Israel in particular, do all of those things, with the exception of links with terrorism and *Al Qaida*, which we all know was simply wrong. Iraq has connections now; the terrorists have filled the vacuum and the war continues.

Many European countries, especially France and to his credit, President Chirac, Russia, the Liberal Democrats, and many Labour MPs opposed the action. It fractured our relationship with the European Union; it nearly

The UN and its Future in the 21st Century

destroyed the UN.

'What must the king do now? must he submit?'[4] In this case it is the UN. What must happen? Should the UN submit? Must it be disposed of? Must it lose – let go?

The United Nations

The world is under huge threat; the UN itself. as well as international organisations, have been attacked by terrorists. The UN must convince world leaders that we cannot fight a 'war' against terrorism; the action against Afghanistan alone showed us this. It must use many more subtle methods, but also address the root causes of terrorism, which have been staring us in the face so long. We must not, above all, allow our free society to be destroyed by the terrorists – that will be their victory indeed.

The UN must encourage information sharing and increase international surveillance and the UN must be involved in these operations. We must address the problem of failed states and poverty, often interchangeable in today's world. To the old maxim, poverty causes war causes poverty causes war; can be added 'and leads to terrorism and the support of terrorist causes'. The example nearest to my heart is of course Palestine, where an occupying force has so reduced the people to poverty and despair that terrorism has increased.

But there are other examples all over Africa and Asia. The UN must enforce its millennium development goals and insist that rich governments pay up. The UK has recently found £3.8 billion for the Iraq war. That amount would have doubled our aid budget and allowed us to reach the UN target for the percentage of Gross National Product to be spent on aid.

The UN must also, with the World Trade Organisation, ensure that the rules of fair trade enable poor countries to make progress, a more important factor than aid. The UN must move to stop the proliferation of nuclear, biological and chemical weapons; for this, India, Pakistan and Israel, as well as Iran and Syria, must come into line. The UN must act to stop the

The UN and its Future in the 21st Century

spread of the greatest weapon of mass destruction of all – the HIV/AIDS pandemic.

It is not good enough for the US to contribute USD15 billion to the fight against AIDS on its own conditions, excluding UN programmes of prevention on religious grounds. The US contribution is becoming a straight donation to the US pharmaceutical industry. The UN must make the nations of the developed world understand that development and relief of poverty, in this world of globalisation and wide communications, is essential if we are to prevent support for terrorism.

Peace-keeping and post-conflict reconstruction is essential if we are to prevent recurring wars and terrorism, and the rich world must be prepared to contribute to this. In this the UK is paramount; perhaps because of our Northern Ireland experience our soldiers are good at this. Wherever I go in the world I hear about their good works, which makes Iraq all the more distressing.

Adherence to international laws and treaties is vital, but in recent years the US have adopted a policy of 'everyone but us' whether in agreements on trade, the Kyoto agreement on greenhouse gas emissions, the International Criminal Court, landmines, nuclear proliferation - the list is endless. The US sticks two fingers up to the rest of the world. No wonder they are hated, and we, the UK, are now included in that hatred. We should be ashamed. Before leaving my list of what needs to be done I must add 'progress on the Middle East Process'. The Road Map is discredited, Israel once again has been allowed to act unilaterally, and the suffering of the Palestinians continues. I repeat that this problem lies at the very root of the world's problems today. Whatever the history for the rights and wrongs of each side, the road to world peace lies through Jerusalem.

The Way Ahead

But how do we achieve any of this? It is all very well saying that the 'UN must', but the UN is sick and has been sorely wounded by the US and the UK. Kofi Annan has already set up a panel to come up with proposals for reform. The Security Council lies at the centre of the UN and was set up

The UN and its Future in the 21st Century

with its present constitution almost sixty years ago. It is ridiculous that this should stay unchanged. Permanent members should include Germany and Japan, and more members from Latin America, Africa and Asia should be added. All members of the Security Council should have a clean bill of health and have complied with UN resolutions. I would like to add that UN funding must be increased and no one should sit on the SC unless they are fully paid up members, and have signed up to major international treaties: is this too much to ask?

In the field of peacekeeping and conflict prevention, the UN member groups should set up regional outposts for these activities based approximately on South American, North American, European, African and Asean blocks. This is already happening, in East Timor and Kosovo, for example. Perhaps we should be encouraging a more formal middle world management in the UN. In addition, these regional outposts should have Human Rights monitors within their reach.

Human Rights abuse is a serious problem for us all. When do we intervene, if ever, when countries' rulers are committing the sorts of human rights abuses perpetrated by Saddam Hussein, the Burmese junta, the Sudanese government in Dafur, and Israel in the occupation of Palestinian territories? The Prime Minister himself said that: 'The most pressing problem we face is to identify the circumstances in which we should get involved in other people's countries'.[5]

Indeed it is. There must be a clear framework for intervention that must be upheld by the UN. We cannot go on ignoring humanitarian crises or acting unilaterally using abuse of human rights as our reason, but really only when it suits our commercial interests. This scenario has been played out by the US and the UK for decades in Iraq.

There is much to do. It has to be done. I will not return to Lord Hannay's reference to Milton in *Paradise Regained,* but quote instead from *Paradise Lost,* a few lines found for me years ago by a brilliant young researcher called Greg Simpson.

> As one who in his journey, bates at noon,
> Though bent on speed, so here the Archangel paused

The UN and its Future in the 21st Century

Betwixt the world destroyed and world restored.[6]

The archangel is waiting, waiting for us to restore International Law and our beloved United Nations Organisation.

References

1. Boswell J. *The Life of Johnson*. London: Wordsworth Editions, 1999.
2. Hannay D. Speech at the Royal Institute of International Affairs, 16 March 2004. At: <http://www.riia.org/pdf/meeting_transcripts/Hannay.pdf> (accessed 29/08/04).
3. Whitaker B. Another fine mess. *Guardian*, 11 September 2003. At: <http://www.guardian.co.uk/elsewhere/journalist/story/0,,1040063,00.html> (accessed 29/08/04).
4. Shakespeare W. *The Complete Works of William Shakespeare: King Richard II, Act 3, Scene 3, line 143*. London: Octopus Books, 1982.
5. Blair T. Speech at the Economic Club, Chicago: 22 April 1999. At: <http://www.pbs.org/newshour/bb/international/jan-june99/blair_doctrine4-23.html> (accessed 29/08/04).
6. Milton J. *Paradise Lost*. Book 12. ed. Fowler A. London: Longmans, 1998.

(Delivered 17 June 2004)

The UN and its Future in the 21st Century

Afterword

Concluding his final book, *Challenges to the United Nations: Building a Safer World* (CIIR/St Martin's Press, 1994) Erskine Childers wrote that:

> It is time, indeed it is overtime, to empower those whom the Charter proclaims to be the first authors of the United Nations – 'We the Peoples'. In addition to the needed strengthening of NGO roles and access, we must press our governments now to do what even in 1945 [UK] Foreign Secretary Ernest Bevin (no 'dreamer') called a necessary 'completion' of the architecture of San Francisco.
>
> We need a United Nations Parliamentary Assembly, where our directly elected representatives can monitor and contribute to the performance of executive governments. They do need help. Those who have been practising double standards need the realisation that the representatives of the citizens of this planet are close by, watching, and alert to expose all unethical international behaviour. Executive governments that wish to follow the Charter and to advance all of its democratic goals need the additional courage that they would derive from such an assembly in session next door to theirs. Creating such an assembly will, of course, be an enormous task, but so have been many of the advances we have managed to make in international relations in the last 50 years.
>
> Despite all the UN System's constraints to date, its research and deliberations have brought us to the point where we know the whole of our world for the first time in human history. We have deprived ourselves of the last excuse, of ignorance of how most of our sisters and brothers have to live out their days. Now, we have to go forward in the giant undertaking of building a democratic United Nations to make the real world safe, just and sustainable, for all its children.

The UN and its Future in the 21st Century

The contributions to this book show that the need for a vibrant UN is greater than ever, and, despite the difficulties, they together outline how it can be achieved. We hope that, in the UN's sixtieth year, these lectures and commentaries will inspire 'We the Peoples' to bring it to pass.

Report of the High-level Panel on Threats, Challenges and Change

Foreword by UN Secretary-General Kofi Annan

Historians may well look back on the first years of the twenty-first century as a decisive moment in the human story. The different societies that make up the human family are today interconnected as never before. They face threats that no nation can hope to master by acting alone - and opportunities that can be much more hopefully exploited if all nations work together.

The purpose of this report is to suggest how nations *can* work together to meet this formidable challenge. It is the work of a panel of sixteen eminent and experienced people, drawn from different parts of the world, whom I asked a year ago to assess current threats to international peace and security; to evaluate how well our existing policies and institutions have done in addressing those threats; and to recommend ways of strengthening the United Nations to provide collective security for the twenty-first century.

The Panel has met, and even surpassed, my expectations. This is a report of great range and depth, which sets out a broad framework for collective security, and indeed gives a broader meaning to that concept, appropriate for the new millennium. It suggests not only ways to deal with particular threats, but also new ways of understanding the connections between them, and explains what this implies in terms of shared policies and institutions. In so doing, it also offers a unique opportunity to refashion and renew the United Nations, which world leaders defined four years ago, in the

Millennium Declaration, as 'the indispensable common house of the entire human family'.

Findings and Recommendations

I wholly endorse the report's core argument that what is needed is a comprehensive system of collective security: one that tackles both new and old threats, and addresses the security concerns of all States - rich and poor, weak and strong. Particularly important is the report's insistence that today's threats to our security are all interconnected. We can no longer afford to see problems such as terrorism, or civil wars, or extreme poverty, in isolation. Our strategies must be comprehensive. Our institutions must overcome their narrow preoccupations and learn to work across the whole range of issues, in a concerted fashion.

The report argues that the front line in today's combat must be manned by capable and responsible *States*. I agree. The task of helping States improve their own capacities to deal with contemporary threats is vital and urgent. The United Nations must be able to do this better. The Panel tells us how.

Other findings of the report that I consider particularly important include the following:

- *Development* and security are inextricably linked. A more secure world is only possible if poor countries are given a real chance to develop. Extreme poverty and infectious diseases threaten many people directly, but they also provide a fertile breeding-ground for other threats, including civil conflict. Even people in rich countries will be more secure if their Governments help poor countries to defeat poverty and disease by meeting the Millennium Development Goals.

- We need to pay much closer attention to *biological security*. Our response to HIV/AIDS was, as the report says, 'shockingly late and shamefully ill-resourced', and donors are still not providing anything like the amount of aid needed to halt the pandemic. But the report goes further. It calls attention to the overall deterioration of our global health system, which is ill-equipped to protect us against existing and emerging infectious diseases; and it highlights both the promise and the peril of advances in biotechnology. It calls for a major initiative to rebuild global public health, beginning with a concerted effort to build public health capacity throughout the developing world, at both local and national levels. This will not only yield direct benefits by preventing and treating disease in the developing world itself, but will also provide the basis for an effective global defence against bio-terrorism and overwhelming natural outbreaks of infectious disease.

- While our principal aim should be to prevent threats from emerging, when they do emerge we must be better prepared to *respond*. Two of the tools we have for this are *sanctions* and *mediation*. The Panel recommends ways to strengthen both. I urge Governments to adopt them.

- When all else fails, it may be necessary and legitimate to *use force*. The report makes a crucial contribution to the search for common criteria, by which to decide when the use of force is justified. I hope Governments will consider its recommendations very carefully. A new consensus on this issue is essential if our collective security system is ever to be truly effective.

- The United Nations must make better use of its assets in the fight against *terrorism*, articulating an effective and principled counter-terrorism strategy that is respectful of the rule of law and universal human rights. One of the obstacles to this up to now has been the inability of United Nations members to agree on a definition of terrorism. The report offers a definition which, I believe, will help build the consensus we need if we are to move forward quickly.

The UN and its Future in the 21st Century

- There is a real danger that we could see a cascade of *nuclear proliferation* in the near future. The report recommends ways of strengthening the non-proliferation regime by creating incentives for States to forego the development of domestic uranium enrichment and reprocessing facilities, and calls for a voluntary time-limited moratorium on the construction of any such facilities. These suggestions, if implemented swiftly and firmly, offer us a real chance to reduce the risk of a nuclear attack, whether by States or non-State actors. They should be put into effect without delay.

- No less important are the recommendations for *adapting the United Nations for the twenty-first century*. The report criticises several areas of the United Nations performance and - however implicitly - United Nations management, for which I take responsibility. These criticisms deserve to be taken seriously, and acted upon.

- All the United Nations principal organs are in need of change, including the Security Council. The report offers two alternative formulae for expanding the Council's membership, which I hope will make it easier for Governments to reach a decision in 2005.

- The report rightly identifies *post-conflict peacebuilding* as an area of vital concern, and offers new ideas for improving our performance in this area - including a new inter-governmental body, the 'Peacebuilding Commission', whose task would be to help States make a successful transition from the immediate post-conflict phase to longer-term reconstruction and development.

- The report also recommends changes to the *Commission on Human Rights*. The Universal Declaration of Human Rights remains one of the United Nations' greatest achievements, and we should all be proud of the Organisation's work in developing international human rights norms and standards. But we cannot move forward without restoring the credibility and effectiveness of our human

- Finally, the report makes recommendations, which I welcome, for *strengthening the Secretariat*. The world needs, and is entitled to expect, an effective United Nations Secretariat, which can attract and retain the best people from all parts of the world.

Conclusion

I hope people all over the world will read this report, discuss it, and urge their Governments to take prompt decisions on its recommendations. I believe the great majority of them will share my feeling that there is an urgent need for the nations of the world to come together and reach a new consensus - both on the future of collective security and on the changes needed if the United Nations is to play its part.

For my part, I will move quickly to consider and implement, as appropriate, those recommendations that are within my purview. I urge the other organs of the United Nations to do the same. And on those issues - such as the rules and norms governing the use of force - which go to the very heart of who we are as the United Nations and what we stand for, I believe decisions should be taken by world leaders next September, when they meet for a special summit at United Nations Headquarters in New York. In March 2005 I shall submit a report of my own, which I hope will help to set the agenda for that summit.

Finally, I would like to express my sincere admiration for the work of the Chair and members of the Panel in producing this report. They did not shrink from tackling the toughest issues that divide us. That such a diverse group, composed of such experienced people, could reach consensus on such farsighted, yet workable, recommendations gives me hope that the nations of the world can do the same, thereby giving new meaning and resonance to the name 'United Nations'.

Summary of Recommendations

Collective Security and the Challenge of Prevention

Poverty, infectious disease and environmental degradation

1. All States must recommit themselves to the goals of eradicating poverty, achieving sustained economic growth and promoting sustainable development.

2. The many donor countries which currently fall short of the United Nations 0.7 per cent gross national product target for official development assistance should establish a timetable for reaching it.

3. World Trade Organization members should strive to conclude the Doha Development Round of multilateral trade negotiations at the latest in 2006.

4. Lender Governments and the international financial institutions should provide highly indebted poor countries with greater debt relief, longer rescheduling and improved access to global markets.

5. Although international resources devoted to meeting the challenge of HIV/AIDS have increased from about $250 million in 1996 to about $2.8 billion in 2002, more than $10 billion annually is needed to stem the pandemic.

6. Leaders of countries affected by HIV/AIDS need to mobilize resources, commit funds and engage civil society and the private sector in disease-control efforts.

7. The Security Council, working closely with UNAIDS, should host a second special session on HIV/AIDS as a threat to international peace and security, to explore the future effects of HIV/AIDS on States and societies,

generate research on the problem and identify critical steps towards a long-term strategy for diminishing the threat.

8. International donors, in partnership with national authorities and local civil society organizations, should undertake a major new global initiative to rebuild local and national public health systems throughout the developing world.

9. Members of the World Health Assembly should provide greater resources to the World Health Organization Global Outbreak Alert and Response Network to increase its capacity to cope with potential disease outbreaks.

10. States should provide incentives for the further development of renewable energy sources and begin to phase out environmentally harmful subsidies, especially for fossil fuel use and development.

11. We urge Member States to reflect on the gap between the promise of the Kyoto Protocol and its performance, re-engage on the problem of global warming and begin new negotiations to produce a new long-term strategy for reducing global warming beyond the period covered by the Protocol (2012).

Conflict between and within States

12. The Security Council should stand ready to use the authority it has under the Rome Statute to refer cases of suspected war crimes and crimes against humanity to the International Criminal Court.

13. The United Nations should work with national authorities, international financial institutions, civil society organizations and the private sector to develop norms governing the management of natural resources for countries emerging from or at risk of conflict.

The UN and its Future in the 21st Century

14. The United Nations should build on the experience of regional organizations in developing frameworks for minority rights and the protection of democratically elected Governments from unconstitutional overthrow.

15. Member States should expedite and conclude negotiations on legally binding agreements on the marking and tracing, as well as the brokering and transfer, of small arms and light weapons.

16. All Member States should report completely and accurately on all elements of the United Nations Register of Conventional Arms, and the Secretary-General should be asked to report annually to the General Assembly and Security Council on any inadequacies in the reporting.

17. A training and briefing facility should be established for new or potential special representatives of the Secretary-General and other United Nations mediators.

18. The Department of Political Affairs should be given additional resources and should be restructured to provide more consistent and professional mediation support.

19. While the details of such a restructuring should be left to the Secretary-General, it should take into account the need for the United Nations to have:
(a) A field-oriented, dedicated mediation support capacity, comprised of a small team of professionals with relevant direct experience and expertise, available to all United Nations mediators;
(b) Competence on thematic issues that recur in peace negotiations, such as the sequencing of implementation steps, the design of monitoring arrangements, the sequencing of transitional arrangements and the design of national reconciliation mechanisms;
(c) Greater interaction with national mediators, regional organizations and non-governmental organizations involved in conflict resolution;

(d) Greater consultation with and involvement in peace processes of important voices from civil society, especially those of women, who are often neglected during negotiations.

20. National leaders and parties to conflict should make constructive use of the option of preventive deployment of peacekeepers.

Nuclear, Radiological, Chemical and Biological Weapons

21. The nuclear-weapon States must take several steps to restart disarmament:
(a) They must honour their commitments under Article VI of the Treaty on the Non-Proliferation of Nuclear Weapons to move towards disarmament and be ready to undertake specific measures in fulfilment of those commitments;
(b) They should reaffirm their previous commitments not to use nuclear weapons against non-nuclear-weapon States.

22. The United States and the Russian Federation, other nuclear-weapon States and States not party to the Treaty on the Non-Proliferation of Nuclear Weapons should commit to practical measures to reduce the risk of accidental nuclear war, including, where appropriate, a progressive schedule for de-alerting their strategic nuclear weapons.

23. The Security Council should explicitly pledge to take collective action in response to a nuclear attack or the threat of such attack on a non-nuclear weapon State.

24. Negotiations to resolve regional conflicts should include confidence-building measures and steps towards disarmament.

25. States not party to the Treaty on the Non-Proliferation of Nuclear Weapons should pledge a commitment to non-proliferation and disarmament, demonstrating their commitment by ratifying the

Comprehensive Nuclear Test Ban Treaty and supporting negotiations for a Fissile Material Cut-off Treaty, both of which are open to nuclear-weapon and non-nuclear-weapon States alike. We recommend that peace efforts in the Middle East and South Asia launch nuclear disarmament talks that could lead to the establishment of nuclear-weapon-free zones in those regions similar to those established for Latin America and the Caribbean, Africa, the South Pacific and South-East Asia.

26. All chemical-weapon States should expedite the scheduled destruction of all existing chemical weapons stockpiles by the agreed target date of 2012.

27. States parties to the Biological and Toxin Weapons Convention should without delay return to negotiations for a credible verification protocol, inviting the active participation of the biotechnology industry.

28. The Board of Governors of the International Atomic Energy Agency (IAEA) should recognize the Model Additional Protocol as today's standard for IAEA safeguards, and the Security Council should be prepared to act in cases of serious concern over non-compliance with non-proliferation and safeguards standards.

29. Negotiations should be engaged without delay and carried forward to an early conclusion on an arrangement, based on the existing provisions of Articles III and IX of the IAEA statute, which would enable IAEA to act as a guarantor for the supply of fissile material to civilian nuclear users.

30. While that arrangement is being negotiated, States should, without surrendering the right under the Treaty on the Non-Proliferation of Nuclear Weapons to construct uranium enrichment and reprocessing facilities, voluntarily institute a time-limited moratorium on the construction of any further such facilities, with a commitment to the moratorium matched by a guarantee of the supply of fissile materials by the current suppliers at market rates.

31. All States should be encouraged to join the voluntary Proliferation Security Initiative.

32. A State's notice of withdrawal from the Treaty on the Non-Proliferation of Nuclear Weapons should prompt immediate verification of its compliance with the Treaty, if necessary mandated by the Security Council. The IAEA Board of Governors should resolve that, in the event of violations, all assistance provided by IAEA should be withdrawn.

33. The proposed timeline for the Global Threat Reduction Initiative to convert highly enriched uranium reactors and reduce HEU stockpiles should be halved from 10 to five years.

34. States parties to the Biological and Toxin Weapons Convention should negotiate a new bio-security protocol to classify dangerous biological agents and establish binding international standards for the export of such agents.

35. The Conference on Disarmament should move without further delay to negotiate a verifiable Fissile Material Cut-off Treaty that, on a designated schedule, ends the production of highly enriched uranium for non-weapon as well as weapons purposes.

36. The Directors-General of IAEA and the Organization for the Prohibition of Chemical Weapons should be invited by the Security Council to report to it twice-yearly on the status of safeguards and verification processes, as well as on any serious concerns they have which might fall short of an actual breach of the Treaty on the Non-Proliferation of Nuclear Weapons and the Chemical Weapons Convention.

37. The Security Council should consult with the Director-General of the World Health Organization to establish the necessary procedures for working together in the event of a suspicious or overwhelming outbreak of

infectious disease.

Terrorism

38. The United Nations, with the Secretary-General taking a leading role, should promote a comprehensive strategy against terrorism, including:
(a) Dissuasion, working to reverse the causes or facilitators of terrorism, including through promoting social and political rights, the rule of law and democratic reform; working to end occupations and address major political grievances; combating organized crime; reducing poverty and unemployment; and stopping State collapse;
(b) Efforts to counter extremism and intolerance, including through education and fostering public debate;
(c) Development of better instruments for global counter-terrorism co-operation, all within a legal framework that is respectful of civil liberties and human rights, including in the areas of law enforcement; intelligence-sharing, where possible; denial and interdiction, when required; and financial controls;
(d) Building State capacity to prevent terrorist recruitment and operations;
(e) Control of dangerous materials and public health defence.

39. Member States that have not yet done so should actively consider signing and ratifying all 12 international conventions against terrorism, and should adopt the eight Special Recommendations on Terrorist Financing issued by the Organization for Economic Co-operation and Development (OECD)-supported Financial Action Task Force on Money-Laundering and the measures recommended in its various best practices papers.

40. The Al-Qaida and Taliban Sanctions Committee should institute a process for reviewing the cases of individuals and institutions claiming to have been wrongly placed or retained on its watch lists.

41. The Security Council, after consultation with affected States, should extend the authority of the Counter-Terrorism Executive Directorate to act

as a clearing house for State-to-State provision of military, police and border control assistance for the development of domestic counter-terrorism capacities.

42. To help Member States comply with their counter-terrorism obligations, the United Nations should establish a capacity-building trust fund under the Counter-Terrorism Executive Directorate.

43. The Security Council should devise a schedule of predetermined sanctions for State non-compliance with the Council's counter-terrorism resolutions.

44. The General Assembly should rapidly complete negotiations on a comprehensive convention on terrorism, incorporating a definition of terrorism with the following elements:
(a) recognition, in the preamble, that State use of force against civilians is regulated by the Geneva Conventions and other instruments, and, if of sufficient scale, constitutes a war crime by the persons concerned or a crime against humanity;
(b) restatement that acts under the 12 preceding anti-terrorism conventions are terrorism, and a declaration that they are a crime under international law; and restatement that terrorism in time of armed conflict is prohibited by the Geneva Conventions and Protocols;
(c) reference to the definitions contained in the 1999 International Convention for the Suppression of the Financing of Terrorism and Security Council resolution 1566 (2004);
(d) description of terrorism as 'any action, in addition to actions already specified by the existing conventions on aspects of terrorism, the Geneva Conventions and Security Council resolution 1566 (2004), that is intended to cause death or serious bodily harm to civilians or non-combatants, when the purpose of such act, by its nature or context, is to intimidate a population, or to compel a Government or an international organization to do or to abstain from doing any act'.

The UN and its Future in the 21st Century

Transnational Organized Crime

45. Member States that have not signed, ratified or resourced the 2000 United Nations Convention against Transnational Organized Crime and its three Protocols, and the 2003 United Nations Convention against Corruption should do so, and all Member States should support the United Nations Office on Drugs and Crime in its work in this area.

46. Member States should establish a central authority to facilitate the exchange of evidence among national judicial authorities, mutual legal assistance among prosecutorial authorities and the implementation of extradition requests.

47. A comprehensive international convention on money-laundering that addresses the issues of bank secrecy and the development of financial havens needs to be negotiated, and endorsed by the General Assembly.

48. Member States should sign and ratify the Protocol to Prevent, Suppress and Punish Trafficking in Persons, Especially Women and Children, and parties to the Protocol should take all necessary steps to effectively implement it.

49. The United Nations should establish a robust capacity-building mechanism for rule-of-law assistance.

The Role of Sanctions

50. The Security Council must ensure that sanctions are effectively implemented and enforced:
(a) When the Security Council imposes a sanctions regime - including arms embargoes - it should routinely establish monitoring mechanisms and provide them with the necessary authority and capacity to carry out high quality, in-depth investigations. Adequate budgetary provisions must be made to implement those mechanisms;

(b) Security Council sanctions committees should be mandated to develop improved guidelines and reporting procedures to assist States in sanctions implementation, and to improve procedures for maintaining accurate lists of individuals and entities subject to targeted sanctions;

(c) The Secretary-General should appoint a senior official with sufficient supporting resources to enable the Secretary-General to supply the Security Council with analysis of the best way to target sanctions and to assist in coordinating their implementation. This official would also assist compliance efforts; identify technical assistance needs and coordinate such assistance; and make recommendations on any adjustments necessary to enhance the effectiveness of sanctions;

(d) Donors should devote more resources to strengthening the legal, administrative, and policing and border-control capacity of Member States to implement sanctions. Capacity-building measures should include efforts to improve air-traffic interdiction in zones of conflict;

(e) The Security Council should, in instances of verified, chronic violations, impose secondary sanctions against those involved in sanctions-busting;

(f) The Secretary-General, in consultation with the Security Council, should ensure that an appropriate auditing mechanism is in place to oversee sanctions administration.

51. Sanctions committees should improve procedures for providing humanitarian exemptions and routinely conduct assessments of the humanitarian impact of sanctions. The Security Council should continue to strive to mitigate the humanitarian consequences of sanctions.

52. Where sanctions involve lists of individuals or entities, sanctions committees should establish procedures to review the cases of those claiming to have been incorrectly placed or retained on such lists.

The UN and its Future in the 21st Century

Collective Security and the Use of Force

Using force: rules and guidelines

53. Article 51 of the Charter of the United Nations should be neither rewritten nor reinterpreted, either to extend its long-established scope (so as to allow preventive measures to non-imminent threats) or to restrict it (so as to allow its application only to actual attacks).

54. The Security Council is fully empowered under Chapter VII of the Charter of the United Nations to address the full range of security threats with which States are concerned. The task is not to find alternatives to the Security Council as a source of authority but to make the Council work better than it has.

55. The Panel endorses the emerging norm that there is a collective international responsibility to protect, exercisable by the Security Council authorizing military intervention as a last resort, in the event of genocide and other large-scale killing, ethnic cleansing or serious violations of humanitarian law which sovereign Governments have proved powerless or unwilling to prevent.

56. In considering whether to authorize or endorse the use of military force, the Security Council should always address - whatever other considerations it may take into account - at least the following five basic criteria of legitimacy:

(a) *Seriousness of threat.* Is the threatened harm to State or human security of a kind, and sufficiently clear and serious, to justify *prima facie* the use of military force? In the case of internal threats, does it involve genocide and other large-scale killing, ethnic cleansing or serious violations of international humanitarian law, actual or imminently apprehended?
(b) *Proper purpose.* Is it clear that the primary purpose of the proposed military action is to halt or avert the threat in question, whatever other purposes or motives may be involved?

(c) *Last resort.* Has every non-military option for meeting the threat in question been explored, with reasonable grounds for believing that other measures will not succeed?

(d) *Proportional means.* Are the scale, duration and intensity of the proposed military action the minimum necessary to meet the threat in question?

(e) *Balance of consequences.* Is there a reasonable chance of the military action being successful in meeting the threat in question, with the consequences of action not likely to be worse than the consequences of inaction?

57. The above guidelines for authorizing the use of force should be embodied in declaratory resolutions of the Security Council and General Assembly.

Peace Enforcement and Peacekeeping Capability

58. The developed States should do more to transform their existing force capacities into suitable contingents for peace operations.

59. Member States should strongly support the efforts of the Department of Peacekeeping Operations, building on the important work of the Panel on United Nations Peace Operations of the United Nations Secretariat, to improve its use of strategic deployment stockpiles, standby arrangements, trust funds and other mechanisms in order to meet the tighter deadlines necessary for effective deployment.

60. States with advanced military capacities should establish standby high readiness, self-sufficient battalions at up to brigade level that can reinforce United Nations missions, and should place them at the disposal of the United Nations.

61. The Secretary-General should recommend and the Security Council should authorize troop strengths for peacekeeping missions that are

sufficient to deter and repel hostile factions.

62. The United Nations should have a small corps of senior police officers and managers (50-100 personnel) who could undertake mission assessments and organize the start-up of police components of peace operations, and the General Assembly should authorize this capacity.

Post-conflict Peacebuilding

63. Special representatives of the Secretary-General should have the authority and guidance to work with relevant parties to establish robust donor-co-ordinating mechanisms, as well as the resources to perform co-ordination functions effectively, including ensuring that the sequencing of United Nations assessments and activities is consistent with Government priorities.

64. The Security Council should mandate and the General Assembly should authorize funding for disarmament and demobilization programmes from assessed budgets for United Nations peacekeeping operations.

65. A standing fund for peacebuilding should be established at the level of at least $250 million that can be used to finance the recurrent expenditures of a nascent Government, as well as critical agency programmes in the areas of rehabilitation and reintegration.

Protecting Civilians

66. All combatants must abide by the Geneva Conventions. All Member States should sign, ratify and act on all treaties relating to the protection of civilians, such as the Genocide Convention, the Geneva Conventions, the Rome Statute of the International Criminal Court and all refugee conventions.

67. The Security Council should fully implement resolution 1265 (1999) on

the protection of civilians in armed conflict.

68. The Security Council, United Nations agencies and Member States should fully implement resolution 1325 (2000) on women, peace and security.

69. Member States should support and fully fund the proposed Directorate of Security and accord high priority to assisting the Secretary-General in implementing a new staff security system in 2005.

A More Effective United Nations for the Twenty-first Century

The General Assembly

70. Members of the General Assembly should use the opportunity provided by the Millennium Review Summit in 2005 to forge a new consensus on broader and more effective collective security.

71. Member States should renew efforts to enable the General Assembly to perform its function as the main deliberative organ of the United Nations. This requires a better conceptualization and shortening of the agenda, which should reflect the contemporary challenges facing the international community. Smaller, more tightly focused committees could help to sharpen and improve resolutions that are brought to the whole Assembly.

72. Following the recommendation of the report of the Panel on Eminent Persons on United Nations-Civil Society Relations, the General Assembly should establish a better mechanism to enable systematic engagement with civil society organizations.

The Security Council

73. Reforms of the Security Council should meet the following principles: (a) They should, in honouring Article 23 of the Charter of the United

The UN and its Future in the 21st Century

Nations, increase the involvement in decision-making of those who contribute most to the United Nations financially, militarily and diplomatically - specifically in terms of contributions to United Nations assessed budgets, participation in mandated peace operations, contributions to the voluntary activities of the United Nations in the areas of security and development, and diplomatic activities

in support of United Nations objectives and mandates. Among developed countries, achieving or making substantial progress towards the internationally agreed level of 0.7 per cent of gross national product for official development assistance should be considered an important criterion of contribution;

(b) They should bring into the decision-making process countries more representative of the broader membership, especially of the developing world;

(c) They should not impair the effectiveness of the Security Council;

(d) They should increase the democratic and accountable nature of the body.

74. A decision on the enlargement of the Council, satisfying these criteria, is now a necessity. The presentation of two clearly defined alternatives, of the kind described below as models A and B, should help to clarify - and perhaps bring to resolution - a debate which has made little progress in the last 12 years.

75. Models A and B both involve a distribution of seats as between four major regional areas, which we identify, respectively, as 'Africa', 'Asia and Pacific', 'Europe' and 'Americas'. We see these descriptions as helpful in making and implementing judgements about the composition of the Security Council, but make no recommendation about changing the composition of the current regional groups for general electoral and other United Nations purposes. Some members of the Panel, in particular our Latin American colleagues, expressed a preference for basing any distribution of seats on the current regional groups.

76. Model A provides for six new permanent seats, with no veto being created, and three new two-year term non-permanent seats, divided among the major regional areas. Model B provides for no new permanent seats, but creates a new category of eight four-year renewable-term seats and one new two-year nonpermanent (and non-renewable) seat, divided among the major regional areas.

77. In both models, having regard to Article 23 of the Charter, a method of encouraging Member States to contribute more to international peace and security would be for the General Assembly, taking into account established practices of regional consultation, to elect Security Council members by giving preference for permanent or longer-term seats to those States that are among the top three financial contributors in their relevant regional area to the regular budget, or
the top three voluntary contributors from their regional area, or the top three troop contributors from their regional area to United Nations peacekeeping missions.

78. There should be a review of the composition of the Security Council in 2020, including, in this context, a review of the contribution (as defined in paragraph 249 of the main report) of permanent and non-permanent members from the point of view of the Council's effectiveness in taking collective action to prevent and remove new and old threats to international peace and security.

79. The Panel recommends that under any reform proposal, there should be no expansion of the veto.

80. A system of 'indicative voting' should be introduced, whereby members of the Security Council could call for a public indication of positions on a proposed action.

81. Processes to improve transparency and accountability in the Security Council should be incorporated and formalized in its rules of procedure.

The UN and its Future in the 21st Century

A Peacebuilding Commission

82. The Security Council, acting under Article 29 of the Charter of the United Nations and after consultation with the Economic and Social Council, should establish a Peacebuilding Commission.

83. The core functions of the Peacebuilding Commission should be to identify countries that are under stress and risk sliding towards State collapse; to organize, in partnership with the national Government, proactive assistance in preventing that process from developing further; to assist in the planning for transitions between conflict and post-conflict peacebuilding; and in particular to
marshal and sustain the efforts of the international community in post-conflict peacebuilding over whatever period may be necessary.

84. While the precise composition, procedures and reporting lines of the Peacebuilding Commission will need to be established, they should take account of the following guidelines:
(a) The Peacebuilding Commission should be reasonably small;
(b) It should meet in different configurations, to consider both general policy issues and country-by-country strategies;
(c) It should be chaired for at least one year and perhaps longer by a member approved by the Security Council;
(d) In addition to representation from the Security Council, it should include representation from the Economic and Social Council;
(e) National representatives of the country under consideration should be invited to attend;
(f) The Managing Director of the International Monetary Fund, the President of the World Bank and, when appropriate, heads of regional development banks should be represented at its meetings by appropriate senior officials;
(g) Representatives of the principal donor countries and, when appropriate, the principal troop contributors should be invited to participate in its deliberations;

(h) Representatives of regional and subregional organizations should be invited to participate in its deliberations when such organizations are actively involved in the country in question.

85. A Peacebuilding Support Office should be established in the Secretariat to give the Peacebuilding Commission appropriate Secretariat support and to ensure that the Secretary-General is able to integrate system-wide peacebuilding policies and strategies, develop best practices and provide cohesive support for field operations.

Regional Organizations

86. In relation to regional organizations:
(a) Authorization from the Security Council should in all cases be sought for regional peace operations;
(b) Consultation and co-operation between the United Nations and regional organizations should be expanded and could be formalized in an agreement, covering such issues as meetings of the heads of the organizations, more frequent exchange of information and early warning, co-training of civilian and military personnel, and exchange of personnel within peace operations;
(c) In the case of African regional and subregional capacities, donor countries should commit to a 10-year process of sustained capacity-building support, within the African Union strategic framework;
(d) Regional organizations that have a capacity for conflict prevention or peacekeeping should place such capacities in the framework of the United Nations Standby Arrangements System;
(e) Member States should agree to allow the United Nations to provide equipment support from United Nations-owned sources to regional operations, as needed;
(f) The rules for the United Nations peacekeeping budget should be amended to give the United Nations the option on a case-by-case basis to finance regional operations authorized by the Security Council with assessed contributions.

The UN and its Future in the 21st Century

The Economic and Social Council

87. The Economic and Social Council should provide normative and analytical leadership in a time of much debate about the causes of, and interconnections between, the many threats we face. To that end, the Economic and Social Council should establish a Committee on the Social and Economic Aspects of Security Threats.

88. The Economic and Social Council should provide an arena in which States measure their commitments to achieving key development objectives in an open and transparent manner.

89. The Economic and Social Council should provide a regular venue for engaging the development community at the highest level, in effect transforming itself into a 'development co-operation forum'. To that end:
(a) A new approach should be adopted within the Economic and Social Council agenda, replacing its current focus on administrative issues and programme coordination with a more focused agenda built around the major themes contained in the Millennium Declaration;
(b) A small executive committee, comprising members from each regional group, should be created in order to provide orientation and direction to the work of the Economic and Social Council and its interaction with principal organs, agencies and programmes;
(c) The annual meetings between the Economic and Social Council and the Bretton Woods institutions should be used to encourage collective action in support of the Millennium Development Goals and the Monterrey Consensus;
(d) The Economic and Social Council, with inputs from its secretariat and the United Nations Development Group, should aim to provide guidance on development co-operation to the governing boards of the United Nations funds, programmes and agencies;
(e) The Economic and Social Council should provide strong support to the efforts of the Secretary-General and the United Nations Development Group to strengthen the coherence of United Nations action at the field

The Commission on Human Rights

90. Membership of the Commission on Human Rights should be made universal.

91. All members of the Commission on Human Rights should designate prominent and experienced human rights figures as the heads of their delegations.

92. The Commission on Human Rights should be supported in its work by an advisory council or panel.

93. The United Nations High Commissioner for Human Rights should be called upon to prepare an annual report on the situation of human rights worldwide.

94. The Security Council and the Peacebuilding Commission should request the High Commissioner for Human Rights to report to them regularly on the implementation of all human rights-related provisions of Security Council resolutions, thus enabling focused, effective monitoring of those provisions.

The Secretariat

95. To assist the Secretary-General, an additional Deputy Secretary-General position should be created, responsible for peace and security.

96. The Secretary-General should be provided with the resources he requires to do his job properly and the authority to manage his staff and other resources as he deems best. To meet the needs identified in the present report, the Panel recommends that:

The UN and its Future in the 21st Century

(a) Member States recommit themselves to Articles 100 and 101 of the Charter of the United Nations;

(b) Member States review the relationship between the General Assembly and the Secretariat with the aim of substantially increasing the flexibility provided to the Secretary-General in the management of his staff, subject always to his accountability to the Assembly;

(c) The Secretary-General's reform proposals of 1997 and 2002 related to human resources should now, without further delay, be fully implemented;

(d) There should be a one-time review and replacement of personnel, including through early retirement, to ensure that the Secretariat is staffed with the right people to undertake the tasks at hand, including for mediation and peacebuilding support, and for the office of the Deputy Secretary-General for peace and security. Member States should provide funding for this replacement as a cost-effective long-term investment;

(e) The Secretary-General should immediately be provided with 60 posts – less than 1 per cent of the total Secretariat capacity – for the purpose of establishing all the increased Secretariat capacity proposed in the present report.

The Charter of the United Nations

97. In addition to any amendment of Article 23 of the Charter of the United Nations required by proposed reform of the Security Council, the Panel suggests the following modest changes to the Charter:

98. Articles 53 and 107 (references to enemy States) are outdated and should be revised.

99. Chapter XIII (The Trusteeship Council) should be deleted.

100. Article 47 (The Military Staff Committee) should be deleted, as should all references to the Committee in Articles 26, 45 and 46.

The UN and its Future in the 21st Century

101. All Member States should rededicate themselves to the purposes and principles of the Charter and to applying them in a purposeful way, matching political will with the necessary resources. Only dedicated leadership within and between states will generate effective collective security for the twenty-first century and forge a future that is both sustainable and secure.

'We the Peoples': Civil Society, the UN and Global Governance

Proposals of the Panel of Eminent Persons on UN-Civil Society Relationships

1. In exercising its convening power, the UN should emphasize inclusion of all constituencies relevant to the issue, recognize that the key actors are different for different issues, foster multi-stakeholder partnerships to pioneer solutions and empower a range of global policy networks to innovate and build momentum on policy options. Member States need opportunities for collective decision-making but they should signal their preparedness to engage other actors in deliberative processes.

2. The UN should embrace an array of forums, each designed to achieve a specific outcome, with participation determined accordingly. The cycle of global debate of an issue should include:
   - Interactive high-level roundtables to survey the framework of issues.
   - Global conferences to define norms and targets.
   - Multi-stakeholder partnerships to put the new norms and targets into practice.
   - Multi-stakeholder hearings to monitor compliance, review experience and revise strategies.

3. The Secretariat should innovate with networked governance, bringing people from diverse backgrounds together to identify possible policy breakthroughs on emerging global priorities. It should experiment with a Global Internet Agora to survey public opinion and raise awareness on emerging issues. The Secretary-General should initiate multi-

stakeholder advisory forums on selected emerging issues and feed their conclusions to appropriate intergovernmental forums.

4. The UN should retain the global conference mechanism but use it sparingly—to address major emerging policy issues that need concerted global action, enhanced public understanding and resonance with global public opinion. The participation of civil society and other constituencies should be planned in collaboration with their networks.

5. The Secretariat should foster multi-constituency processes as new conduits for voice on UN priorities, redirecting resources now used for single constituency forums covering multiple issues. The UN Secretariat and the secretariats of Specialized Agencies should convene public hearings to review progress in meeting globally agreed commitments. Being technical and concerned with implementation rather than new global policies, the Secretary-General could convene them on his own authority. Proceedings should be transmitted through the Secretary-General to relevant intergovernmental forums.

6. The General Assembly should permit the carefully planned participation of other actors besides central governments in its processes. In particular, General Assembly Committees and Special Sessions should regularly invite contributions by those offering high-quality independent inputs. The participation arrangements should be made in collaboration with the relevant constituency networks. The UN Secretariat should help plan innovative interactive sessions linked to the formal meetings but outside them.

7. To mainstream partnerships, the Secretary-General should, with Member States' approval and donor support:
    - Establish a Partnership Development Unit, headed by a high-level staff member to help incubate and decentralise the partnership approach, guide the needed management shifts, ensure sound evaluations and provide support services throughout the UN.

- Identify partnership focal points throughout all UN organs and agencies.
- Review partnership issues in coordination forums, such as the High Level Committee on Programmes and the Chief Executives Board.
- Ensure systematic learning from partnership efforts by creating a multistakeholder Partnership Assessment Forum, with UN staff, governments, civil society organizations and others.
- Provide training in partnership development to governments, civil society and other constituencies, as well as to UN staff.
- Periodically review the effectiveness of these efforts.

8. The proposed Partnership Development Unit should ensure that lessons of practice are fully internalized in operational and management approaches, conduct rigorous evaluations to learn about the full costs and development impacts of multi-sectoral partnerships and inform the debate about the institutional implications of the approach.

9. The Secretariat should strengthen its relationship with different actors in the private sector by:
   - Incorporating the Global Compact under the proposed Office of Constituency Engagement and Partnerships (see Proposal 24).
   - Engaging with small and medium businesses and their national associations and helping build the capacity and competitiveness of micro and small businesses.
   - Strengthening the Global Compact's capacity for—and contribution to— enhancing corporate responsibility.

10. The UN Development Group (UNDG) should ensure that the rhetoric of country leadership, coordination and partnership is put into effective practice, to open space for all constituencies to contribute to UN goals.

   At the country level this entails:
   - Enhancing the capacity of country offices (UN Houses) to identify, convene and broker the partnerships needed to meet the main

The UN and its Future in the 21st Century

challenges and build consensus on country-specific goals (see Proposal 11).
- Conveying systematic messages to country staff about learning from and providing support to civil society and other actors, using the rubric of the Millennium Development Goals and other globally agreed goals as reference points.
- Ensuring that UN Houses work with Regional Commissions to inject the experience of country level actors into regional and global deliberative processes.

At the global level this entails:
- Identifying and rewarding Participation Pioneers within the UN system, by establishing, with donor support, a global fund to support UN innovations in partnership development at country level.
- Identifying and disseminating lessons from innovative partnership and countries where co-operation with non-State actors is strongest.
- Assessing partnership qualities in the annual performance appraisals of Resident Coordinators and other country-level staff.
- Persuading donors to support the extra cost of being an effective networking organization, including the greater investment in coordination that this requires.

11. The Resident Coordinators and UNDG agencies at the country level should undertake the necessary restructuring, coordination and investment to enable the UN to meet the networking challenges by:
    - Initially appointing local constituency engagement specialists in 30-40 countries, with facilitation skills and knowledge of civil society in the country (see Proposal 25).
    - Reviewing the effectiveness of current country-level information and communications resources, redirecting them to support strategies and partnerships to achieve globally agreed goals.

- Establishing Civil Society Advisory Groups in a pilot range of countries to guide the UN's strategy; similar advisory groups could be considered for business and other constituencies.

12. Security Council members should further strengthen their dialogue with civil society—supported by the Secretary-General—by:
    - Improving the planning and effectiveness of the Arria formula meetings by lengthening lead times and covering travel costs to increase the participation of actors from the field. UN country staff should assist in identifying civil society interlocutors.
    - Ensuring that Security Council field missions meet regularly with appropriate local civil society leaders, international humanitarian NGOs and perhaps others, such as business leaders. UN HQ and field staff should facilitate these meetings.
    - Installing an experimental series of Security Council Seminars to discuss issues of emerging importance to the Council. Serviced by the Secretariat, these would include presentations by civil society and other constituencies as well as UN specialists such as Special Rapporteurs.
    - Convening independent Commissions of Inquiry after Council-mandated operations. A Global Public Policy Committee connecting national Foreign Affairs committees could serve as such a commission (Proposal 15).

13. The UN should routinely encourage national parliaments to hold debates on major matters coming up in the UN and to to discuss these matters with relevant ministers. To facilitate this, relevant draft documents, including progress on the MDGs and other globally agreed goals, should be made available to parliaments when they are transmitted to governments. The Secretary-General should seek the co-operation of the Inter-Parliamentary Union (IPU) and parliamentarian associations. Member States should regularly consult MPs on UN matters and debrief them after major UN meetings.

The UN and its Future in the 21st Century

14. Member States should more regularly include MPs in their delegations to major UN meetings, while taking care to avoid compromising the independence of those parliamentarians. The UN Secretariat should test opportunities for MPs to contribute as parliamentarians, including in parliamentary debates before a General Assembly session on a major topic. MPs specializing in a subject could also be invited to speak in relevant General Assembly committees and Special Sessions, particularly when these review progress towards meeting the MDGs and other agreed global goals.

15. Member States should make way for an enhanced role for parliamentarians in global governance. They should instruct the Secretariat to work with national parliaments and the Inter-Parliamentary Union, as appropriate, to convene one or more experimental Global Public Policy Committees (GPPC) to discuss emerging priorities on the global agenda. These committees would comprise parliamentarians from the most relevant functional committee in a globally representative range of countries. In an experimental five-year period, different organizational arrangements could be tested and, through periodic review, refined over time.

16. The Secretary-General should form a small Elected Representative Liaison Unit, based on the Non-Governmental Liaison Service, to:
    - Provide a dedicated information service for parliaments and MP associations, including a dedicated web-based information service for MPs.
    - Encourage greater attention to UN processes in national parliaments.
    - Help create more effective opportunities for MPs to take part in UN forums.
    - Organize Global Public Policy Committees, working closely with national parliaments, the IPU, specialized agencies, and other organizations as appropriate.

The UN and its Future in the 21st Century

- Foster debate within the UN system about new or improved strategies for engaging MPs and parliaments.

17. The General Assembly should debate a resolution affirming and respecting local autonomy as a universal principle.

18. The Elected Representative Unit (see Proposal 16) should liaise with local authorities and their new world association and disseminate lessons of good practice. The UN should regard United Cities and Local Governments as an advisory body on governance matters. The Secretary-General should also require UN bodies with national presence to build close contacts with local authorities and their national and regional associations. Specifically, Resident Coordinators should interact regularly with local authorities to inform them of UN programmes and processes and to encourage partnerships with them.

19. The UN should realign accreditation with its original purpose— an agreement between civil society actors and Member States based on the applicants' expertise, competence and skills. To achieve this, Member States should agree to merge the current procedures at UN Headquarters for ECOSOC, the Department of Public Information, conferences and their follow-up into a single UN accreditation process, with responsibility for this assumed by the General Assembly.

20. Member States should shift the task of reviewing applications to the Secretariat to reduce time inefficiencies and to increase the technical focus of the review. An Accreditation Unit should be established within the General Assembly Secretariat, incorporating staff now responsible for accreditation in different UN departments (therefore budget neutral). This Unit would help set up the advisory body to offer guidance on whether applications should be recommended or not. A designated General Assembly committee would decide on accreditation, based on this guidance. The Secretariat should ensure increased use of information technologies to manage the accreditation

process. The S-G should encourage the UN agencies, country offices and others to cooperate in a system-wide effort.

21. The Secretary-General should foster enhanced coordination and support for the accreditation process by:
    - Instructing national and regional offices of the UN to facilitate applications.
    - Using the Chief Executives Board processes to foster closer coordination among UN agencies, funds, programmes and regional commissions.
    - Ensuring wider availability of information on the rights and responsibilities related to accreditation (say, through booklets aimed at civil society and UN staff).

22. The Secretary-General should initiate a consultative review, to be finished within three years, whereupon proposals would be submitted to the General Assembly for revising the accreditation categories to align them better with today's practices and priorities.

23. The Secretariat should encourage the main constituencies the UN works with to form broad networks to help it with selection and quality assurance. But the UN should not demand this or stipulate how it is to be done. Networks would be encouraged to advise secretariats and Bureaux on the participation of their constituencies in intergovernmental processes and help monitor practices and revise strategies, perhaps evolving into recognized 'advisory groups.' The UN Secretariat should discuss with these groups possible codes of conduct and 'self-policing' mechanisms to heighten disciplines of quality, governance and balance.

24. With Member States' approval, the Secretary-General should appoint an Under-Secretary-General in charge of a new Office of Constituency Engagement and Partnerships. This office would be responsible for formulating and implementing the strategy for the UN's engagement

with all constituencies beyond its formal membership of central governments. It would monitor engagements throughout the UN system and provide advice and good practice lessons. It could comprise the following:

- A Civil Society Unit, to absorb the Non-Governmental Liaison Service.
- A Partnership Development Unit, to absorb the UN Fund for International Partnerships.
- An Elected Representative Liaison Unit.
- The Global Compact Office.
- The Secretariat of the Permanent Forum on Indigenous Issues.

25. With Member States' approval, the Secretary-General should initiate a programme to appoint 30-40 constituency engagement specialists in UN Houses to help the UN and the wider system enhance engagement with a diversity of constituencies. He should invite contributions from bilateral donors and foundations to a trust fund to finance these appointments for a trial four-year period.

26. The Secretary-General should make redressing North-South imbalances a priority in enhancing UN-civil society relations. He should enlist donor support for enhancing UN capacity to identify and work with local actors, establishing a fund to build southern civil society capacity to participate and ensuring that country-level engagement feeds into the global deliberative processes.

27. The UN should establish a fund to enhance the capacity of civil society in developing countries to engage in UN processes and partnerships. The Secretariat should seek contributions from governments, foundations, UN sources and elsewhere. And it should establish an administration and governance structure for the fund that puts maximum emphasis on decision-making at the country level.

The UN and its Future in the 21st Century

28. The Secretary-General and other top UN managers should use frequent opportunities to convey to staff the importance they ascribe to constituency engagement and partnership. These issues should feature prominently in all human resource processes, including recruitment, promotion and annual appraisal. Staff throughout the system, including managers, should be given training in such matters.

29. The Secretary-General should use his capacity as chairman of the wider UN system coordination mechanism to encourage all agencies, including the Bretton Woods Institutions, to enhance their engagement with civil society and other actors and to cooperate with one another across the UN system to promote this, with periodic progress reviews.

30. Member States should encourage, through the forums of the UN, an enabling policy environment for civil society throughout the world and expanded dialogue and partnership opportunities in development processes. The Secretariat leadership, Resident Coordinators and governance specialists should use their dialogues with governments to similar effect.

Charter of the United Nations

WE THE PEOPLES OF THE UNITED NATIONS DETERMINED
➤ to save succeeding generations from the scourge of war, which twice in our lifetime has brought untold sorrow to mankind, and
➤ to reaffirm faith in fundamental human rights, in the dignity and worth of the human person, in the equal rights of men and women and of nations large and small, and
➤ to establish conditions under which justice and respect for the obligations arising from treaties and other sources of international law can be maintained, and
➤ to promote social progress and better standards of life in larger freedom,
AND FOR THESE ENDS
➤ to practice tolerance and live together in peace with one another as good neighbours, and
➤ to unite our strength to maintain international peace and security, and
➤ to ensure, by the acceptance of principles and the institution of methods, that armed force shall not be used, save in the common interest, and
➤ to employ international machinery for the promotion of the economic and social advancement of all peoples,
HAVE RESOLVED TO COMBINE OUR EFFORTS TO ACCOMPLISH THESE AIMS
Accordingly, our respective Governments, through representatives assembled in the city of San Francisco, who have exhibited their full powers found to be in good and due form, have agreed to the present Charter of the United Nations and do hereby establish an international organization to be known as the United Nations.

CHAPTER I
PURPOSES AND PRINCIPLES

Article 1
The Purposes of the United Nations are:
1. To maintain international peace and security, and to that end: to take effective collective measures for the prevention and removal of threats to the peace, and for the suppression of acts of aggression or other breaches of the peace, and to bring about by peaceful means, and in conformity with the principles of justice and international law, adjustment or settlement of international disputes or situations which might lead to a breach of the peace;
2. To develop friendly relations among nations based on respect for the principle of equal rights and self-determination of peoples, and to take other appropriate measures to strengthen universal peace;
3. To achieve international co-operation in solving international problems of an economic, social, cultural, or humanitarian character, and in promoting and encouraging respect for human rights and for fundamental freedoms for all without distinction as to race, sex, language, or religion; and
4. To be a centre for harmonizing the actions of nations in the attainment of these common ends.

Article 2
The Organization and its Members, in pursuit of the Purposes stated in Article 1, shall act in accordance with the following Principles.
1. The Organization is based on the principle of the sovereign equality of all its Members.
2. All Members, in order to ensure to all of them the rights and benefits resulting from membership, shall fulfill in good faith

the obligations assumed by them in accordance with the present Charter.
3. All Members shall settle their international disputes by peaceful means in such a manner that international peace and security, and justice, are not endangered.
4. All Members shall refrain in their international relations from the threat or use of force against the territorial integrity or political independence of any state, or in any other manner inconsistent with the Purposes of the United Nations.
5. All Members shall give the United Nations every assistance in any action it takes in accordance with the present Charter, and shall refrain from giving assistance to any state against which the United Nations is taking preventive or enforcement action.
6. The Organization shall ensure that states which are not Members of the United Nations act in accordance with these Principles so far as may be necessary for the maintenance of international peace and security.
7. Nothing contained in the present Charter shall authorize the United Nations to intervene in matters which are essentially within the domestic jurisdiction of any state or shall require the Members to submit such matters to settlement under the present Charter; but this principle shall not prejudice the application of enforcement measures under Chapter VlI.

CHAPTER II
MEMBERSHIP

Article 3
The original Members of the United Nations shall be the states which, having participated in the United Nations Conference on International Organization at San Francisco, or having previously signed the Declaration by United Nations of 1 January 1942, sign the present Charter and ratify it in accordance with Article 110.

Article 4
1. Membership in the United Nations is open to all other peace-loving states which accept the obligations contained in the present Charter and, in the judgment of the Organization, are able and willing to carry out these obligations.
5. The admission of any such state to membership in the United Nations will be effected by a decision of the General Assembly upon the recommendation of the Security Council.

Article 5
A Member of the United Nations against which preventive or enforcement action has been taken by the Security Council may be suspended from the exercise of the rights and privileges of membership by the General Assembly upon the recommendation of the Security Council. The exercise of these rights and privileges may be restored by the Security Council.

Article 6
A Member of the United Nations which has persistently violated the Principles contained in the present Charter may be expelled from the Organization by the General Assembly upon the recommendation of the Security Council.

CHAPTER III
ORGANS

Article 7
1. There are established as the principal organs of the United Nations:
   a General Assembly
   a Security Council
   an Economic and Social Council
   a Trusteeship Council
   an International Court of Justice
   and a Secretariat.
2. Such subsidiary organs as may be found necessary may be established in accordance with the present Charter.

Article 8
The United Nations shall place no restrictions on the eligibility of men and women to participate in any capacity and under conditions of equality in its principal and subsidiary organs.

CHAPTER IV
THE GENERAL ASSEMBLY

COMPOSITION

Article 9
1. The General Assembly shall consist of all the Members of the United Nations.
2. Each Member shall have not more than five representatives in the General Assembly.

FUNCTIONS and POWERS

Article 10
The General Assembly may discuss any questions or any matters within the scope of the present Charter or relating to the powers and functions of any organs provided for in the present Charter, and, except as provided in Article 12, may make recommendations to the Members of the United Nations or to the Security Council or to both on any such questions or matters.

Article 11
1. The General Assembly may consider the general principles of co-operation in the maintenance of international peace and security, including the principles governing disarmament and the regulation of armaments, and may make recommendations with regard to such principles to the Members or to the Security Council or to both.
2. The General Assembly may discuss any questions relating to the maintenance of international peace and security brought before it by any Member of the United Nations, or by the Security Council, or by a state which is not a Member of the United Nations in accordance with Article 35, paragraph 2, and, except as provided in Article 12, may make

recommendations with regard to any such questions to the state or states concerned or to the Security Council or to both. Any such question on which action is necessary shall be referred to the Security Council by the General Assembly either before or after discussion.
3. The General Assembly may call the attention of the Security Council to situations which are likely to endanger international peace and security.
4. The powers of the General Assembly set forth in this Article shall not limit the general scope of Article 10.

Article 12
1. While the Security Council is exercising in respect of any dispute or situation the functions assigned to it in the present Charter, the General Assembly shall not make any recommendation with regard to that dispute or situation unless the Security Council so requests.
2. The Secretary-General, with the consent of the Security Council, shall notify the General Assembly at each session of any matters relative to the maintenance of international peace and security which are being dealt with by the Security Council and shall similarly notify the General Assembly, or the Members of the United Nations if the General Assembly is not in session, immediately the Security Council ceases to deal with suchmatters.

Article 13
1. The General Assembly shall initiate studies and make recommendations for the purpose of:
a. promoting international co-operation in the political field and encouraging the progressive development of international law and its codification;
b. promoting international co-operation in the economic, social, cultural, educational, and health fields, and assisting in the

realization of human rights and fundamental freedoms for all without distinction as to race, sex, language, or religion.
2. The further responsibilities, functions and powers of the General Assembly with respect to matters mentioned in paragraph 1 (b) above are set forth in Chapters IX and X.

Article 14
Subject to the provisions of Article 12, the General Assembly may recommend measures for the peaceful adjustment of any situation, regardless of origin, which it deems likely to impair the general welfare or friendly relations among nations, including situations resulting from a violation of the provisions of the present Charter setting forth the Purposes and Principles of the United Nations.

Article 15
1. The General Assembly shall receive and consider annual and special reports from the Security Council; these reports shall include an account of the measures that the Security Council has decided upon or taken to maintain international peace and security.
2. The General Assembly shall receive and consider reports from the other organs of the United Nations.

Article 16
The General Assembly shall perform such functions with respect to the international trusteeship system as are assigned to it under Chapters XII and XIII, including the approval of the trusteeship agreements for areas not designated as strategic.

Article 17
1. The General Assembly shall consider and approve the budget of the Organization.
2. The expenses of the Organization shall be borne by the Members as apportioned by the General Assembly.

3. The General Assembly shall consider and approve any financial and budgetary arrangements with specialized agencies referred to in Article 57 and shall examine the administrative budgets of such specialized agencies with a view to making recommendations to the agencies concerned.

VOTING

Article 18
1. Each member of the General Assembly shall have one vote.
2. Decisions of the General Assembly on important questions shall be made by a two-thirds majority of the members present and voting. These questions shall include: recommendations with respect to the maintenance of international peace and security, the election of the non-permanent members of the Security Council, the election of the members of the Economic and Social Council, the election of members of the Trusteeship Council in accordance with paragraph 1 (c) of Article 86, the admission of new Members to the United Nations, the suspension of the rights and privileges of membership, the expulsion of Members, questions relating to the operation of the trusteeship system, and budgetary questions.
3. Decisions on other questions, including the determination of additional categories of questions to be decided by a two-thirds majority, shall be made by a majority of the members present and voting.

Article 19
A Member of the United Nations which is in arrears in the payment of its financial contributions to the Organization shall have no vote in the General Assembly if the amount of its arrears equals or exceeds the amount of the contributions due from it for the preceding two full years. The General Assembly may, nevertheless, permit such a Member to vote if it is satisfied that the failure to pay is due to

conditions beyond the control of the Member.

PROCEDURE

Article 20
The General Assembly shall meet in regular annual sessions and in such special sessions as occasion may require. Special sessions shall be convoked by the Secretary-General at the request of the Security Council or of a majority of the Members of the United Nations.

Article 21
The General Assembly shall adopt its own rules of procedure. It shall elect its President for each session.

Article 22
The General Assembly may establish such subsidiary organs as it deems necessary for the performance of its functions.

CHAPTER V
THE SECURITY COUNCIL

COMPOSITION

Article 23
1. The Security Council shall consist of fifteen Members of the United Nations. The Republic of China, France, the Union of Soviet Socialist Republics, the United Kingdom of Great Britain and Northern Ireland, and the United States of America shall be permanent members of the Security Council. The General Assembly shall elect ten other Members of the United Nations to be non-permanent members of the Security Council, due regard being specially paid, in the first instance to the contribution of Members of the United Nations to the maintenance of international peace and security and to the other purposes of the Organization, and also to equitable geographical distribution.
2. The non-permanent members of the Security Council shall be elected for a term of two years. In the first election of the non-permanent members after the increase of the membership of the Security Council from eleven to fifteen, two of the four additional members shall be chosen for a term of one year. A retiring member shall not be eligible for immediate re-election.
3. Each member of the Security Council shall have one representative.

FUNCTIONS and POWERS

Article 24
1. In order to ensure prompt and effective action by the United Nations,its Members confer on the Security Council primary responsibility for the maintenance of international peace and

security, and agree that in carrying out its duties under this responsibility the Security Council acts on their behalf.
2. In discharging these duties the Security Council shall act in accordance with the Purposes and Principles of the United Nations. The specific powers granted to the Security Council for the discharge of these duties are laid down in Chapters VI, VII, VIII, and XII.
3. The Security Council shall submit annual and, when necessary, special reports to the General Assembly for its consideration.

Article 25
The Members of the United Nations agree to accept and carry out the decisions of the Security Council in accordance with the present Charter.

Article 26
In order to promote the establishment and maintenance of international peace and security with the least diversion for armaments of the world's human and economic resources, the Security Council shall be responsible for formulating, with the assistance of the Military Staff Committee referred to in Article 47, plans to be submitted to the Members of the United Nations for the establishment of a system for the regulation of armaments.

VOTING

Article 27
1. Each member of the Security Council shall have one vote.
2. Decisions of the Security Council on procedural matters shall be made by an affirmative vote of nine members.

3. Decisions of the Security Council on all other matters shall be made by an affirmative vote of nine members including the concurring votes of the permanent members; provided that, in decisions under Chapter VI, and under paragraph 3 of Article 52, a party to a dispute shall abstain from voting.

PROCEDURE

Article 28
1. The Security Council shall be so organized as to be able to function continuously. Each member of the Security Council shall for this purpose be represented at all times at the seat of the Organization.
2. The Security Council shall hold periodic meetings at which each of its members may, if it so desires, be represented by a member of the government or by some other specially designated representative.
3. The Security Council may hold meetings at such places other than the seat of the Organization as in its judgment will best facilitate its work.

Article 29
The Security Council may establish such subsidiary organs as it deems necessary for the performance of its functions.

Article 30
The Security Council shall adopt its own rules of procedure, including the method of selecting its President.

Article 31
Any Member of the United Nations which is not a member of the Security Council may participate, without vote, in the discussion of any question brought before the Security Council whenever the latter considers that the interests of that Member are specially affected.

Article 32

Any Member of the United Nations which is not a member of the Security Council or any state which is not a Member of the United Nations, if it is a party to a dispute under consideration by the Security Council, shall be invited to participate, without vote, in the discussion relating to the dispute. The Security Council shall lay down such conditions as it deems just for the participation of a state which is not a Member of the United Nations.

CHAPTER VI

PACIFIC SETTLEMENT OF DISPUTES

Article 33
1. The parties to any dispute, the continuance of which is likely to endanger the maintenance of international peace and security, shall, first of all, seek a solution by negotiation, enquiry, mediation, conciliation, arbitration, judicial settlement, resort to regional agencies or arrangements, or other peaceful means of their own choice.
2. The Security Council shall, when it deems necessary, call upon the parties to settle their dispute by such means.

Article 34
The Security Council may investigate any dispute, or any situation which might lead to international friction or give rise to a dispute, in order to determine whether the continuance of the dispute or situation is likely to endanger the maintenance of international peace and security.

Article 35
1. Any Member of the United Nations may bring any dispute, or any situation of the nature referred to in Article 34, to the attention of the Security Council or of the General Assembly.
2. A state which is not a Member of the United Nations may bring to the attention of the Security Council or of the General Assembly any dispute to which it is a party if it accepts in advance, for the purposes of the dispute, the obligations of pacific settlement provided in the present Charter.
3. The proceedings of the General Assembly in respect of matters brought to its attention under this Article will be subject to the provisions of Articles 11 and 12.

Article 36
1. The Security Council may, at any stage of a dispute of the nature referred to in Article 33 or of a situation of like nature, recommend appropriate procedures or methods of adjustment.
2. The Security Council should take into consideration any procedures for the settlement of the dispute which have already been adopted by the parties.
3. In making recommendations under this Article the Security Council should also take into consideration that legal disputes should as a general rule be referred by the parties to the International Court of Justice in accordance with the provisions of the Statute of the Court.

Article 37
1. Should the parties to a dispute of the nature referred to in Article 33 fail to settle it by the means indicated in that Article, they shall refer it to the Security Council.
2. If the Security Council deems that the continuance of the dispute is in fact likely to endanger the maintenance of international peace and security, it shall decide whether to take action under Article 36 or to recommend such terms of settlement as it may consider appropriate.

Article 38
Without prejudice to the provisions of Articles 33 to 37, the Security Council may, if all the parties to any dispute so request, make recommendations to the parties with a view to a pacific settlement of the dispute.

CHAPTER VII
ACTION WITH RESPECT TO THREATS TO THE PEACE, BREACHES OF THE PEACE, AND ACTS OF AGGRESSION

Article 39
The Security Council shall determine the existence of any threat to the peace, breach of the peace, or act of aggression and shall make recommendations, or decide what measures shall be taken in accordance with Articles 41 and 42, to maintain or restore international peace and security.

Article 40
In order to prevent an aggravation of the situation, the Security Council may, before making the recommendations or deciding upon the measures provided for in Article 39, call upon the parties concerned to comply with such provisional measures as it deems necessary or desirable. Such provisional measures shall be without prejudice to the rights, claims, or position of the parties concerned. The Security Council shall duly take account of failure to comply with such provisional measures.

Article 41
The Security Council may decide what measures not involving the use of armed force are to be employed to give effect to its decisions, and it may call upon the Members of the United Nations to apply such measures. These may include complete or partial interruption of economic relations and of rail, sea, air, postal, telegraphic, radio, and other means of communication, and the severance of diplomatic relations.

Article 42
Should the Security Council consider that measures provided for in Article 41 would be inadequate or have proved to be inadequate, it

may take such action by air, sea, or land forces as may be necessary to maintain or restore international peace and security. Such action may include demonstrations, blockade, and other operations by air, sea, or land forces of Members of the United Nations.

Article 43
1. All Members of the United Nations, in order to contribute to the maintenance of international peace and security, undertake to make available to the Security Council, on its call and in accordance with a special agreement or agreements, armed forces, assistance, and facilities, including rights of passage, necessary for the purpose of maintaining international peace and security.
2. Such agreement or agreements shall govern the numbers and types of forces, their degree of readiness and general location, and the nature of the facilities and assistance to be provided.
3. The agreement or agreements shall be negotiated as soon as possible on the initiative of the Security Council. They shall be concluded between the Security Council and Members or between the Security Council and groups of Members and shall be subject to ratification by the signatory states in accordance with their respective constitutional processes.

Article 44
When the Security Council has decided to use force it shall, before calling upon a Member not represented on it to provide armed forces in fulfilment of the obligations assumed under Article 43, invite that Member, if the Member so desires, to participate in the decisions of the Security Council concerning the employment of contingents of that Member's armed forces.

Article 45
In order to enable the United Nations to take urgent military measures, Members shall hold immediately available national air-force contingents for combined international enforcement action. The strength and degree of readiness of these contingents and plans for their combined action shall be determined within the limits laid down in the special agreement or agreements referred to in Article 43, by the Security Council with the assistance of the Military Staff Committee.

Article 46
Plans for the application of armed force shall be made by the Security Council with the assistance of the Military Staff Committee.

Article 47
1. There shall be established a Military Staff Committee to advise and assist the Security Council on all questions relating to the Security Council's military requirements for the maintenance of international peace and security, the employment and command of forces placed at its disposal, the regulation of armaments, and possible disarmament.
2. The Military Staff Committee shall consist of the Chiefs of Staff of the permanent members of the Security Council or their representatives. Any Member of the United Nations not permanently represented on the Committee shall be invited by the Committee to be associated with it when the efficient discharge of the Committee's responsibilities requires the participation of that Member in its work.
3. The Military Staff Committee shall be responsible under the Security Council for the strategic direction of any armed forces placed at the disposal of the Security Council. Questions relating to the command of such forces shall be worked out subsequently.

4. **The Military Staff Committee, with the authorization of the Security Council and after consultation with appropriate regional agencies, may establish regional sub-committees.**

Article 48
1. **The action required to carry out the decisions of the Security Council for the maintenance of international peace and security shall be taken by all the Members of the United Nations or by some of them, as the Security Council may determine.**
2. **Such decisions shall be carried out by the Members of the United Nations directly and through their action in the appropriate international agencies of which they are members.**

Article 49
The Members of the United Nations shall join in affording mutual assistance in carrying out the measures decided upon by the Security Council.

Article 50
If preventive or enforcement measures against any state are taken by the Security Council, any other state, whether a Member of the United Nations or not, which finds itself confronted with special economic problems arising from the carrying out of those measures shall have the right to consult the Security Council with regard to a solution of those problems.

Article 51
Nothing in the present Charter shall impair the inherent right of individual or collective self-defence if an armed attack occurs against a Member of the United Nations, until the Security Council has taken measures necessary to maintain international peace and security. Measures taken by Members in the exercise of this right of self-defence shall be immediately reported to the Security Council and shall not in any way affect the authority and responsibility of the Security Council under the present Charter to take at any time such action as it deems necessary in order to maintain or restore international peace and security.

CHAPTER VIII
REGIONAL ARRANGEMENTS

Article 52
1. Nothing in the present Charter precludes the existence of regional arrangements or agencies for dealing with such matters relating to the maintenance of international peace and security as are appropriate for regional action provided that such arrangements or agencies and their activities are consistent with the Purposes and Principles of the United Nations.
2. The Members of the United Nations entering into such arrangements or constituting such agencies shall make every effort to achieve pacific settlement of local disputes through such regional arrangements or by such regional agencies before referring them to the Security Council.
3. The Security Council shall encourage the development of pacific settlement of local disputes through such regional arrangements or by such regional agencies either on the initiative of the states concerned or by reference from the Security Council.
4. This Article in no way impairs the application of Articles 34 and 35.

Article 53
1. The Security Council shall, where appropriate, utilize such regional arrangements or agencies for enforcement action under its authority. But no enforcement action shall be taken under regional arrangements or by regional agencies without the authorization of the Security Council, with the exception of measures against any enemy state, as defined in paragraph 2 of this Article, provided for pursuant to Article 107 or in regional arrangements directed against renewal of aggressive policy on

the part of any such state, until such time as the Organization may, on request of the Governments concerned, be charged with the responsibility for preventing further aggression by such a state.

2. The term enemy state as used in paragraph 1 of this Article applies to any state which during the Second World War has been an enemy of any signatory of the present Charter.

Article 54

The Security Council shall at all times be kept fully informed of activities undertaken or in contemplation under regional arrangements or by regional agencies for the maintenance of international peace and security.

CHAPTER IX
INTERNATIONAL ECONOMIC AND SOCIAL CO-OPERATION

Article 55
With a view to the creation of conditions of stability and well-being which are necessary for peaceful and friendly relations among nations based on respect for the principle of equal rights and self-determination of peoples, the United Nations shall promote:
a. higher standards of living, full employment, and conditions of economic and social progress and development;
b. solutions of international economic, social, health, and related problems; and international cultural and educational co-operation; and
c. universal respect for, and observance of, human rights and fundamental freedoms for all without distinction as to race, sex, language, or religion.

Article 56
All Members pledge themselves to take joint and separate action in co-operation with the Organization for the achievement of the purposes set forth in Article 55.

Article 57
1. The various specialized agencies, established by intergovernmental agreement and having wide international responsibilities, as defined in their basic instruments, in economic, social, cultural, educational, health, and related fields, shall be brought into relationship with the United Nations in accordance with the provisions of Article 63.
2. Such agencies thus brought into relationship with the United Nations are hereinafter referred to as specialized agencies.

Article 58
The Organization shall make recommendations for the co-ordination of the policies and activities of the specialized agencies.

Article 59
The Organization shall, where appropriate, initiate negotiations among the states concerned for the creation of any new specialized agencies required for the accomplishment of the purposes set forth in Article 55.

Article 60
Responsibility for the discharge of the functions of the Organization set forth in this Chapter shall be vested in the General Assembly and, under the authority of the General Assembly, in the Economic and Social Council, which shall have for this purpose the powers set forth in Chapter X.

CHAPTER X
THE ECONOMIC AND SOCIAL COUNCIL

COMPOSITION

Article 61
1. The Economic and Social Council shall consist of fifty-four Members of the United Nations elected by the General Assembly.
2. Subject to the provisions of paragraph 3, eighteen members of the Economic and Social Council shall be elected each year for a term of three years. A retiring member shall be eligible for immediate re-election.
3. At the first election after the increase in the membership of the Economic and Social Council from twenty-seven to fifty-four members, in addition to the members elected in place of the nine members whose term of office expires at the end of that year, twenty-seven additional members shall be elected. Of these twenty-seven additional members, the term of office of nine members so elected shall expire at the end of one year, and of nine other members at the end of two years, in accordance with arrangements made by the General Assembly.
4. Each member of the Economic and Social Council shall have one representative.

FUNCTIONS and POWERS

Article 62
1. The Economic and Social Council may make or initiate studies and reports with respect to international economic, social, cultural, educational, health, and related matters and may make recommendations with respect to any such matters to the General Assembly to the Members of the United Nations, and to the specialized agencies concerned.

2. It may make recommendations for the purpose of promoting respect for, and observance of, human rights and fundamental freedoms for all.
3. It may prepare draft conventions for submission to the General Assembly, with respect to matters falling within its competence.
4. It may call, in accordance with the rules prescribed by the United Nations, international conferences on matters falling within its competence.

Article 63
1. The Economic and Social Council may enter into agreements with any of the agencies referred to in Article 57, defining the terms on which the agency concerned shall be brought into relationship with the United Nations. Such agreements shall be subject to approval by the General Assembly.
2. It may co-ordinate the activities of the specialized agencies through consultation with and recommendations to such agencies and through recommendations to the General Assembly and to the Members of the United Nations.

Article 64
1. The Economic and Social Council may take appropriate steps to obtain regular reports from the specialized agencies. It may make arrangements with the Members of the United Nations and with the specialized agencies to obtain reports on the steps taken to give effect to its own recommendations and to recommendations on matters falling within its competence made by the General Assembly.
2. It may communicate its observations on these reports to the General Assembly.

Article 65
The Economic and Social Council may furnish information to the Security Council and shall assist the Security Council upon its request.

Article 66
1. The Economic and Social Council shall perform such functions as fall within its competence in connexion with the carrying out of the recommendations of the General Assembly.
2. It may, with the approval of the General Assembly, perform services at the request of Members of the United Nations and at the request of specialized agencies.
3. It shall perform such other functions as are specified elsewhere in the present Charter or as may be assigned to it by the General Assembly.

VOTING

Article 67
1. Each member of the Economic and Social Council shall have one vote.
2. Decisions of the Economic and Social Council shall be made by a majority of the members present and voting.

PROCEDURE

Article 68
The Economic and Social Council shall set up commissions in economic and social fields and for the promotion of human rights, and such other commissions as may be required for the performance of its functions.

Article 69
The Economic and Social Council shall invite any Member of the United Nations to participate, without vote, in its deliberations on any matter of particular concern to that Member.

Article 70
The Economic and Social Council may make arrangements for representatives of the specialized agencies to participate, without vote, in its deliberations and in those of the commissions established by it, and for its representatives to participate in the deliberations of the specialized agencies.

Article 71
The Economic and Social Council may make suitable arrangements for consultation with non-governmental organizations which are concerned with matters within its competence. Such arrangements may be made with international organizations and, where appropriate, with national organizations after consultation with the Member of the United Nations concerned.

Article 72
1. The Economic and Social Council shall adopt its own rules of procedure, including the method of selecting its President.
2. The Economic and Social Council shall meet as required in accordance with its rules, which shall include provision for the convening of meetings on the request of a majority of its members.

CHAPTER XI
DECLARATION REGARDING NON-SELF-GOVERNING TERRITORIES

Article 73
Members of the United Nations which have or assume responsibilities for the administration of territories whose peoples have not yet attained a full measure of self-government recognize the principle that the interests of the inhabitants of these territories are paramount, and accept as a sacred trust the obligation to promote to the utmost, within the system of international peace and security established by the present Charter, the well-being of the inhabitants of these territories, and, to this end:
a. to ensure, with due respect for the culture of the peoples concerned, their political, economic, social, and educational advancement, their just treatment, and their protection against abuses;
b. to develop self-government, to take due account of the political aspirations of the peoples, and to assist them in the progressive development of their free political institutions, according to the particular circumstances of each territory and its peoples and their varying stages of advancement;
c. to further international peace and security;
d. to promote constructive measures of development, to encourage research, and to co-operate with one another and, when and where appropriate, with specialized international bodies with a view to the practical achievement of the social, economic, and scientific purposes set forth in this Article; and
e. to transmit regularly to the Secretary-General for information purposes, subject to such limitation as security and constitutional considerations may require, statistical and other information of a technical nature relating to economic, social, and educational conditions in the territories for which they are respectively responsible other than those territories to which Chapters XII and XIII apply.

Article 74

Members of the United Nations also agree that their policy in respect of the territories to which this Chapter applies, no less than in respect of their metropolitan areas, must be based on the general principle of good-neighbourliness, due account being taken of the interests and well-being of the rest of the world, in social, economic, and commercial matters.

CHAPTER XII
INTERNATIONAL TRUSTEESHIP SYSTEM

Article 75
The United Nations shall establish under its authority an international trusteeship system for the administration and supervision of such territories as may be placed thereunder by subsequent individual agreements. These territories are hereinafter referred to as trust territories.

Article 76
The basic objectives of the trusteeship system, in accordance with the Purposes of the United Nations laid down in Article 1 of the present Charter, shall be:
a. to further international peace and security;
b. to promote the political, economic, social, and educational advancement of the inhabitants of the trust territories, and their progressive development towards self-government or independence as may be appropriate to the particular circumstances of each territory and its peoples and the freely expressed wishes of the peoples concerned, and as may be provided by the terms of each trusteeship agreement;
c. to encourage respect for human rights and for fundamental freedoms for all without distinction as to race, sex, language, or religion, and to encourage recognition of the interdependence of the peoples of the world; and
d. to ensure equal treatment in social, economic, and commercial matters for all Members of the United Nations and their nationals, and also equal treatment for the latter in the administration of justice, without prejudice to the attainment of the foregoing objectives and subject to the provisions of Article 80.

Article 77
1. The trusteeship system shall apply to such territories in the following categories as may be placed thereunder by means of trusteeship agreements:
   a. territories now held under mandate;
   b. territories which may be detached from enemy states as a result of the Second World War; and
   c. territories voluntarily placed under the system by states responsible for their administration.
2. It will be a matter for subsequent agreement as to which territories in the foregoing categories will be brought under the trusteeship system and upon what terms.

Article 78
The trusteeship system shall not apply to territories which have become Members of the United Nations, relationship among which shall be based on respect for the principle of sovereign equality.

Article 79
The terms of trusteeship for each territory to be placed under the trusteeship system, including any alteration or amendment, shall be agreed upon by the states directly concerned, including the mandatory power in the case of territories held under mandate by a Member of the United Nations, and shall be approved as provided for in Articles 83 and 85.

Article 80
1. Except as may be agreed upon in individual trusteeship agreements, made under Articles 77, 79, and 81, placing each territory under the trusteeship system, and until such agreements have been concluded, nothing in this Chapter shall be construed in or of itself to alter in any manner the rights whatsoever of any states or any peoples or the terms of existing

international instruments to which Members of the United Nations may respectively be parties.
2. Paragraph 1 of this Article shall not be interpreted as giving grounds for delay or postponement of the negotiation and conclusion of agreements for placing mandated and other territories under the trusteeship system as provided for in Article 77.

Article 81

The trusteeship agreement shall in each case include the terms under which the trust territory will be administered and designate the authority which will exercise the administration of the trust territory. Such authority, hereinafter called the administering authority, may be one or more states or the Organization itself.

Article 82

There may be designated, in any trusteeship agreement, a strategic area or areas which may include part or all of the trust territory to which the agreement applies, without prejudice to any special agreement or agreements made under Article 43.

Article 83

1. All functions of the United Nations relating to strategic areas, including the approval of the terms of the trusteeship agreements and of their alteration or amendment shall be exercised by the Security Council.
2. The basic objectives set forth in Article 76 shall be applicable to the people of each strategic area.
3. The Security Council shall, subject to the provisions of the trusteeship agreements and without prejudice to security considerations, avail itself of the assistance of the Trusteeship Council to perform those functions of the United Nations under the trusteeship system relating to political, economic, social, and educational matters in the strategic areas.

Article 84

It shall be the duty of the administering authority to ensure that the trust territory shall play its part in the maintenance of international peace and security. To this end the administering authority may make use of volunteer forces, facilities, and assistance from the trust territory in carrying out the obligations towards the Security Council undertaken in this regard by the administering authority, as well as for local defence and the maintenance of law and order within the trust territory.

Article 85
1. **The functions of the United Nations with regard to trusteeship agreements for all areas not designated as strategic, including the approval of the terms of the trusteeship agreements and of their alteration or amendment, shall be exercised by the General Assembly.**
2. **The Trusteeship Council, operating under the authority of the General Assembly shall assist the General Assembly in carrying out these functions.**

CHAPTER XIII
THE TRUSTEESHIP COUNCIL

COMPOSITION

Article 86
1. The Trusteeship Council shall consist of the following Members of the United Nations:
    a. those Members administering trust territories;
    b. such of those Members mentioned by name in Article 23 as are not administering trust territories; and
    c. as many other Members elected for three-year terms by the General Assembly as may be necessary to ensure that the total number of members of the Trusteeship Council is equally divided between those Members of the United Nations which administer trust territories and those which do not.
2. Each member of the Trusteeship Council shall designate one specially qualified person to represent it therein.

FUNCTIONS and POWERS

Article 87
The General Assembly and, under its authority, the Trusteeship Council, in carrying out their functions, may:
a. consider reports submitted by the administering authority;
b. accept petitions and examine them in consultation with the administering authority;
c. provide for periodic visits to the respective trust territories at times agreed upon with the administering authority; and
d. take these and other actions in conformity with the terms of the trusteeship agreements.

Article 88
The Trusteeship Council shall formulate a questionnaire on the political, economic, social, and educational advancement of the inhabitants of each trust territory, and the administering authority for each trust territory within the competence of the General Assembly shall make an annual report to the General Assembly upon the basis of such questionnaire.

VOTING

Article 89
1. Each member of the Trusteeship Council shall have one vote.
2. Decisions of the Trusteeship Council shall be made by a majority of the members present and voting.

PROCEDURE

Article 90
1. The Trusteeship Council shall adopt its own rules of procedure, including the method of selecting its President.
2. The Trusteeship Council shall meet as required in accordance with its rules, which shall include provision for the convening of meetings on the request of a majority of its members.

Article 91
The Trusteeship Council shall, when appropriate, avail itself of the assistance of the Economic and Social Council and of the specialized agencies in regard to matters with which they are respectively concerned.

CHAPTER XIV

THE INTERNATIONAL COURT OF JUSTICE

Article 92

The International Court of Justice shall be the principal judicial organ of the United Nations. It shall function in accordance with the annexed Statute, which is based upon the Statute of the Permanent Court of International Justice and forms an integral part of the present Charter.

Article 93
1. All Members of the United Nations are *ipso facto* parties to the Statute of the International Court of Justice.
2. A state which is not a Member of the United Nations may become a party to the Statute of the International Court of Justice on conditions to be determined in each case by the General Assembly upon the recommendation of the Security Council.

Article 94
1. Each Member of the United Nations undertakes to comply with the decision of the International Court of Justice in any case to which it is a party.
2. If any party to a case fails to perform the obligations incumbent upon it under a judgment rendered by the Court, the other party may have recourse to the Security Council, which may, if it deems necessary, make recommendations or decide upon measures to be taken to give effect to the judgment.

Article 95
Nothing in the present Charter shall prevent Members of the United Nations from entrusting the solution of their differences to other tribunals by virtue of agreements already in existence or which may be concluded in the future.

Article 96
1. **The General Assembly or the Security Council may request the International Court of Justice to give an advisory opinion on any legal question.**
2. **Other organs of the United Nations and specialized agencies, which may at any time be so authorized by the General Assembly, may also request advisory opinions of the Court on legal questions arising within the scope of their activities.**

CHAPTER XV

THE SECRETARIAT

Article 97
The Secretariat shall comprise a Secretary-General and such staff as the Organization may require. The Secretary-General shall be appointed by the General Assembly upon the recommendation of the Security Council. He shall be the chief administrative officer of the Organization.

Article 98
The Secretary-General shall act in that capacity in all meetings of the General Assembly, of the Security Council, of the Economic and Social Council, and of the Trusteeship Council, and shall perform such other functions as are entrusted to him by these organs. The Secretary-General shall make an annual report to the General Assembly on the work of the Organization.

Article 99
The Secretary-General may bring to the attention of the Security Council any matter which in his opinion may threaten the maintenance of international peace and security.

Article 100
1. In the performance of their duties the Secretary-General and the staff shall not seek or receive instructions from any government or from any other authority external to the Organization. They shall refrain from any action which might reflect on their position as international officials responsible only to the Organization.

2. Each Member of the United Nations undertakes to respect the exclusively international character of the responsibilities of the Secretary-General and the staff and not to seek to influence them in the discharge of their responsibilities.

Article 101
1. The staff shall be appointed by the Secretary-General under regulations established by the General Assembly.
2. Appropriate staffs shall be permanently assigned to the Economic and Social Council, the Trusteeship Council, and, as required, to other organs of the United Nations. These staffs shall form a part of the Secretariat.
3. The paramount consideration in the employment of the staff and in the determination of the conditions of service shall be the necessity of securing the highest standards of efficiency, competence, and integrity. Due regard shall be paid to the importance of recruiting the staff on as wide a geographical basis as possible.

CHAPTER XVI

MISCELLANEOUS PROVISIONS

Article 102
1. Every treaty and every international agreement entered into by any Member of the United Nations after the present Charter comes into force shall as soon as possible be registered with the Secretariat and published by it.
2. No party to any such treaty or international agreement which has not been registered in accordance with the provisions of paragraph 1 of this Article may invoke that treaty or agreement before any organ of the United Nations.

Article 103
In the event of a conflict between the obligations of the Members of the United Nations under the present Charter and their obligations under any other international agreement, their obligations under the present Charter shall prevail.

Article 104
The Organization shall enjoy in the territory of each of its Members such legal capacity as may be necessary for the exercise of its functions and the fulfilment of its purposes.

Article 105
1. The Organization shall enjoy in the territory of each of its Members such privileges and immunities as are necessary for the fulfilment of its purposes.
2. Representatives of the Members of the United Nations and officials of the Organization shall similarly enjoy such privileges and immunities as are necessary for the independent exercise of their functions in connexion with the Organization.
3. The General Assembly may make recommendations with a view to determining the details of the application of paragraphs 1 and 2 of this Article or may propose conventions to the Members of the United Nations for this purpose.

CHAPTER XVII

TRANSITIONAL SECURITY ARRANGEMENTS

Article 106
Pending the coming into force of such special agreements referred to in Article 43 as in the opinion of the Security Council enable it to begin the exercise of its responsibilities under Article 42, the parties to the Four-Nation Declaration, signed at Moscow, 30 October 1943, and France, shall, in accordance with the provisions of paragraph 5 of that Declaration, consult with one another and as occasion requires with other Members of the United Nations with a view to such joint action on behalf of the Organization as may be necessary for the purpose of maintaining international peace and security.

Article 107
Nothing in the present Charter shall invalidate or preclude action, in relation to any state which during the Second World War has been an enemy of any signatory to the present Charter, taken or authorized as a result of that war by the Governments having responsibility for such action.

CHAPTER XVIII

AMENDMENTS

Article 108
Amendments to the present Charter shall come into force for all Members of the United Nations when they have been adopted by a vote of two thirds of the members of the General Assembly and ratified in accordance with their respective constitutional processes by two thirds of the Members of the United Nations, including all the permanent members of the Security Council.

Article 109
1. A General Conference of the Members of the United Nations for the purpose of reviewing the present Charter may be held at a date and place to be fixed by a two-thirds vote of the members of the General Assembly and by a vote of any nine members of the Security Council. Each Member of the United Nations shall have one vote in the conference.
2. Any alteration of the present Charter recommended by a two-thirds vote of the conference shall take effect when ratified in accordance with their respective constitutional processes by two thirds of the Members of the United Nations including all the permanent members of the Security Council.
3. If such a conference has not been held before the tenth annual session of the General Assembly following the coming into force of the present Charter, the proposal to call such a conference shall be placed on the agenda of that session of the General Assembly, and the conference shall be held if so decided by a majority vote of the members of the General Assembly and by a vote of any seven members of the Security Council.

CHAPTER XIX

RATIFICATION AND SIGNATURE

Article 110
1. The present Charter shall be ratified by the signatory states in accordance with their respective constitutional processes.
2. The ratifications shall be deposited with the Government of the United States of America, which shall notify all the signatory states of each deposit as well as the Secretary-General of the Organization when he has been appointed.
3. The present Charter shall come into force upon the deposit of ratifications by the Republic of China, France, the Union of Soviet Socialist Republics, the United Kingdom of Great Britain and Northern Ireland, and the United States of America, and by a majority of the other signatory states. A protocol of the ratifications deposited shall thereupon be drawn up by the Government of the United States of America which shall communicate copies thereof to all the signatory states.
4. The states signatory to the present Charter which ratify it after it has come into force will become original Members of the United Nations on the date of the deposit of their respective ratifications.

Article 111
The present Charter, of which the Chinese, French, Russian, English, and Spanish texts are equally authentic, shall remain deposited in the archives of the Government of the United States of America. Duly certified copies thereof shall be transmitted by that Government to the Governments of the other signatory states.
IN FAITH WHEREOF the representatives of the Governments of the United Nations have signed the present Charter.
DONE at the city of San Francisco the twenty-sixth day of June, one thousand nine hundred and forty-five.

Universal Declaration of Human Rights

Adopted and proclaimed by General Assembly resolution 217 A (III) of 10 December 1948

On December 10, 1948 the General Assembly of the United Nations adopted and proclaimed the Universal Declaration of Human Rights the full text of which appears in the following pages. Following this historic act the Assembly called upon all Member countries to publicize the text of the Declaration and 'to cause it to be disseminated, displayed, read and expounded principally in schools and other educational institutions, without distinction based on the political status of countries or territories.'

PREAMBLE

Whereas recognition of the inherent dignity and of the equal and inalienable rights of all members of the human family is the foundation of freedom, justice and peace in the world,

Whereas disregard and contempt for human rights have resulted in barbarous acts which have outraged the conscience of mankind, and the advent of a world in which human beings shall enjoy freedom of speech and belief and freedom from fear and want has been proclaimed as the highest aspiration of the common people,

Whereas it is essential, if man is not to be compelled to have recourse, as a last resort, to rebellion against tyranny and oppression, that human rights should be protected by the rule of law,

Whereas it is essential to promote the development of friendly relations between nations,

Whereas the peoples of the United Nations have in the Charter reaffirmed their faith in fundamental human rights, in the dignity and worth of the human person and in the equal rights of men and women and have determined to promote social progress and better standards of life in larger freedom,

Whereas Member States have pledged themselves to achieve, in co-operation with the United Nations, the promotion of universal respect for and observance of human rights and fundamental freedoms,

Whereas a common understanding of these rights and freedoms is of the greatest importance for the full realization of this pledge,

Now, Therefore THE GENERAL ASSEMBLY proclaims THIS UNIVERSAL DECLARATION OF HUMAN RIGHTS as a common standard of achievement for all peoples and all nations, to the end that every individual and every organ of society, keeping this Declaration constantly in mind, shall strive by teaching and education to promote respect for these rights and freedoms and by progressive measures, national and international, to secure their universal and effective recognition and observance, both among the peoples of Member States themselves and among the peoples of territories under their jurisdiction.

Article 1.

All human beings are born free and equal in dignity and rights.They are endowed with reason and conscience and should act towards one another in a spirit of brotherhood.

Article 2.

Everyone is entitled to all the rights and freedoms set forth in this Declaration, without distinction of any kind, such as race, colour, sex, language, religion, political or other opinion, national or social origin, property, birth or other status. Furthermore, no distinction shall be made on the basis of the political, jurisdictional or international status of the country or territory to which a person belongs, whether it be independent, trust, non-self-governing or under any other limitation of sovereignty.

Article 3.
Everyone has the right to life, liberty and security of person.
Article 4.
No one shall be held in slavery or servitude; slavery and the slave trade shall be prohibited in all their forms.
Article 5.
No one shall be subjected to torture or to cruel, inhuman or degrading treatment or punishment.
Article 6.
Everyone has the right to recognition everywhere as a person before the law.
Article 7.
All are equal before the law and are entitled without any discrimination to equal protection of the law. All are entitled to equal protection against any discrimination in violation of this Declaration and against any incitement to such discrimination.
Article 8.
Everyone has the right to an effective remedy by the competent national tribunals for acts violating the fundamental rights granted him by the constitution or by law.
Article 9.
No one shall be subjected to arbitrary arrest, detention or exile.
Article 10.
Everyone is entitled in full equality to a fair and public hearing by an independent and impartial tribunal, in the determination of his rights and obligations and of any criminal charge against him.
Article 11.
(1) Everyone charged with a penal offence has the right to be presumed innocent until proved guilty according to law in a public trial at which he has had all the guarantees necessary for his defence.
(2) No one shall be held guilty of any penal offence on account of any act or omission which did not constitute a penal offence, under national or international law, at the time when it was committed.

Nor shall a heavier penalty be imposed than the one that was applicable at the time the penal offence was committed.

Article 12.

No one shall be subjected to arbitrary interference with his privacy, family, home or correspondence, nor to attacks upon his honour and reputation. Everyone has the right to the protection of the law against such interference or attacks.

Article 13.

(1) Everyone has the right to freedom of movement and residence within the borders of each state.

(2) Everyone has the right to leave any country, including his own, and to return to his country.

Article 14.

(1) Everyone has the right to seek and to enjoy in other countries asylum from persecution.

(2) This right may not be invoked in the case of prosecutions genuinely arising from non-political crimes or from acts contrary to the purposes and principles of the United Nations.

Article 15.

(1) Everyone has the right to a nationality.

(2) No one shall be arbitrarily deprived of his nationality nor denied the right to change his nationality.

Article 16.

(1) Men and women of full age, without any limitation due to race, nationality or religion, have the right to marry and to found a family. They are entitled to equal rights as to marriage, during marriage and at its dissolution.

(2) Marriage shall be entered into only with the free and full consent of the intending spouses.

(3) The family is the natural and fundamental group unit of society and is entitled to protection by society and the State.

Article 17.

(1) Everyone has the right to own property alone as well as in association with others.

(2) No one shall be arbitrarily deprived of his property.

Article 18.

Everyone has the right to freedom of thought, conscience and religion; this right includes freedom to change his religion or belief, and freedom, either alone or in community with others and in public or private, to manifest his religion or belief in teaching, practice, worship and observance.

Article 19.

Everyone has the right to freedom of opinion and expression; this right includes freedom to hold opinions without interference and to seek, receive and impart information and ideas through any media and regardless of frontiers.

Article 20.

(1) Everyone has the right to freedom of peaceful assembly and association.

(2) No one may be compelled to belong to an association.

Article 21.

(1) Everyone has the right to take part in the government of his country, directly or through freely chosen representatives.

(2) Everyone has the right of equal access to public service in his country.

(3) The will of the people shall be the basis of the authority of government; this will shall be expressed in periodic and genuine elections which shall be by universal and equal suffrage and shall be held by secret vote or by equivalent free voting procedures.

Article 22.

Everyone, as a member of society, has the right to social security and is entitled to realization, through national effort and international co-operation and in accordance with the organization and resources of each State, of the economic, social and cultural rights indispensable for his dignity and the free development of his personality.

Article 23.

(1) Everyone has the right to work, to free choice of employment, to just and favourable conditions of work and to protection against unemployment.

(2) Everyone, without any discrimination, has the right to equal pay for equal work.

(3) Everyone who works has the right to just and favourable remuneration ensuring for himself and his family an existence worthy of human dignity, and supplemented, if necessary, by other means of social protection.

(4) Everyone has the right to form and to join trade unions for the protection of his interests.

Article 24.

Everyone has the right to rest and leisure, including reasonable limitation of working hours and periodic holidays with pay.

Article 25.

(1) Everyone has the right to a standard of living adequate for the health and well-being of himself and of his family, including food, clothing, housing and medical care and necessary social services, and the right to security in the event of unemployment, sickness, disability, widowhood, old age or other lack of livelihood in circumstances beyond his control.

(2) Motherhood and childhood are entitled to special care and assistance. All children, whether born in or out of wedlock, shall enjoy the same social protection.

Article 26.

(1) Everyone has the right to education. Education shall be free, at least in the elementary and fundamental stages. Elementary education shall be compulsory. Technical and professional education shall be made generally available and higher education shall be equally accessible to all on the basis of merit.

(2) Education shall be directed to the full development of the human personality and to the strengthening of respect for human rights and fundamental freedoms. It shall promote understanding,

tolerance and friendship among all nations, racial or religious groups, and shall further the activities of the United Nations for the maintenance of peace.

(3) Parents have a prior right to choose the kind of education that shall be given to their children.

Article 27.

(1) Everyone has the right freely to participate in the cultural life of the community, to enjoy the arts and to share in scientific advancement and its benefits.

(2) Everyone has the right to the protection of the moral and material interests resulting from any scientific, literary or artistic production of which he is the author.

Article 28.

Everyone is entitled to a social and international order in which the rights and freedoms set forth in this Declaration can be fully realized.

Article 29.

(1) Everyone has duties to the community in which alone the free and full development of his personality is possible.

(2) In the exercise of his rights and freedoms, everyone shall be subject only to such limitations as are determined by law solely for the purpose of securing due recognition and respect for the rights and freedoms of others and of meeting the just requirements of morality, public order and the general welfare in a democratic society.

(3) These rights and freedoms may in no case be exercised contrary to the purposes and principles of the United Nations.

Article 30.

Nothing in this Declaration may be interpreted as implying for any State, group or person any right to engage in any activity or to perform any act aimed at the destruction of any of the rights and freedoms set forth herein.

The UN and its Future in the 21st Century

UN Millennium Development Goals

Goal 1: Eradicate extreme poverty and hunger

Target 1: Halve, between 1990 and 2015, the proportion of people whose income is less than one dollar a day

1. Proportion of population below $1 per day
2. Poverty gap ratio [incidence x depth of poverty]
3. Share of poorest quintile in national consumption

Target 2: Halve, between 1990 and 2015, the proportion of people who suffer from hunger
4. Prevalence of underweight children (under-five years of age)
5. Proportion of population below minimum level of dietary energy consumption

Goal 2: Achieve universal primary education

Target 3: Ensure that, by 2015, children everywhere, boys and girls alike, will be able to complete a full course of primary schooling
6. Net enrolment ratio in primary education
7. Proportion of pupils starting grade 1 who reach grade 5
8. Literacy rate of 15-24 year olds

Goal 3: Promote gender equality and empower women

Target 4: Eliminate gender disparity in primary and secondary education preferably by 2005 and to all levels of education no later than 2015
9. Ratio of girls to boys in primary, secondary and tertiary education
10. Ratio of literate females to males of 15-24 year olds
11. Share of women in wage employment in the nonagricultural sector

12. Proportion of seats held by women in national parliament

Goal 4: Reduce child mortality

Target 5: Reduce by two-thirds, between 1990 and 2015, the under-five mortality rate
13. Under-five mortality rate
14. Infant mortality rate
15. Proportion of 1 year old children immunised against measles

Goal 5: Improve maternal health

Target 6: Reduce by three-quarters, between 1990 and 2015, the maternal mortality ratio
16. Maternal mortality ratio
17. Proportion of births attended by skilled health personnel

Goal 6: Combat HIV/AIDS, malaria and other diseases

Target 7: Have halted by 2015, and begun to reverse, the spread of HIV/AIDS
18. HIV prevalence among 15-24 year old pregnant women
19. Contraceptive prevalence rate
20. Number of children orphaned by HIV/AIDS

Target 8: Have halted by 2015, and begun to reverse, the incidence of malaria and other major diseases
21. Prevalence and death rates associated with malaria
22. Proportion of population in malaria risk areas using effective malaria prevention and treatment measures
23. Prevalence and death rates associated with tuberculosis
24. Proportion of TB cases detected and cured under DOTS (Directly Observed Treatment Short Course)

Goal 7: Ensure environmental sustainability

Target 9: Integrate the principles of sustainable development into country policies and programmes and reverse the loss of environmental resources
25. Proportion of land area covered by forest
26. Land area protected to maintain biological diversity
27. GDP per unit of energy use (as proxy for energy efficiency)
28. Carbon dioxide emissions (per capita)
[Plus two figures of global atmospheric pollution: ozone depletion and the accumulation of global warming gases]

Target 10: Halve, by 2015, the proportion of people without sustainable access to safe drinking water
29. Proportion of population with sustainable access to an improved water source

Target 11: By 2020, to have achieved a significant improvement in the lives of at least 100 million slum dwellers
30. Proportion of people with access to improved sanitation
31. Proportion of people with access to secure tenure
[Urban/rural disaggregation of several of the above indicators may be relevant for monitoring improvement in the lives of slum dwellers]

Goal 8: Develop a Global Partnership for Development

Target 12: Develop further an open, rule-based, predictable, non-discriminatory trading and financial system. Includes a commitment to good governance, development, and poverty reduction – both nationally and internationally

Target 13: Address the Special Needs of the Least Developed Countries
Includes: tariff and quota free access for LDC exports; enhanced programme of debt relief for HIPC and cancellation of official bilateral

debt; and more generous ODA for countries committed to poverty reduction

Target 14: Address the Special Needs of landlocked countries and small island developing states (through Barbados Programme and 22nd General Assembly provisions)

Target 15: Deal comprehensively with the debt problems of developing countries through national and international measures in order to make debt sustainable in the long term
Some of the indicators listed below will be monitored separately for the Least Developed Countries (LDCs), Africa, landlocked countries and small island developing states. Official Development Assistance
32. Net ODA as percentage of DAC donors' GNI [targets of 0.7% in total and 0.15% for LDCs]
33. Proportion of ODA to basic social services (basic education, primary health care, nutrition, safe water and sanitation)
34. Proportion of ODA that is untied
35. Proportion of ODA for environment in small island developing states
36. Proportion of ODA for transport sector in land-locked countries
Market Access
37. Proportion of exports (by value and excluding arms) admitted free of duties and quotas
38. Average tariffs and quotas on agricultural products and textiles and clothing
39. Domestic and export agricultural subsidies in OECD countries
40. Proportion of ODA provided to help build trade capacity
Debt Sustainability
41. Proportion of official bilateral HIPC debt cancelled
42. Debt service as a percentage of exports of goods and services
43. Proportion of ODA provided as debt relief
44. Number of countries reaching HIPC decision and completion points

The UN and its Future in the 21st Century

Target 16: In co-operation with developing countries, develop and implement strategies for decent and productive work for youth
45. Unemployment rate of 15-24 year olds

Target 17: In co-operation with pharmaceutical companies, provide access to affordable, essential drugs in developing countries
46. Proportion of population with access to affordable essential drugs on a sustainable basis

Target 18: In co-operation with the private sector, make available the benefits of new technologies, especially information and communications
47. Telephone lines per 1000 people
48. Personal computers per 1000 people

The Hague Agenda for Peace and Justice for the 21st Century

The Hague Agenda for Peace and Justice for the 21st Century has emerged from an intensive democratic process of consultation among the members of the Hague Appeal for Peace Organizing and Co-ordinating Committees, and the hundreds of organisations and individuals that have actively participated in the Hague Appeal process. The Agenda represents what these civil society organisations and citizens consider as some of the most important challenges facing humankind as it embarks upon a new millennium.

The Agenda reflects the four major strands of the Hague Appeal:

1. Root Causes of War/Culture of Peace
2. International Humanitarian and Human Rights Law and Institutions
3. Prevention, Resolution and Transformation of Violent Conflict
4. Disarmament and Human Security

Preamble

The world is emerging from the bloodiest, most war-ridden century in history. On the eve of the new century, it is time to create the conditions in which the primary aim of the United Nations, 'to save succeeding generations from the scourge of war', can be realised. This is the goal of The Hague Appeal for Peace.

Sceptics will say that it cannot be done. The Hague Appeal challenges this assumption. This century has seen unimagined changes. Society now has the means to cure disease and eliminate poverty and starvation. The twentieth century has also seen the creation of a set of universal norms that, if implemented, would go a long way toward making war unnecessary and impossible. We have witnessed inspiring and successful experiments with active non-violence in struggles for independence and civil rights by unarmed peoples' movements. And this century has seen the replacement of authoritarian forms of government by democratic governance and the increasing role of civil society in the affairs of humanity.

Recent years have seen outbreaks of genocide in Cambodia, Bosnia, Rwanda and Kosovo, brutal attacks against civilians and the spread of horrendous weapons of mass destruction capable of ending life on much or all of the planet. Indigenous populations continue to be denied their rights to self-determination. In a great many cases, the world's governments have manifestly failed to fulfil their responsibility to prevent conflict, protect civilians, end war, eradicate colonialism, guarantee human rights and create the conditions of permanent peace.

Therefore, this historic mission and responsibility cannot be entrusted solely to governments. The Hague Appeal proposes a Citizens' Agenda for Peace and Justice for the 21st Century. This will entail a fundamentally new approach, building on the recent model of New Diplomacy in which citizen advocates, progressive governments and international organisations have worked together for common goals. We will embrace the moral imagination and courage necessary to create a 21st century culture of peace and to develop national and supranational institutions that ultimately must be the guarantors of peace and justice in this world.

There is already much to choose from. Civil society has flourished since the end of the Cold War and launched campaigns aimed at eradicating landmines, reducing the traffic in small arms, alleviating third world debt, ending violence against women, abolishing nuclear weapons, protecting the rights of children, stopping the use of child soldiers and building an independent International Criminal Court. These grassroots efforts are having a major impact. They are succeeding because they mobilise ordinary people, because they integrate different sectors (human rights, the environment, humanitarian assistance, disarmament, sustainable development, etc.) and because they invite the full participation of women, youth, indigenous peoples, minorities, the disabled and other affected groups.

These campaigns have generated unity and cohesion and demonstrate what can be done when people are listened to instead of talked at. The Hague Appeal for Peace intends to listen, learn and then to build. Out of this process will emerge a new Citizens' Agenda for Peace and Justice for the 21st Century. It is a vital and realisable goal.

The components of the Hague Appeal for Peace are motivated by the following main themes:

Traditional Failure

Traditional approaches to preventing war and building peace have by and large failed disastrously. This is evidenced by the growing brutality of warfare, and the callous disregard for civilian life in such conflicts as the Congo, Sierra Leone and Kosovo. Impunity for ethnic cleansing and for crimes against humanity is not compatible with international law. Big-power bullying tactics are not diplomacy. Sanctions that starve the poor are not solidarity. Fire-brigade peacekeeping efforts are no substitute for sophisticated early warning and conflict prevention.

Human Security

It is time to redefine security in terms of human and ecological needs instead of national sovereignty and national borders. Redirecting funding from armaments to human security and sustainable development will establish new priorities leading to the construction of a new social order which ensures the equal participation of marginalised groups, including women and indigenous people, restricts use of military force, and moves towards collective global security.

The UN and its Future in the 21st Century

Soft Power

We are profoundly encouraged that civil society and progressive governments are choosing 'soft power' paths, utilising negotiation, coalition building and new diplomacy methods of settling disputes, while rejecting the 'hard power' dictates of major powers, militaries and economic conglomerates.

All Human Rights for All

The violation of human rights is one of the root causes of war. These violations include the denial of economic, social and cultural rights, as well as political and civil rights. The artificial distinction between these two sets of rights can no longer be tolerated. We affirm the universality and indivisibility of human rights and call for stronger mechanisms to implement and enforce human rights treaties and to afford redress to victims for the violation of their rights.

Replacing the Law of Force with the Force of Law

The rule of law has been contemptuously ignored in contemporary conflicts. The Hague Appeal seeks to develop and promote universal adherence to and implementing of international law. It also seeks to invigorate existing institutions of international law like the International Court of Justice and the International Criminal Court. Knowledge of and recourse to international law must also be made more accessible to individuals.

Taking the Initiative

It is time for people to assert their commitment to peace and- if necessary- to wrest peace-making away from the exclusive control of politicians and military establishments. Too often, peace initiatives are proposed as a last resort, with negotiations restricted to the warmongers, and imposed on

The UN and its Future in the 21st Century

those most affected, particularly women and children. Those who have suffered the most must have a place at the table when peace agreements are drawn up, with equal representation for women. If necessary, civil society should also convene peace initiatives before crises get out of control and lives are lost. This can help to turn early warning from a slogan into a reality.

Bottom-Up Globalisation

The alarming concentration of economic power and the irresponsible imposition of neo-liberal, macro-economic policies are destroying the environment, generating poverty and desperation, widening divisions and fomenting war. The Hague Appeal encourages efforts to challenge this destructive model of globalisation through community-based coalitions such as the Jubilee 2000 call for debt forgiveness and through campaigns to eradicate poverty and economically empower women.

Democratic International Decision-Making

The United Nations system and other multilateral institutions have the capacity to be a unique and universal force for peace. Too often, however, they have been treated with cynicism, politicised, and under-funded. The international system must be revived, democratised and provided with resources if it is realise its potential in peace-building. In particular, we call for a Security Council that can serve human security rather then Great Power interests, and for a radical reorientation of international financial institutions to make them more transparent and accountable and to serve human rather then corporate needs.

Humanitarian Interventions

The Hague Appeal demands the speedy and effective intervention of humanitarian forces, subject to the prescriptions of the United Nations Charter, when civilians are threatened by genocide, war crimes, crimes

The UN and its Future in the 21st Century

against humanity and extreme national disasters. It is extraordinary that so little attention has been paid to the idea of establishing a standing intervention force. Civil society should consider new forms of civilian intervention as a matter of urgency.

Finding the Money for Peace and Starving the Funds for War

The allocation of resources is seriously distorted. Many of today's conflicts are fuelled by economic greed and the grab for raw materials, while billions are spent on the arms trade and other forms of militarisation. At the same time, many worthwhile peace initiatives and programmes for human security suffer from a lack of funds even though governments have adopted an extraordinary series of global action plans at the historic world conferences convened during the last decade of the 20th century. These priorities must be reversed. In addition to eliminating weapons of mass destruction and drastically curbing the arms trade, military budgets must be progressively reduced.

Further Reading

Kofi Annan. 'Problems Without Passport'. *Foreign Policy,* September/October 2002.

Dean Acheson. *Present at the Creation: My Years in the State Department.* New York: Norton, 1969.

Boutros Boutros-Ghali. *Unvanquished: A U.S.-U.N. Saga,* New York: Random House, 1999.

Kevin M. Cahill, (ed). *A Framework for Survival: Health, Human Rights, and Humanitarian Assistance in Conflicts and Disasters.* New York/London: HarperCollins, 1993.

Erskine Childers with Brian Urquhart. Renewing the United Nations System. *Development Dialogue,* Dag Hammarskjöld Foundation, Uppsala: 1994; No. 1.

Erskine Childers, (ed). *Challenges to the United Nations: Building a Safer World.* London: Catholic Institute for International Relations/ New York: St Martin's Press, 1994.

Peter Donaldson. *Worlds Apart: The Development Gap and what it Means.* Harmondsworth: Pelican, 1986.

Angela Drakulich. *A Global Agenda: Issues before the United Nations.* New York: United Nations Association of the United States of America, 2004

Louis Emmerij, Richard Jolly, and Thomas G. Weiss. *Ahead of the Curve? UN Ideas and Global Challenges.* Bloomington: Indiana University Press, 2001.

Gareth Evans. *Cooperating for Peace. London:* Allen & Unwin, 1993.

Richard A. Falk, Samuel S. Kim, Saul H. Medlovitz, (eds). *The United Nations and a Just World Order.* Boulder Co/Oxford: Westview Press, 1991.

Ford Foundation. *Financing an Effective United Nations.* New York: Ford Foundation, 1993.

Paul Kennedy, Dirk Messner, and Franz Nuscheler, (eds). *Global Trends and Global Governance.* Vancouver: University of British Columbia Press/London: Pluto Press, 2002.

Stanley Meisler. *United Nations: The First Fifty Years.* New York: Atlantic Monthly Press, 1995.

Julius Nyerere and South Centre. *Facing the Challenge.* London: Zed Books, 1993.

Stephen Schlesinger. *Act of Creation: The Founding of the United Nations.* Boulder Co/Oxford: Westview Press, 2003.

South Commission, *The Challenge to the South.* Oxford: OUP, 1990.

Ramesh Thakur and Edward Newman, (eds). *New Millennium, New Perspectives: The United Nations, Security and Governance.* New York: United Nations University Press, 2000.

United Nations. *Everyone's United Nations*. New York: UN (recurring updated handbook of the UN system, available at UN Sales Agents).

Brian Urquhart and Erskine Childers. A World in Need of Leadership: Tomorrow's United Nations: *Development Dialogue*, Dag Hammarskjöld Foundation, 1990: No. 1-2.

Barbara Walker, (ed). *Uniting the Peoples and Nations*. New York: World Federalist Association, 1993.

The UN and its Future in the 21st Century

Some Useful Web Sites

Action for UN Renewal (Act-UN)
www.action-for-un-renewal.org.uk

Hague Appeal for Peace
www.haguepeace.org

High-level Panel on Threats, Challenges and Change
www.un.org.secureworld/

International Court of Justice (ICJ)
www.icj-cij.org

International Criminal Court (ICC)
www.un.org/law/icc/

Panel of Eminent Persons on UN - Civil Society Relations
www.un.org/reform/panel.htm

UK Network for Civil Society Link with UN General Assembly (UNGA-Link UK) www.ungalink.org.uk

United Nations Association UK (UNA-UK)
www.una-uk.org

The UN and its Future in the 21st Century

United Nations Organization
www.un.org

Universal Declaration of Human Rights
www.unhchr.ch/udhr.index.htm

VM Centre for Peace
www.vmpeace.org

INDEX

Aegean Sea, 92, 98
Afghanistan, 6, 72, 79, 125, 129-30, 135, 137-8, 140, 148, 158-62
Africa, 6, 14, 71, 73, 83, 117-9, 142, 159, 162, 164, 177, 187, 190, 261
Agenda 21, 56, 69, 76
Agenda for Peace, 59, 263-8
Aid, 73, 106, 110, 122-3, 129, 160-3, 170
AIDS, see HIV/AIDS
Aiken, Frank, 71
Albania, 87-8, 93
Algeria, 116
al Qaida, 27, 160-1
Amnesty International, 77, 144
Amsterdam Treaty, 71, 80
Andrews, Mr, 71
Angola, 104-6
Annan, Kofi, 2, 11, 14, 17-19, 22, 47, 67, 82, 108, 163
Antiballistic Missile (ABM) Treaty, 31, 128
Aouzou Strip, 92
Asia, 24-6, 34, 41, 58, 61, 74, 117-9, 125, 142, 148, 162, 164, 177, 187
Association of South-East Asian Nations (ASEAN), 58, 164
Axis Powers, 86
Azerbaijan, 148

Bahrain, 90
Balkans, 119
Bakassi Peninsula, 91-2
Bangkok, 134
Basra, 140
Belgium, 94
Benin, 86
Berlin, 84
    Wall, 79
bin Laden, Osama, 129, 160-1
Biological agents and weapons, 5, 117, 176, 178
Biological and Toxin Weapons Convention (BTWC), 125, 141, 177, 178
Biological diversity, 260

Biological security, 8, 165, 169
Blair, Tony, 80, 161, 165
Boland, Frederick, 13
Bosnia & Herzegovina, 59, 91, 93, 105, 147, 159
Botswana, 92
Brahimi Panel / Report, 43, 112
Brazil, 71, 83, 85, 156
Britain, see United Kingdom
Bretton Woods system, 34, 56, 74, 191-2, 204
Brooks, Edwin, 121, 128
Brundtland, Gro Harlem, 3
Bush administration, 31, 124-5, 129, 130, 146
Bush doctrine, 128
Bush, Pres. George W, 160-1

Cambodia, 73, 79, 104-5, 159, 264
Cameroon, 86, 91-2
Canada, 30, 58, 87, 94
Caucasus, 116, 119
Central America, 104
Central Intelligence Agency, 123
Chad, 89, 92, 98
Charter, see UN Charter
Chechnya, 60, 140
Chemical weapons, 27, 162, 177-8
Chemical Weapons Convention, 178
China, 28, 30, 85, 94, 146-8, 153, 215, 250
Childers, Erskine, 13, 17, 32-3, 35-7, 45, 52, 64-5, 67-8, 70-1, 75, 78, 82-3, 110-1, 134, 141, 143-4, 154, 166
Childers, Erskine (father), 32, 64-5
Childers, Erskine (grandfather), 32, 64-5
Child mortality, 259
Chirac, Pres. Jacques, 161
Chlorofluorocarbons (CFCs), 120, 127
Chomsky, Noam, 74
Civil Society Forum (see also People's Assembly), 77
Climate change (see also Global warming, 49, 102, 120, 122, 130, 146
Clinton administration, 29
Clinton, Pres. Bill, 147

INDEX

Cluster bombs, 117
Cold War, 1, 23, 28, 30-1, 37-40, 43, 50, 53, 54, 79, 81, 85-6, 102, 104, 115, 117, 123-4, 144, 149, 155, 158, 264
Collective security, 2, 5, 8, 12, 18-20, 41, 54, 59, 114, 168-70, 172-3, 183, 186, 194
Collins, Michael, 65
Colombia, 86, 116
Commission on Human Rights, 4, 8, 127, 171, 192
Common Foreign and Security Policy (CFSP), 71, 149, 150
Comprehensive Test Ban Treaty (CTBT), 23, 30
Conference on Disarmament (CD), 27, 178
Convention on Certain Conventional Weapons (CCW), 29
Convention on the Rights of the Child, 141
Conflict resolution, 64, 78, 175
Corfu Channel, 87
Congo, 32, 86, 101, 265
Cook, Robin, 158
Counter-Terrorism-Committee, 24, 29, 170, 179, 180
Counter-insurgency, 124
Crime, 2, 5-8, 40, 58, 69, 91, 98, 102, 110, 139-40, 146, 156, 174, 179-81, 254, 265, 267
Cuba, 60, 72, 129, 196
Culture of Peace, 1, 263-4
Cyprus, 59

Dafur, 164
Danube, 87, 92
Debt/debt relief, 64, 67, 73-4, 122, 125, 126, 173, 261, 264, 267
de Mello, Sergio Viera, 113
Democratic People's Republic of Korea, 24, 25, 129
Democratic Republic of Congo, see Congo, Zaire
Department for International Development (DfID), 161

Department of Peacekeeping Operations, 184
Department of Political Affairs, 175
Depleted uranium, 138, 140
Development, 4, 7-9, 14-17, 21, 25-6, 30-2, 34, 37-8, 41, 43-4, 47, 52-3, 56, 58, 60-1, 67, 69, 73, 75-6, 80, 84-5, 102, 124-7, 115-9, 122-3, 126-9, 134, 137, 144, 151, 159, 161-3, 169, 171, 173-4, 179-81, 187, 189, 191, 196-8, 203-4, 211, 226, 228, 234, 236, 251, 255-8, 260-1, 264-5
De Villepin, Dominique, 155
Disarmament Commission (see also ENDC), 29
Doha Development Round, 7, 173
Dublin, 33, 65, 83

Earth Summit 56, 77
East Timor, 44, 105, 108, 164
Economic and Social Council (ECOSOC), 8, 21, 23, 44-5, 50, 53, 68, 70, 76, 77, 137, 189, 191, 201, 209, 213, 229-33, 241, 244-5
Education, 73, 107, 118, 137-8, 179, 211, 228, 230, 234, 236, 238, 240, 251-2, 256-8
Egypt, 71, 83, 85
Eighteen Nation Disarmament Commission (ENDC), 28
El Salvador, 73, 79, 86, 106, 159
Equality, 15, 20, 57, 68, 154, 206, 209, 237, 253, 258
Ethics, 13, 14, 17, 18
Europe, 54, 69, 81, 115, 122, 125, 142, 146, 149, 150, 152, 159, 187
European Community/Union (EU), 33, 58, 64, 66-7, 70-1, 75, 80, 146-7, 149-53, 161, 178, 181-2, 144, 152-3
European Parliament, 68, 70-1, 75, 78, 82, 151-2

Fissile material, 60, 177
Fissile Material Cutoff Treaty (FMCT), 28, 177-8
Food and Agriculture Organisation (FAO),

INDEX

34
Former Yugoslavia, 73, 81, 110, 116
France, 71, 78, 85-6, 94, 149, 153-5, 161, 215, 248, 250
Freedom, 1, 15, 17, 19, 72, 85, 90, 105, 154, 205-6, 212, 228, 231, 234, 251-2, 254-7
Free market, 61, 115-6, 118, 124
Fuel-air explosives, 117

Gender equality, 258
General Agreement on Tariffs and Trade (GATT), 74
General and Complete Disarmament, 82, 83
General Assembly, 13, 17-8, 22, 27-9, 44-6, 50-1, 55-6, 64, 66, 68, 70, 76, 77, 85, 100, 103, 132, 137, 139, 142, 175, 180-1, 184-6, 188, 193, 196, 200-2, 108-19, 229-32, 239-41
Geneva, 3, 27, 108
Geneva Convention(s), 80, 140, 180, 185
Genoa, 116
Genocide, 3, 5, 6, 38, 43, 50, 94-5, 133, 138-9, 159, 183, 264, 267
Genocide Convention, 91, 93, 185
Germany, 30, 57, 85-6, 94, 149, 164
Glasnost, 85
Global governance/government, 9-11, 41, 76, 195, 200
Globalisation, 5, 7, 16, 47, 66, 72-3, 77-8. 83, 102-3, 115-6, 133, 148, 151, 154, 163, 267
Global warming (see also Climate change), 7, 41, 102, 174, 260
Gothenburg, 152
Greece, 98
Green Party, 66, 70, 80
Greenpeace, 77
Gross National Product (GNP), 17, 69, 75, 106, 162, 173, 187
Group of Seven, 56
Guantanamo, 129
Guinea, 86
Gulf – see Persian Gulf
Gulf War, 33, 116, 119, 140

Hague Agenda/Appeal for Peace, 82-3, 263-7
Hague, The, 76, 84
Haiti, 59, 79
Hamburg, 101
Hammarskjöld, Dag, 73
Hannay, Lord, 158, 164-5
Helms, Senator Jesse, 103
High-Level Panel, 2, 5, 10, 17, 50, 168, 272
HIV/AIDS, 6-8, 21, 39, 41, 44, 46, 163, 169, 173, 259
Honduras, 86
Human Development Index (HDI), 17
Humanitarian intervention, 19, 42, 103, 138, 267
Human Rights (see also Universal Declaration of Human Rights, UN Commission on Human Rights), 1, 4, 5, 8, 14, 16, 20, 34, 39-40, 42, 46-8, 56, 58, 60-1, 64, 69, 72-3, 82, 85, 101, 107, 125, 127, 135, 137-8, 140, 142-4, 150, 156, 161, 164, 170-2, 179, 192, 205-6, 212, 228, 231-2, 236, 251-7, 263-4, 266

India, 24, 30, 71, 77-8, 81, 116, 153, 162
Indonesia, 86, 116, 119, 129
Intermediate Nuclear Forces (INF) Treaty, 23
International Atomic Energy Agency (IAEA), 25, 177-8
International Campaign to Ban Landmines, 29, 76, 264
International Commission on Intervention and State Security, 19
International Court of Justice (World Court, ICJ), 30, 37, 55, 60, 68, 71, 76, 80-1, 80-6, 93, 96, 98-9, 101, 132, 137, 139, 142, 209, 220, 242-3, 266,
International Criminal Court (ICC), 82, 101, 110, 125, 141, 145, 163, 174, 185, 264, 266
International Labour Organization (ILO), 34

INDEX

International Law, 1-2, 16, 19, 22, 37, 48, 54, 58, 60, 76, 80, 85-6, 88-91, 93-4, 96-9, 132-6, 141-5, 163, 165, 180, 205-6, 211, 253, 265-6
International Monetary Fund (IMF), 34, 56, 64, 74, 106, 152, 154
Iran, 25, 86, 88, 90, 93, 98, 129, 148, 162
Iraq, 18, 26, 28, 33, 49, 79, 82, 103, 112, 113, 116, 129-30, 135, 139, 144-8, 154, 158-64
Ireland, 32-3, 64-6, 71-2, 75, 78-9, 81, 83, 116, 152
Israel/Israelis, 24, 100, 116, 140, 161-4
Italy, 58, 94

Japan, 57, 85, 164
Jenin, 135, 140
Johnson, Samuel, 158, 165
Jordan, 85

Kabul, 161
Kagan, Robert, 151
Karadzic, Radovan, 104
Karzai, Pres. Hamid, 161
Kazakhstan, 148
Kenya, 129
Khan, A.Q., 25
Khan, Irene, 144
Korea, North, see Democratic People's Republic of Korea
Kosovo, 44, 93-5, 105, 108, 135, 147, 158-9, 164, 264-5
Kosovo Liberation Army (KLA), 159
Krauthammer, Charles, 124, 128
Kuwait, 105, 140, 159
Kyoto Protocol, 7, 77, 123, 125-6, 128, 141, 146, 163, 174

Lake Chad, 89, 92, 98
Landmine Convention, 29, 141
Landmines, 29, 39, 76, 163, 264
Latin America, 164, 177, 187
Laser-guided bombs, 117
Law of the Sea Tribunal, 101, 141
League of Nations, 84, 136

Least developed countries, 61, 260-1
Lebanon, 140
Libya, 25, 89, 92, 98-100
Liechtenstein, 86
Lisbon, 151
Lockerbie, 98
London, 84
Luxembourg, 32, 65

Maastricht Treaty, 71
Madagascar, 85
Madrid, 129
Malaria, 86
Malaysia, 86
Mali, 88
Mediation, 9, 59, 84, 170, 175, 193, 219
Melanesia, 26
Mercusor, 58
Mexico, 58, 71, 74, 83, 116, 118
Middle East, 100, 118, 125, 139, 142, 163, 177
Millennium Declaration, 8, 12, 14, 15, 17, 18, 46, 169, 191
Millennium Development Goals, 7, 14, 21, 162, 169, 191, 198, 258-62
Milton, John, 164-5
Mladic, Ratko, 104
Monsanto, 75
Montenegro, 93, 96
Montreal Convention, 99
Monterrey Conference/Consensus, 8, 44, 191
Morocco, 119, 129
Moscow, 23, 38, 109, 248
Mozambique, 73, 79, 104, 159
Multilateral Agreement on Investment (MAI), 74-5
Mutual Assured Destruction (MAD), 30

Naipaul, V.S., 26
Nairobi, 108
Namibia, 92, 104-5, 159
NATO, 28, 30, 64, 80-1, 86, 93-5, 135, 144, 149-50, 159
Neo-colonialism, 103

INDEX

Netherlands, 85, 94, 100
New Agenda Coalition (NAC), 71, 83
Newfoundland, 87
New International Economic Order, 103
New York, 12, 14, 107-8, 119, 134, 160, 172
New Zealand, 58, 71, 83
Nicaragua, 86, 89, 98
Nice Treaty, 152
Niger, 86
Nigeria, 86, 91-2
Nobel Peace Prize, 76
Non-Aligned Movement (NAM), 28
Non-Proliferation Treaty (NPT), 4-5, 13, 24-5, 71, 81, 171, 176-8
Non-Governmental Organisations (NGOs), 34, 47, 52, 63-4, 67, 76, 111, 150, 175, 233
North American Free Trade Area (NAFTA), 74
Northern Ireland, 116, 163
North Korea, see Democratic People's Republic of Korea
North-South axis/divide/imbalances/relations, 11, 45, 203
North-South dialogue, 103
North-South trade, 125
Nuclear Non-Proliferation Treaty, see Non-Proliferation Treaty
Nuclear Posture Review, 30
Nuclear proliferation, 11, 25, 163, 171
Nuclear weapons, 5, 14, 23-7, 30-1, 71, 76, 80-1, 96-7, 117, 176-7, 264

O'Brien, Conor Cruise, 13
Omagh, 80
Omar, Mullah, 29
Operation Desert Storm, 79
Organization for Economic Co-operation and Development (OECD), 56, 179
Organization for the Prohibition of Chemical Weapons (OPCW), 178
Organization for Security and Co-operation in Europe (OSCE), 81, 150
Ozone layer, 120

Palestine/Palestinians, 135, 137-8, 140, 162
[Palestinian] wall, 100
Pakistan, 24-5, 71, 81, 116, 129, 162
Pan Am, 98
Panyarachun, Anand, 2
Paris, 84, 119
Partnership for Peace (PfP), 81
Peacebuilding, 4, 6, 9, 39, 43, 171, 188-90, 193
Peacebuilding Commission, 3, 171, 189-90, 192
Peacekeeping, 34, 42-4, 48, 52-3, 57-60, 66-8, 71, 79-80, 102, 102-8, 110, 112, 127, 164, 184-5, 188, 190, 265
People's Assembly, see also Civil Society Forum, 64, 66, 78, 82
Perestroika, 85
Pentagon, 145, 160
Perle, Richard, 145, 155
Permanent Court of International Justice, 84, 86
Permanent Five (P5), 132, 141
Persian Gulf, 119, 122, 125
Peru, 116, 118
Petersburg Tasks, 80
Polisario, 119
Pollution, 58, 102, 127, 260
Porto Alegre, 156
Portobello Barracks, 65
Portugal, 94
Post-conflict peacebuilding, 6, 107, 123, 127, 163, 171, 185, 189
Poverty, 1-2, 5-8, 10, 14-15, 39, 41, 47, 52, 61, 63, 74, 106-7, 113, 115-6, 126, 127, 137, 154, 162-3, 169, 173, 179, 258, 260-1, 263
Prague, 116
Project for a New American Century, 148, 156

Qatar, 90

Rambouillet, 93
Real IRA, 80
Regional Organisations, 8, 92

INDEX

Republic of Congo, (see also Zaire), 86
Rio de Janeiro, 69, 76-7
Robinson, Mary, 72, 82
Romania, 86
Roosevelt, Pres. Franklin D, 11
Russia/Russian Federation, 30, 68, 81, 84, 85, 94, 96, 146-8, 153, 161, 176, 250
Rwanda, 6, 43, 50, 74, 79, 86, 104, 110, 139, 159, 264

Saddam Hussein, 129, 145, 147, 160-1, 164
Sanctions, 42, 75, 79, 99, 104-5, 139, 170, 179-82, 187
San Francisco, 136, 166, 205, 250
Savimbi, Jonas, 104
Seattle, 116
Scotland, 99-100,
Security Council, 1-4, 11, 19, 20-24, 28- 30, 42, 44-6, 50, 52-4, 57-8, 60, 64, 66, 68, 70-2, 79, 85, 87, 94-5, 97-100, 103-5, 109, 112-13, 132-7, 139-43, 146-7, 153, 155, 163-4, 171, 173-190, 192-3, 199, 208-25, 238-9, 242-4, 248-9, 267
Secretary General (see also Annan, Kofi), 2, 7, 9, 13-14, 17-20, 22-3, 32-3, 35, 43, 46-7, 50-1, 55, 60, 72, 79, 100, 103, 105, 109, 111, 132, 134-5, 142, 144, 168, 175, 179, 182, 184-6, 190-3, 196, 199-204
September 11 2001 (9/11), 18, 21-2, 24, 27, 112, 115-6, 119, 125-6, 137, 144, 148
Severe Acute Respiratory Syndrome (SARS), 5
Serbia, 93, 96, 103
Shakespeare, William, 48, 165
Shiva, Vandana, 78
Sierra Leone, 44, 85, 106, 265
Single European Act, 71
Singapore, 86
Slovakia, 85-7, 92
Solzhenitsyn, Alexander, 36
Somalia, 74, 79, 104, 116, 159

South Africa, 71, 73, 83, 159
Sovereignty, 19, 26, 38, 41, 58-9, 61, 88-91, 102-3, 107, 110, 112, 114, 151, 252, 265
Soviet Union (see also Russia), 27, 107, 149
Spain, 58, 87, 94-5, 116
Srebrenica, 43
Sri Lanka, 116
Stanford, Ca, 33
Strategic Arms Reduction Treaties (START), 21
Structural Adjustment Programs (SAPs), 73, 107
Sub-Saharan Africa, 142
Sudan, 72, 79, 160, 164
Sweden, 35, 71, 83
Switzerland, 136
Syria, 162

Taliban, 125, 129, 160, 179
Tehran, 88, 93
Terrorism, 1-3, 5-8, 11, 17, 21-4, 29, 40-1, 46, 79, 99, 102, 112, 119, 125, 137, 139-40, 144, 160-3, 169-70, 179-80
Thailand, 2, 134
The Hague, see Hague, The,
Tokyo, 108
Tolerance, 15, 78, 179, 205, 257
Trinity College Dublin, 32
Turkey, 98, 129
Turkmenistan, 148
Tuvalu, 153
Twin Towers, 160

Uganda, 86, 101
Ukraine, 86
UN Charter, 18, 20, 33, 36, 41-2, 54, 60, 64-6, 70, 73, 75, 78-80, 82, 84-5, 96-100, 105, 132-140, 142-3, 166, 183, 186, 188-9, 193-4, 205-250
UN Commission on Human Rights (UNHCR), 4, 8, 72, 127, 171, 192

INDEX

UN Conference on Trade and
 Development (UNCTAD), 104,
 127-8
UN Development Programme
 (UNDP), 7, 25-6, 32, 34, 67, 73,
 106, 127, 134
UNESCO, 34, 73
UNICEF, 34, 67, 70, 79
UN Register of Conventional Arms,
 175
UNITA, 105
United Kingdom, 85, 87-8, 158, 215,
 250
United States, 1, 7, 21, 33, 54-5, 64,
 68, 78-80, 85-6, 88-91, 93, 95,
 98, 109, 112, 116, 123-4, 128,
 130, 136, 144, 147, 156, 158,
 176, 215, 250
Universal Declaration of Human
 Rights, 137-8, 142, 171, 251-7
UNSCOM, 135
Uranium, 25, 171, 177-8
Urquhart, Sir Brian, 13, 17, 33, 35,
 103, 105, 110-11, 134, 143
Uruguay, 77
US Space Command, 148, 157
USSR (Union of Soviet Socialist
 Republics), 27, 30, 36, 107, 149,
 215, 250
U Thant, 32

Venezuela, 85,
Vereshchetin, Judge, 96
Veto, 4, 42, 52, 57, 66, 70-1, 87,
 134, 136, 141-2, 147, 153, 187-9
Vienna Convention on Diplomatic
 Relations, 93

War Crimes Tribunal, 110, 146
War on Terror, 125, 129-30, 138
Washington, 37-8, 83-4, 109, 116,
 130, 135, 148, 151, 155, 157,
 160
Weapons of Mass Destruction
 (WMD), 2-3, 18-19, 23-29, 268
Western Sahara, 59, 92, 119

Woolsey, James, 123, 128
World Bank, 34, 56, 64, 73-4, 76,
 106, 137, 152, 189
World Court, see International Court of
 Justice
World Court Project, 76
World Federation of United Nations
 Associations, 32
World Trade Organization (WTO), 56, 74,
 76, 101, 106, 111, 155, 162, 173
World War II, 18, 39, 54, 136, 159
World Health Organization (WHO), 5, 34,
 79, 127, 174, 178
World Health Assembly, 174

Yugoslavia, 73, 79, 81, 86, 91, 94-5, 110,
 116, 147

Zaire (see also Congo), 74
Zapatistas, 118
Zimbabwe, 77

The UN and its Future in the 21st Century

Action for UN Renewal

Action for UN Renewal (ACT-UN) is a network of organisations and individuals campaigning for a more effective United Nations. We co-operate with other UN-related NGOs, in particular the United Nations Association, and our primary role is to monitor and enhance the United Kingdom's contribution to the renewal and reform of the United Nations system. As one of the five permanent Members of the Security Council, with one of the world's richest economies, this country has particular responsibilities for the United Nations.

Our aims are:

- to see greater transparency and public accountability in the way the UK government carries out its responsibilities within the UN system with respect for international law and the UN Charter.

- to see that the United Nations is at the centre of all government decisions involving security, economic and social justice, environmental protection and human rights at the international level

- to promote wider knowledge and understanding of the UN Charter; and of the functions and activities of the UN system with its Commissions, Programmes and Specialised Agencies all working for a fairer and better world

- to explore and publicise proposals for UN reform and renewal, so that the Organisation can more effectively promote peace and human rights for all peoples, and equitable access to the world's resources

The UN and its Future in the 21st Century

We are working toward the reforms of the United Nations that can fulfil its Charter promises for ALL the world's people:

- Peace
- Human Rights
- International Law
- Social Justice
- Better Living Standards
- Freedom

Why not join Action for UN Renewal? Subscription only £5 (plus donation if possible) Tel: 020 8399 2547 www.action-for-un-renewal.org.uk

Please make your cheques payable to Action for UN Renewal and send to Action for UN Renewal, 3 Whitehall Court, London, SW1A 2EL

Name..
Address..
....

Notes

Notes

Notes